RESTLESS CITIES

RESTLESS CITIES

EDITED BY
MATTHEW BEAUMONT
AND GREGORY DART

VERSO

London • New York

for
Clara Dart
and
Amelia Beaumont

First published by Verso 2010
© the collection Verso 2010
© individual contributions the contributors 2010

1 3 5 7 9 10 8 6 4 2

Verso
UK: 6 Meard Street, London W1F 0EG
US: 20 Jay Street, Suite 1010, Brooklyn, NY 11201
www.versobooks.com

Verso is the imprint of New Left Books

ISBN-13: 978-1-84467-405-3

British Library Cataloguing in Publication Data
A catalogue record for this book is available from the British Library

Library of Congress Cataloging-in-Publication Data
A catalog record for this book is available from the Library of Congress

Typeset by MJ Gavan, Truro, Cornwall
Printed in the US by Worldcolor/Fairfield

Contents

CONTENTS

Preface

In his notations on the theory and practice of 'rhythmanalysis', composed as an old man, Henri Lefebvre, the celebrated French philosopher of urban life, stated that 'in order to grasp and analyse rhythms', particularly those of the street, 'it is necessary to get outside them, but not completely: be it through illness or a technique'. Rhythms must be objectified without thereby becoming de-subjectified. 'A certain exteriority enables the analytic intellect to function', he explains; 'however, to grasp a rhythm it is necessary to have been *grasped* by it; one must *let oneself go*, give oneself over, abandon oneself to its duration'. In order to understand the city, and its ceaseless contrapuntal rhythms, one must 'situate oneself simultaneously inside and outside it'. For Lefebvre, approaching his ninetieth birthday, the balcony of his apartment, directly above the street, provided the liminal perspective he needed. From there, looking onto the rue Rambuteau, opposite the Pompidou Centre, he felt he could separate out some of the sights and noises that from the street itself seem simply to be chaos. The traffic on the road beneath him, for example, stopping and abruptly starting again in an elaborate urban choreography, fascinates him:

> Towards the right, below, a traffic light. On red, cars at a standstill, the pedestrians cross, feeble murmurings, footsteps, confused voices. One does not chatter while crossing a dangerous junction under the threat of wild cats and elephants ready to charge forward, taxis, buses,

lorries, various cars. Hence the relative silence in this crowd. A kind of soft murmuring, sometimes a cry, a call. Therefore the people produce completely different noises when the cars stop: feet and words. From right to left and back again. And on the pavements along the perpendicular street. At the green lights, steps and words stop. A second of silence and then it's the rush, the starting up of tens of cars, the rhythms of the old bangers speeding up as quickly as possible. At some risk: passersby to the left, buses cutting across, other vehicles. Whereby a slowing down and restart (stage one: starting up—stage two: slowing down for the turn—stage three: brutal restart, foot down, top speed, excluding traffic jams…). The harmony between what one sees and what one hears (from the window) is remarkable.

Restless Cities, a collection of essays exploring aspects of the metropolitan city since the nineteenth century, aims to occupy the contradictory space inhabited by Lefebvre. It inhabits the inside and the outside of the city. It attempts to apprehend the characteristic rhythms of the city, for analytical purposes; but at the same time it abandons itself to them. Both melancholic and celebratory in spirit, the book might therefore be conceptualized as a series of brief 'city symphonies' (in the cinematic tradition that runs from Walter Ruttmann via Dziga Vertov to Terence Davies) transposed into print. Its contributors drift through the cities they reconstruct, moving at different rhythms, in multifarious directions, tracing trajectories that are at once geographical, historical and psychological, and crisscrossing one another's paths. The book's title is intended to evoke a sense of the metropolis as a site of endless making and unmaking; one in which, under the ceaseless influence of capitalist development, identities of all kinds are constantly solidifying, constantly liquefying. It is also intended to communicate the peculiar combination of innervation and enervation, the restless and the restive, which often typifies people's relationship to the metropolis: the city as a state of delirium so habitual as to be almost unnoticeable.

Restless Cities thus represents an attempt both to identify some of the patterns that have defined everyday life in the modern city and to observe their constitutive or transformative effects on individuals. Its chapters interweave the analytical and the experiential, the abstract and the concrete, in the hope of evoking an imaginative as well as a cognitive understanding of the city. The rhythmanalyst, according to Lefebvre, 'will come to "listen" to a house, a street, a town, as an audience listens to a symphony'. The study of the city, then, both as a technique and a kind of illness.

The editors would like to record their gratitude to Tom Penn, for his commitment to this book, and to Tim Clark and Mark Martin, for their technical expertise. The financial support provided by the Chambers Fund in the Department of English at UCL, which paid for the costs of the images that have been commissioned or reproduced, is also gratefully acknowledged. Finally, many thanks to Matt Stuart for his photographs, particularly those that head up each chapter (but also for those on pages 26, 186 and 209). Unless otherwise indicated, the photographs embedded in the text of chapters were taken by the authors of those chapters themselves.

Matthew Beaumont
Gregory Dart

Archiving

Michael Sheringham

One of the city's archives is its detritus: hieroglyphic blobs of gum splattering the sidewalk, runic streaks and crevices on pavements or blank façades, encampments of bottle banks, hoppers for supplements to supplements and household non-desiderata. Georges Perec aspired to be a Linnaeus of flyers. He wanted to classify every specimen of street bumph: prostitutes' cards in phone-boxes, missing pet ads pasted to lampposts, offers of manicure or babysitting sellotaped to drainpipes, tessellated with tear-off phone numbers. The whole lot. Brassaï's photographs of scrunched tube tickets, and the ripped-poster art of Raymond Hains and Jacques Villeglé, pay homage to this papery profusion. The place to look, though, is in the gutter. Paris in the early morning, when the taps are on and the city's entrails bob in clear water streaming down imperceptible gradients, marshalled by bundles of rags or carpet off-cuts held together by loops of string. All day we can admire the craft of the street-cleaners: they know just how to angle these probosces of fabric, shag and twist, which regulate the flow of water and gunge, then sprawl at dried-up intersections tripping nonchalant passers-by. For years I thought I was the sole aficionado of these bulbous packages in paisley pinks and dodgy mustards, like monstrous big toes or swaddled foundlings, which are party to the city's pristine aspirations yet bespeak its abjection. Until I discovered Steve McQueen's exquisite ektachromes (his *Barrage* series)—where my beloved bundles seem to pose for their portraits—and Georges Didi-Huberman's *Ninfa Moderna*, an erudite study where these emblems of the city, photographed by Atget, Moholy-Nagy and Fleischer, stand for Benjamin's loss of aura, and Aby Warburg's eternal nymph dragged down into modernity's dust. In Italo Calvino's *Invisible Cities* (1972), the citizens of Leonia live under constant threat of burial under a landslide of rubbish. In Leonia everything is box-fresh every day, and the profligate joys of expelling, discarding and liquidating generate the ominous mountains of garbage that ring the city in ever-widening circles. In Victor Hugo's *Les Misérables* (1862) the threat comes from down below, from Paris's stercoraceous under-layer, the 'Leviathan's intestine', an ever-growing pool of shit and piss, expanding with the city since the Middle Ages, inadequately canalized by an unregulated labyrinth of stone-built sewers which, by the early nineteenth century, for example in the great floods of 1802, regularly failed to prevent overflow. Then, as Hugo puts it, the *cloacae* found their Christopher Columbus—in the person of Bruneseau, precursor of London's Bazalgette.

Situating a key episode of his great archive-novel in the sewers allowed Hugo to develop his vision of Paris as a vast ocean into which we can suddenly vanish. Following Jean Valjean's desperate plunge, Hugo deluges us in digressive detail. Bruneseau's initial reconnaissances allegedly took seven years, and among the articles the explorer found were a rag-picker's shoulder-basket, a Huguenot medal with the effigy of a pig wearing a cardinal's cap, and numerous jewels and coin hoards. The most surprising find was a dirty piece of cloth, caught on a rusty hinge, bearing a monogram with the letters LAVBESP: a relic of Marat's love affair with a *grande dame* that had served for a shroud after his assassination.

Hugo wasn't the first writer to see the city as an archive. Defoe's *Journal of the Plague Year*, written in 1722 a few decades after the catastrophe that had occurred in his youth, uses statistics and facsimiled documents in ways that later writers, including Joyce and Perec, will make more familiar. Jean-Sébastien Mercier's multivolume *Tableau de Paris*, from the late eighteenth century, on which Walter Benjamin drew frequently in the *Arcades Project*, is an astonishing compilation of urban fact. Calvino admired Balzac's early novel *Ferragus* (1833) as a topographical epic where streets and *quartiers* determined actions and events, bearing out Balzac's contention that 'the physiognomy of the street imprints ideas in our minds against which we are defenceless'. Hugo had a similar feeling for the power of the streets and *Les Misérables* may be the European novel where street names are the most abundant. (He notes in passing that Paris in the 1830s had 2,200 streets, and I wouldn't be surprised if most got a mention. I gave up counting). Like *Ulysses* (1922), *Les Misérables* was written largely in exile from the city that was its muse, and is set in the period of the author's youth. Hugo noted that the places he wrote about came back like melancholy apparitions. But *Les Misérables* is not a lifeless gazetteer. As in the novels of Dickens in the same period, the city is brought to life through itineraries, trajectories and destinies played out on the field of play defined by the street map, stretching out of the medieval centre into the working-class *faubourgs* and beyond. Hugo devotes some remarkable pages to what he calls the 'amphibious' realm of Paris's *banlieues*—surrounding villages that were being absorbed into the metropolis via an intermediate sprawl he calls 'limbo'. Making a litany of their names, from Arcueil to Vanves, via Drancy and Gonesse, he comments on the forlorn *tristesse* of this ring of appendages tainted by the capital's miasma but representing the limits of the known universe for its children.

Like Dickens, Hugo was haunted by the figure of the street urchin, and the pages on the Parisian *gamin*, emblematized by Gavroche, are justly famous. Carving out a persona as a social historian-cum-philosopher (philosophers deal in the microscopic he claimed), Hugo's narrator, like Defoe's 'H. F.', devises a form of city writing where fiction and documentary interweave. Gavroche is viewed in terms of statistics (as a foundling), of natural history (as a species of the city's fauna), of social stratification (the *gaminerie* as a caste), and above all in terms of sociolinguistics (as the exponent of a particularly rich brand of *argot*). Although relatively short, as in Defoe's case, the geographical and temporal distance at which Hugo wrote allowed him to present himself as an urban archaeologist, bent on communicating his perception of Paris as 'un total', a totality. Part of this discourse is founded on comparison: as later writing will confirm, seeing a city

3

archivally, as layer upon layer of compacted material detail, is often best achieved by looking at one city through the prism of another. For Hugo, Rome is a regular foil and *Les Misérables* contains passages that overlay Parisian and Roman topographies in a manner that anticipates Michel Butor's tale of these two cities, *La Modification* (1957). In *Les Misérables* London is also in the frame, and this raises the question of how far the vision of Paris we find in mid-nineteenth-century French literature was inflected by imaginings of a city ten times as big. I've long felt that in Baudelaire's case 'London' provided the code through which he deciphers 'Paris'. After all, in the reflections on the city in essays such as 'The Painter of Modern Life' (1863), it is essentially De Quincey's *Confessions of an English Opium-Eater* (1821) and Poe's 'The Man of the Crowd' (1840), both set in London, which Baudelaire cites. The 'fourmillante cité', a vision of Paris which, after its transmutation by the Surrealists and Situationists, was to have such an enduring impact on the way the Anglo-Saxon imagination construes London—from T. S. Eliot to Iain Sinclair and Patrick Keiller—may in fact have been concocted from London ingredients in the first place. Writing in Guernsey, reading the *Illustrated London News*, Hugo's retrospective view of Paris, with its mixture of the miniature and the gigantic, the sublime and the grotesque, was probably infiltrated by the city then being mythologized by Dickens and Doré. Hugo calls Paris a cosmos: Athens, Rome and Jerusalem rolled into one; a dark forest without limits. Its unfathomable and innumerable pockets and recesses are the product of infinite poverty and deprivation. For him it is the duty of the 'social observer' to visit these shadowy realms, and the emphasis he places on the underground world of the sewers, on cemeteries and desolate suburbs, allegorizes the persistence of the human soul in the city's filth. Hugo's novel is written 'according to the ethics of the archive', as Adam Thirlwell puts it in the introduction to a new translation: 'the archive', he adds, 'believes in the refusal of selection. It believes that everything, at some point, can return to haunt the powerful'.

Hugo's archive-novel has an afterlife in Patrick Modiano's *Dora Bruder* (1997), translated by Joanna Kilmartin as *The Search Warrant*, which documents the author's attempt to discover what happened to Dora, a 16-year-old Jewish girl who vanished from the streets of Paris during the Occupation, and whose name features in Serge Klarsfeld's archive of convoys from Paris, via Drancy, to the death camp at Auschwitz. Modiano is a novelist whose work is haunted by the Occupation, but *Dora Bruder*, which contains numerous documents and facsimiles, is an autobiographical record of a journey into the archives of the city where nearly all his works are set. Modiano knows Paris like the back of his hand and when one day in the archives he came across an old issue of *Paris-Soir* dated 31 December 1941, carrying a small ad with a description of a missing teenager, inserted by Dora's desperate parents, he was immediately struck by the address given in the eighteenth *arrondissement*, an area that had played a significant part in a period of his own life. Initially Modiano wasn't sure he would be able to find out much more about Dora, and after a while he wrote a novel in which, despite the entry in Klarsfeld's haunting *Memorial to the French Children of the Holocaust* (1995), he imagined she had escaped deportation. But that didn't settle anything; so after three or four years he began painstakingly following up every possible lead, seeking permission to consult numerous official archives, meeting with the usual obstruction on the part of officious 'sentinels of oblivion', while also following his own intuitive pathways. He finds out quite a bit about her parents, immigrants from central Europe who lived in one small hotel room, and discovers that, in trying to shelter her from the anti-Jewish laws, they had sent Dora to board at a convent in another part of Paris. When they placed the missing person ad it was because she had run away from school for a second time, and it is quite likely that she was picked up in a raid by the French Occupation police during this second *fugue*.

Modiano is fascinated by Dora's bids for freedom and spends days pacing the Paris streets, retracing the itineraries he thinks she would have taken 50 years earlier, and hanging around the places he thinks were familiar to her. He becomes a kind of somnambulist, walking the streets in the 1990s but along trajectories dating from the 1940s. As he walks 'with' Dora, memories of his own adolescence, when he had also run away, keep superimposing other trajectories in the same streets over hers, and so another time band, the early 1960s, gradually interweaves with the earlier and later ones. In *Dora Bruder*, archival journeying becomes a kind of time-travelling.

As he walks, ghost-like, in Dora's and his own past footsteps, Modiano's pedestrian itineraries in the Paris of the 1990s turn the city into a palimpsest, a multi-decked set of archival traces relating to various points in the history of the city's streets and monuments. Infiltrated by memories of the past, Paris becomes a ghost city where Modiano repeatedly experiences an uncanny sense of emptiness, as if Dora's absence, and his inability to bring more than a small portion of her life back to the surface, voided Paris of its living reality. At other times Modiano finds himself noting strange echoes, coincidences and convergences, as his life and Dora's interpenetrate, and as (in the absence of any hard facts) he comes increasingly to identify with her.

One coincidence involves *Les Misérables*, a literary text that, along with many other pieces of evidence, Modiano's speculations weave into the fabric of Dora's Paris archive. When he visits the location of Dora's convent school, now replaced by ugly offices, which had stood on the corner of 60–64 rue de Picpus, on the corner with the rue de la Gare-de-Reuilly in the twelfth *arrondissement*, Modiano realises that it had been sited more or less exactly where Hugo placed the convent school in which Jean Valjean and Cosette find sanctuary when in desperation they climb over a garden wall with the policeman Javert hot on their heels. On looking up the passage, which he quotes in his text, adding to the archival materials, Modiano realises that Hugo, after giving precise details of Jean Valjean's itinerary, up to the point where he and Cosette cross over to the Right Bank via the Austerlitz Bridge, had invented a fantasy topography, making up an imaginary *quartier* he called the Petit-Picpus and locating the convent at no. 62 rue du Petit-Picpus. The area in question had in fact been razed and remodelled between the 1830s and the 1860s, and Hugo presents it as part of the 'old Paris' now swept away by progress and to which, he claims, only a map dated 1727 now attests. And he refers to old street names surviving in a new Paris even though the Paris in question was one he had invented.

Modiano is moved and troubled to find that Dora's vanished school (he finds only a pamphlet about the Mother Superior in Dora's day), stood in the heart of a *quartier* Hugo grafted, for practical reasons to do with the novelist's trade and the exigencies of fiction, onto the map of Paris, knowing that the rebuilding of the area meant that his readers would not be able to check without archival investigations of their own. It's somehow fitting that the quiet haven in the twelfth *arrondissement*, where Dora could have been safe had she not chosen to run away, should be tinged with the imaginary, and should enter a chain of substitutions where real and fictive documents, traces and identities, should be set in a restless motion like that of the city. For Dora's story, like Jean Valjean's, is part of the archive of Paris, and in doing the legwork for *Dora Bruder*, pounding the pavements and communing with Dora in her absence, and then writing his book—her book—Modiano injects himself into the veins of his city, becoming a wraith haunting the eternal and ever-changing streets.

Like *Dora Bruder*, W. G. Sebald's *Austerlitz* (2001) reconfigures our vision of familiar spaces by seeing cities as archives: repositories of written traces enshrined in topographies. Sebald, like Modiano, suggests a connection between accepting to lose the outlines of one's familiar identity and gaining access to a hidden dimension of urban reality. The novel charts the gradual re-emergence of buried experience—translation from Czechoslovakia to Britain as part of the humanitarian *Kindertransport* missions that rescued many Jewish children just before the start of the Second World War. The protagonist, Jacques Austerlitz, an architectural historian, meets the unnamed narrator, a figure clearly based on Sebald himself, in the waiting room, the *Salle des Pas Perdus*, of the central station in Antwerp, and from thereon railway stations and other monuments in a number of cities, principally Brussels, Paris, London and Prague, will recur repeatedly in the narrative. In the painfully slow process of recollection and reconstruction recounted by Austerlitz, in a series of meetings in London and Paris, these cities tend to merge and separate as parallels and echoes between them, rooted in the shared history of twentieth-century Europe, keep emerging. The monuments are objective features of their respective cityscapes, and reflect discrete architectural histories, as in the case of the old and new national library buildings in Paris. But the memories and associations these buildings possess, by virtue of the role they have played as the setting for key events in both personal and collective histories and destinies, involves them in a play of similarities and differences that opens them up to subjective appropriation. So that, as in the case of the Antwerp *Nocturama*, which the narrator visits at the beginning of *Austerlitz*, where infra-red lighting enables the visitor to see owls, bats and other creatures of the night, the city streets and monuments exist in a twilight zone between objective and subjective realms. Moreover, the layout and material fabric of each of these labyrinthine buildings have complex histories of their own that have led to areas of disuse, neglect, abandonment or total erasure. On more or less every page of Sebald's novel buildings stand as the materialization of mental landscapes, and countless attributes of urban monuments— for example, the way they may incorporate a patchwork of styles, or have been used successively for different purposes—reflect disturbances in the spheres of memory and inner reality.

Austerlitz is framed by descriptions of two fortresses, one at Breendonk in Belgium, the other, described by Dan Jacobson in his book, *Hershel's Kingdom* (1998), which retraces his Jewish grandfather's life story in South Africa. Beyond Austerlitz's own story, these fortresses—associated with *The Empty Fortress* (1967), Bruno Bettelheim's study of autistic children, locked into themselves—are described in ways that set up parallels with a whole series of buildings that appear within his narrative, particularly railway stations, and especially both Liverpool Street in London, where he eventually realises he first arrived as a child, and the Gare d'Austerlitz in Paris, associated with the life he discovers his father had led after fleeing Prague. We also encounter zoos, archival repositories, libraries, museums and hospitals—particularly the vast hospital complex of La Salpêtrière in Paris, the size of a small town. The Salpêtrière has strong echoes of the Theresienstadt ghetto to which Austerlitz's mother was sent, but also fits into the topography of his father's traces in Paris prior to his deportation. Ultimately, all these monuments are set in restless motion, through connections that are deeply rooted in historical realities but also serve to dissolve time.

To expose the hidden histories of familiar monuments is to defamiliarize the city we thought we knew, and to wrench us out of the present, into an intermediate zone of overlapping timescales. As he and the narrator walk through Greenwich Park, Austerlitz observes that 'even in a metropolis ruled by time like London it's still possible to be outside time'. Later, Austerlitz reflects that we don't understand the laws governing the return of the past, and that he feels more and more that time doesn't exist, only 'spaces interlocking according to rules of a higher form of stereometry, between which the living and the dead can move back and forth as they like'. Like Modiano in *Dora Bruder*, in order to try to connect with a past whose traces still seem present in the recesses of the city, Austerlitz feels driven to sever his ties with the ordinary existence that keeps us in the here and now, where our lives are dominated by the single track of the immediate future. He burns his notes for a work of architectural history and embarks on a series of nocturnal wanderings through London, where he often meets other 'spectres' as he surrenders to the 'vortex of past time'. Living in extreme solitude, as a kind of spectre, he exposes himself to the city's capacity to release the ghosts harboured by its monuments. In doing so, he resists the amnesia represented by the new Bibliothèque nationale in Paris, which can be seen as 'the official manifestation of the increasingly importunate urge to break with everything which still has some living connection to the past'. As in Modiano, the vision of city-as-archive works not only through a constant interaction of inner and outer topographies but through the interplay of a variety of archival strata including networks of literary and cultural allusion and references to numerous creatures, object and images. The reconfiguration of urban space in this novel, as in Modiano's, involves the creation of a complex literary structure that places the archival at its centre, both in the way that cities are represented (or rather apprehended) as multiple archives, and in the way in which the protagonists are primarily involved in forms of archival journey and activity: going back and forth between past and present via thought processes that, however subjective, never lose track of material traces. And it is through this vision of the city as archive that Modiano and Sebald enact particular modes or visions of subjectivity, different no doubt, but comparable in their questioning of settled forms of identity.

A city is a memory machine. Cities need their histories as proof of their dynamism. Outside cities, in forests and plains, myths hold sway: places acquire legendary associations; hallowed sites engender pilgrimages or mirror cosmic forces. A city on the other hand comprises an accumulation of events that are converted into symbols in the collective memory of the inhabitants. The city itself is a microcosmos, a totality, and it has its own history, interiorized by its inhabitants. Names—of streets, squares, monuments and districts—play a key role in this process. This is partly because names often commemorate signal events, or key players in the city's destiny, but it is also because these objective features of the urban landscape can ferry deeply personal associations.

In his books on the Paris underground the anthropologist Marc Augé suggests that the names of métro stations often serve as nodal points where personal memory and social memory converge. Our own private associations, connected with habitual trajectories that change in the course of our lives, as we move house or change jobs, interweave with the historical, topographic or biographical memories enshrined in the names of the stations. Where logically, Augé notes, the names of the stations derive from the streets and intersections above ground, for him, since childhood, it has been the reverse: the particular sonority or semantic aura of the name of the underground station 'colours' his picture of the neighbourhood in which he finds himself at the exit—just as Proust's image of Vitré or Florence was tinged with the sounds of their names. In Moscow Benjamin had the feeling that every step he took was on named ground, 'and in a flash imagination builds a whole quarter out of the sound'. A city's names build a world within a world, creating pathways of reverie that may distance us from actuality, but connect us to the living fabric of the city. For Jean-Christophe Bailly, 'Fleet Street', parallel to the Thames, conjures up images of England's maritime history, the whiff of tar commingling with printer's ink, and the flapping of ensigns merging with the whirr of rotary presses. Benjamin, on spying the name 'Barnabe' on a tram in Marseilles, reflects that the 'sad, confused story of Barnabas' was not inappropriate for a streetcar heading out into the city's forlorn hinterland.

In the *Arcades Project* Benjamin often refers to street names, calling them 'intoxicating substances' that can generate what Michel de Certeau, another enthusiast, calls 'semantic pathways'. Street names can evoke all kinds of feelings in us, relating to our memories of the locations themselves, or to associations we may have with the name by virtue of its referent or of the sound and shape of the words. In his essay on Berlin, Benjamin talks of the extraordinary resonance that the name *Brauhausberg* held for him. In the *Arcades Project* he cites a number of reformers who had sought at various times to rid Paris of what they considered to be ungracious or inappropriate names (rue du Petit-Musc and the like), and had urged the municipal authorities to adopt a rational and educative system based for instance on place names that would be allocated according to the location of the street. Thus a certain J. B. Pujoulx suggested that streets in the north of Paris could be named after towns in the north of France, and so forth (a system that was in fact later adopted in Maurepas, one of Paris's new satellite towns). For Benjamin this kind of proposal, however whimsical—and undesirable, since it would purge the city of the archival humus compacted in its names—pays tribute to the power of names in the city. And so does the politics of urban naming, demonstrated by the use of commemoration as an arm of state propaganda, and by the frequent changes of name that occur in French or Russian cities. Raymond Queneau wrote a wonderful sequence of poems based on Paris street names, deriving comic effects from the frequent lack of fit between the street and the individual or entity referred to by its name. Later, Jacques Roubaud revisited many of these locations and provided an update on the senior poet-archivist's findings.

The archival dimension of the city is not confined to the past. For Foucault, the archive is above all a field of discourses where utterances are anonymized and de-temporalized. What count are networks of lateral connection and the meanings they make possible at a given time. For Derrida, the archive is first of all a physical location, a place of deposit—like the *Archivo de los Indios* in the heart of Seville, the National Archives at Kew, or the edifice in Paris that stands in the rue des Archives. Secondly, for Derrida, the archive is the site of a conflict between the urge to preserve and the urge to destroy, between remembering and forgetting. Archival action consists in the activities of accumulation, classification and consultation: it happens in the present, but its true time-frame is the future. Archives are always of the future; what we make of the pasts that we are made of. The cityscape, its streets, monuments and open spaces, its slums and *beaux quartiers*, are all the product of accretion, juxtaposition and transformation, but this history is made available to us at the surface. The city wears its heart on its sleeve. It is now, and we are part of it. 'Time flaps on the mast' wrote Virginia Woolf in *Mrs Dalloway* (1925).

In the *Philosophical Investigations* (1953), Wittgenstein compares language to an ancient city, 'a maze of little streets and squares, of old and new houses, and of houses with additions from various periods ... surrounded by a multitude of new boroughs with straight regular streets and uniform houses'. To turn this around, as Jacques Roubaud does in *The Great Fire of London* (1989), and see the city as a language, is to open up a field of possibilities, corresponding to different facets of language itself. If we privilege enunciation, the pragmatics of utterance, where language as system (*langue*) is set in motion by one-off activations (*parole*), we can follow Barthes and de Certeau and see walking in the city as an activation of the urban grid, a 'generative grammar of the legs' as Bailly puts it, that sidesteps the planners, and the remit of official histories, and creates a city cast in our own image, a micro-history of personal trajectories where chance encounters are the fruit of what the Surrealists called *errance* and the Situationists *dérive*. Or we can think of the city as a library, an aggregation of reading material. This is what London is for Roubaud: its

Squares, Crescents, Mews, Places, Gardens, Circuses and Closes (Perec once noted the richness of the English urban lexicon compared with that of French) are suffused by the sounds of spoken English—a language he understands, but which still envelops him in foreignness. His London archive is also constructed out of London's literary archive through the novels he devours (by Trollope, Murdoch, or his favourite writer, Sylvia Townsend Warner) during his regular solitary sojourns at the Crescent Hotel in Cartwright Gardens. One of Roubaud's finest city-poems, in *The Plurality of Worlds of Lewis* (1991), is called 'Cartwright Gardens: a Meditation'.

One source of the uncanny temper of Paul Auster's *New York Trilogy* (1986) is the way his New York is shot through with European references and resonances. Even when Auster recycles Poe, Hawthorne and Melville, it feels as if these American figures have returned to us via the European literary imaginary they helped to fashion. In 'City of Glass' there is a clear link with the Baudelairean *flâneur* and its embedding in Poe, but Auster's *flânerie* is steeped in Benjamin, and further overlayed by the footsteps of other European writers: Beckett, Blanchot, Jabès. As in Roubaud and Sebald, literary palimpsest and urban palimpsest go hand in hand. The narrator of 'City of Glass' is a detective writer called Quinn, a name with an Irish ring and echoes of the Algonquin Hotel (where a scene of the *Trilogy* is set), a shrine of the American literary archive, its name evoking the verdant Mannahatta of the Algonquin Indians whose dispossession and disappearance are also referred to in Auster's story. Like Modiano's Paris and Iain Sinclair's London, Auster's New York is a 'City of Disappearances': as so often, the archive, despite its plenitude and profusion, invokes what is missing rather than what is present. For Quinn, aimless city wandering is part of a euphoric practice of existential estrangement. By 'flooding himself with externals' and 'drowning himself out of himself', he turns New York into a 'nowhere'. Listening to the music of some street performers, he aspires to be 'drawn into the circle of its repetitions' and to disappear (he thinks of Baudelaire's prose poem, from *Paris Spleen*, called 'Anywhere out of this world'). Quinn follows a man who behaves like 'an archaeologist inspecting a shard in some prehistoric ruin'; but the things the man picks up from the sidewalk are stray bits of dirt and junk. When questioned he avers, 'my motives are lofty but my work now takes place in the realm of the everyday'. Resembling the Baudelairean rag-picker, whom Benjamin made an emblematic city figure indexing the endless heterogeneity of urban space, Auster's character is a scavenger, like the urban gleaners Agnès Varda tracked down in her documentary film, *The Gleaners and I* (2000). Although every city has its own archive, the archival, in its materiality, its layeredness, its endless transformations, is a dimension that cities have in common, and that we access by consenting to let go of our familiar reference points in personal and collective time and space.

To construe the city as a language can also be to cast oneself as a kind of philologist, attentive to shifts and slides, bifurcations and compressions. In this vein the archive-city is constructed through the figure of the amateur urban explorer. This is usually someone who devises a project that may look sociological but in fact has less to do with hard knowledge than with encountering hidden dimensions of the city. When he wrote *The People of the Abyss* (1903), his exposé of East End poverty, Jack London boned up on relevant statistical information. But his account of the way he carried out his investigation, with its echoes of De Quincey's and Dickens's forays, and of Charles Booth's notorious mappings of London poverty, takes on a different complexion when he describes the outfit he devised to pass himself off as a typical dosser, and the measures he took in case of emergencies (he rented a safe house to which he could repair after his nights in flea-ridden hostels and had a sovereign sewn into the lining of his carefully distressed jacket). The contemporary French writer François Bon paid homage to Jack London in his own project, recorded in *La Douceur dans l'abîme* (1999). Bon is an exponent of the writing workshop—in prisons, hospital and schools—and a collector of life histories. Invited to run sessions in a shelter for the homeless in the eastern industrial town of Nancy, he made a weekly trip over a period of several months, getting the lost men and women to talk, and capturing their stories in their own words, while the photographer Jérôme Schlomoff worked on their portraits. The project culminated in a live performance featuring the participants and their texts and images. Lives and their histories, including those of the departed and the missing, are one of the city's archives.

In his *Attempt to Exhaust a Parisian Space* (1976) Georges Perec spent three days trying to get down everything he could see in a Paris square, the Place Saint-Sulpice, logging the passage of buses, pedestrians and pigeons, listing, categorizing, classifying, and by this method constituting an archive of the present. In *Roissy-Express* (1990) François Maspero and his companion, the photographer Anaïk Frantz, spent a month on line B of the Paris suburban railway, the RER, devoting a day and a night to each station on the line, checking into a hotel and then going out to talk to the locals and observing their environment. Whilst compiled over three years, Thomas Clerc's book on the French capital's tenth *arrondissement*, entitled *Paris, Museum of the Twenty-first Century* (2007), presents itself as a continuous walk covering each of the district's 155 streets, with observations classified under some 60 rubrics, including 'Site poems', 'Incidents', 'Gestures', and, for architectural monstrosities, 'Should be blown up as soon as possible'. The rubric 'Archive' includes written or illustrated texts and objects encountered in various locales, including a box of CDs spilt on the pavement, a stray page from a film script, a defaced legal notice about a derelict building, and a set of photographs pinned up outside a nursery school commemorating a parent-teacher outing.

These Parisian projects have their counterpart in works on London and its environs, wonderfully scrutinized by Iain Sinclair, including *London Orbital* (2002), and *Hackney, That Rose-Red Empire* (2009), in both of which, like Maspero, Sinclair maintains a productive tension between surface and depth, the subjective and the objective, the past and the present. In *Rodinsky's Room* (1999), Sinclair's collaboration with Rachel Lichtenstein, another kind of balance is struck, between the verbal extravagance of the compulsive fabulist and myth-monger (Sinclair) and the earnest directness of a young woman haunted by her own origins (Lichtenstein). Lichtenstein's chapters, alternating with Sinclair's, build up an antiphonal and eventually polyphonic mosaic of voices, as documents offering potential witness to the fate of a vanished synagogue janitor progressively return to the surface. Like Modiano's *Dora Bruder*, *Rodinsky's Room* is a record of archival journeying, where legwork, ratiocination and the decrypting of traces produce haunting new geographies of places we thought we knew. In *Brick Lane* (2007), Rachel Lichtenstein continues the journey, archiving another stretch of London territory.

Lost in the city, lost in the archive. Benjamin claimed you couldn't know a city until you had lost yourself in it. For the Surrealists the trick was not more control but less: the displacement of purpose by submission to chance, and the invention of protocols to record chance's bounty. Louis Aragon's *Paris Peasant* (1926), to which Benjamin owed so much, archives an arcade that had disappeared by the time the book was published. Aragon does all the voices: archaeologist, private dick, shrink, *homme moyen sensuel*; but it's really all dictation: he takes down what the arcade tells him. Cities change, more quickly than we mortals, as Baudelaire lamented, and the processes through which a city endlessly mutates—planning, unplanning, demolition, infilling, renovation, gentrification, migration: the list needs to be much longer—are the outcome of our industry, but cannot be fully known or stabilized. We change too, and a city's archive comprises shifts in population, economic twists and crashes, and the impact of increasingly global histories. The city is its own archivist, piling 'document' onto 'document'; we have to find ways of being its amanuensis. Benjamin observed that we succumb to the power of the street by 'submitting to the monotonous fascination of the unfurling band of asphalt'. Let us add the poet Jacques Réda to those who have taken this to heart. Inspired by Baudelaire and Borges (transmitter of the 'fervour' of his native Buenos Aires), *The Ruins of Paris* (1977) launched a succession of books in which Réda constantly invents new ways of responding to the messages of the streets. In prose, verse, prose poems, fake guidebooks and faux 'How-to' manuals, the aim is the same: to reach a point where the boot is on the other foot, a state of grace where it is the city that walks the walker, making the archivist a part of its ever-expanding archive.

Reading

Augé, Marc, *In the Metro*, trans. Tom Conley (Minneapolis: University of Minnesota Press, 2002).

Auster, Paul, *New York Trilogy* (Harmondsworth: Penguin, 1987).

Bailly, Jean-Christophe, *La Ville à l'œuvre* (Paris: Jacques Bertoin, 1992).

Benjamin, Walter, *The Arcades Project*, trans. Howard Eiland and Kevin McLaughlin (Harvard: Harvard University Press, 1999).

Bon, François, *La Douceur dans l'Abîme* (Strasbourg: La Nuée bleue, 1999).

Calvino, Italo, *Invisible Cities*, trans. William Weaver (London: Vintage, 1997).

Clerc, Thomas, *Paris, Musée du XXIe siècle: le 10e arrondissement* (Paris: Gallimard, 2007).

Didi-Huberman, Georges, *Ninfa Moderna: essai sur le drapé tombé* (Paris: Gallimard, 2002).

Hugo, Victor, *Les Misérables*, trans. Julie Rose (London: Vintage, 2008).

Klarsfeld, Serge, *Mémorial des enfants juifs deportés de France* (Paris: Klarsfeld Foundation, 1995).

Lichtenstein, Rachel and Iain Sinclair, *Rodinsky's Room* (London: Granta, 1999).

London, Jack, *The People of the Abyss* (London: Pluto, 1998).

Modiano, Patrick, *The Search Warrant*, trans. Joanna Kilmartin (London: Harvill, 2000).

Perec, Georges, *Species of Spaces and Other Places*, trans. John Sturrock (Harmondsworth: Penguin, 1997).

Réda, Jacques, *The Ruins of Paris*, trans. Mark Treharnes (London: Reaktion, 1996).

Roubaud, Jacques, *The Plurality of Worlds of Lewis*, trans. Rosemarie Waldrop (London: Dalkey Archive Press, 1995).

Sebald, W. G., *Austerlitz*, trans. Anthea Bell (London: Hamish Hamilton, 2001).

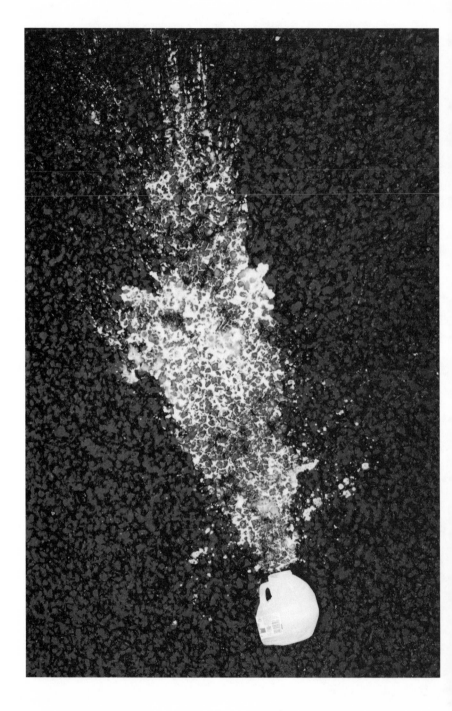

Bombing

Chris Petit

The border of the City of London where I live was flattened in the Second World War by a German V2 rocket landing in Smithfield. This resulted in the post-war construction of Chamberlain, Powell and Bonn's Golden Lane and Barbican estates when the municipal dream was still alive. During the war, architects, with little to do, drew up *The London County Council Bomb Damage Maps 1939–45*, colour-coding individual buildings black for total destruction, purple for beyond repair, right down to yellow for light damage. The beautiful colours and geometry of these maps were in stark contrast to the actual chaos and rubble, but architects dreaming of a modern future saw such wholesale destruction as a saving on demolition costs and slum clearance, making redevelopment inevitable without the usual problems of planning committees.

In the long run English modernism failed, as people grew afraid of the future, preferring renovation and doing up old homes. But modernism's failure was not one of design, rather of maintenance. One need look no further than London's ailing infrastructure to see that the problem of the war was that the Germans didn't bomb enough.

The River Thames made London an easy target from the air, even at night, but the Germans never embraced aerial bombardment with the enthusiasm of the British, perhaps because their army had the war in hand, perhaps because the British, in a series of colonial wars, had already seen what could be achieved. As early as 1924 the future head of Bomber Command Sir Arthur 'Bomber' Harris was advocating the conversion of transport planes into heavy bombers, and, after drop-ping incendiaries on villages in Iraq, noted how fire was more destructive than explosives, a lesson that would result in the annihila-tion of Hamburg and Dresden two decades later. The Germans never developed anything as efficient as the four-engined Lancaster. After 1941 their best efforts were reserved for the Eastern front, leaving them too reliant on scientific gamble and the sort of secret weapons that fed the imaginations of post-war boys' comics. Although the V1 had an unsettling psychological effect, because once the drone of the rocket's engine was heard to stop everyone knew it was over its target, the terror anticipated by the Germans failed to materialize. My mother tells of having received her commission and going to London to collect her WRNS officer's uniform and wearing it for the first time when a V1 cut out over Sloane Square, and she thought she'd be damned if she was going to throw herself in the gutter and ruin her new uniform. Nor was the V1 economical. The project cost the equivalent of 24,000 fighter planes.

The British turned bombing into a comprehensive but futile weapon that failed to break German civilian morale as Harris had predicted it would. A poster from 1943 lists Bomber Command's several hundred raids on German cities, claiming hammer blows to key Nazi industries. The number would increase hugely towards the end of the war when the western Allies introduced round-the-clock bombing. In 1945 Bomber Command flew over 60,000 missions, dropping more than 180,000 tons of bombs, a daily average that was 30 times higher than in 1942. Official talk was of military targets, but area bombing, as practiced by the RAF (the Americans, operating by day, adopted 'precision' bombing), was a war on civilians, to which Churchill put an end only when victory had become inevitable and concern was growing about insufficient accommodation for the victors.

In a neat act of recycling that smacked of poetic justice, the rubble from London's Blitz was transported east to form the core of the wartime runways for the Allied bomber fleets to return the compli-ment. At one stage of the war there was an airfield every eight miles in East Anglia. By 1942 many were being built to accommodate

American B17 Flying Fortresses, a phenomenal construction task requiring miles of runways, hangars, drainage, plumbing, wiring, prefabricated Nissan and Quonset huts, and millions of bricks.

After the first bomb was dropped from a plane in 1911 it was inevitable, given military thinking and the stalemates of the First World War, that the battlefield as a place where representatives of warring nations went to fight would be superseded. War conducted from the air sought out civilians and, by extension, the places where they were gathered in the highest density: cities.

In the 1920s and '30s the British had thought nothing of using aerial bombardment to keep the natives in line. Given the sparse terrain of the colonial Near and Middle East, what needed hitting stood out, but a notable failure occurred in Burma where, in a foretaste of the US experience in Vietnam, bombs proved ineffective in the jungle. In the Second World War both English and Germans brought pigeons home to roost by importing methods previously reserved for business outside Europe. Hitler's attitude to Poland was colonial. By invading he saw his actions as similar to those of Italy, Spain, the United States, Belgium, Holland, France and England during several centuries of territorial expansion. According to F. P. J. Veale in *Advance to Barbarism* (1948), the British public was conned into blaming the Blitz on the Germans, since the first raids had been carried out by the RAF with the aim of inviting reprisals, 'thus keeping alive the British will to fight', which, for Veale, turned the bombing war into an enormous experiment in psychological engineering.

In 1943 the Ministry of Economic Warfare issued *The Bomber's Baedeker: Guide to the Economic Importance of German Towns and Cities*, with a second edition in 1944, listing the most important economic targets of the Third Reich in terms of spatial distribution and priority targets, very often located in areas of residential density. What started on the part of the RAF as an inability to hit anything of significance had by 1943 developed into a pervasive technology: cities became targets because they were there. Given the difficulty of sighting at night, and in blackout, let alone hitting anything, the RAF broadened its scope, aiming to fulfil Harris's vision of whole cities in flames. Harris, a literal, coarse man, regarded himself as an agent of justice and retribution. To him the July 1943 firestorms of Hamburg were just desserts, justifying the operation's code name, Gomorrah. The firestorms, helped by climactic conditions, were no fluke. Tests had been conducted on replica German houses, down to the contents of an average attic, to find out what burned best. (The Americans would have an easier time with Japanese houses because they were so highly combustible.) German cities of the oldest heritage were most at risk, with their crowded, wooden medieval centres. In Hamburg the munitions were unloaded in 43 minutes, followed by what Jorg Friedrich in *The Fire* (2006) described as 'atmospheric reactions that raged for three hours with the force of a Pacific hurricane' and left 40,000 dead. There was talk afterwards among the Allies of the Hamburgization of Berlin, except that Berlin refused to burn, 'honey-combed' as it was (according to Friedrich), 'with parapeted firewalls'. Fire insurance maps were consulted to no avail.

The bombing war was argued in technocratic terms, as a series of practical solutions, to distract from wider moral issues. Scruples, or LMF (lack of moral fibre) were dealt with harshly by the RAF, whereas the Nazis, by contrast, excused without punishment those who had no stomach for their extermination programme. The British bombing war and German mass murders started as ramshackle affairs but ended as huge killing machines. The German situation was pre-meditated, the British one reactive and counter-tactical, but there were uncomfortable overlaps. Freeman Dyson, a leading nuclear physicist after the war, and before that a civilian operations analyst in Harris's office (which gave him access to information on civilian bombing kept from the public), later compared himself to the German organizers of mass extermination. 'They had sat in their offices, writing memoranda and calculating how to murder people efficiently, just like me. The main difference was that they were sent to jail or hanged as war criminals, while I went free.'

The first shock of Auschwitz is its location. The original camp, where the gassing was first done, is not hidden away as you might expect, but on the town's ring road, where a retail park might be today. As for the camp itself, the shock is one of institutional familiarity, an unsettling combination of the uncanny and the homely, an association that the Nazis were to play on, in their heavy-handed way, with their wrought-iron mottos, flower beds, and the camp orchestra sending labour gangs off to work. What struck me most about this original camp, as opposed to the adjacent Birkenau with its familiar tower and rail tracks, was how the regulation brick buildings and wide paths don't even look much like the concentration camp of collective imagination (previously it had been a Polish barracks). Even more remarkable was the self-conscious pretence at ordinariness, sentimentality even, in the artless Teutonic numerals painted on the domestic-looking lanterns hanging outside each barracks' door, as though these vernacular details might persuade the perpetrators that what they were doing was either useful or normal. Primo Levi made the same point, writing that it was important to look back at these camps not as hellish zones where all signposts had been lost but as grotesque extensions of recognisable institutions, the lesson being that the familiar is what we should fear most because the gap between genocide and the ordinary is not a great one, and can and will be accommodated, as history continues to show.

In her exemplary book *Auschwitz* (2005), Sybille Steinbacher shows how much attention was paid to German leisure and well-being. It was a family posting notable for its modern comforts, educational facilities and medical care. Travelling players put on shows in the theatre inside the camp grounds: popular farces, and a generic evening under the title *Attack of the Comics*, as well as classics such as the Dresden State Theatre's presentation in February 1943 of *Goethe Then and Now*. This domestic peace 'did not contradict the professional everyday life of the SS members', Steinbacher notes. It may have contributed to their psychological stability, as shown by the Solahutte photographs taken of camp staff relaxing at a nearby leave centre, with no shadow of doubt in evidence, just randiness, certainty of gesture and amiable mugging to the camera.

Prefabricated wartime architecture finds a successor in the new shed estates and their adjuncts, the industrial zone and retail park. These are usually located in a similar flat and featureless terrain, occupying hinterlands that are neither urban, suburban nor rural and far from anything picturesque that might block planning permission. These non-residential estates function as displaced satellite hubs, making cities, of which they are an expansion, redundant, and they represent the sort of non-space in which so much contemporary life happens. For an advanced school of writers and philosophers that includes J. G. Ballard and Paul Virilio, this supermodernity reduces the city to a shell, invaded by new forms of tribalism, of which financial hooliganism is one example, no longer a measure of civilization but an invitation to apocalypse. 'A few atrophied cities pride themselves on being the epicentre of the world,' Virilio writes in *City of Panic* (2004), 'when they are merely lost citadels—in other words, targets, for firestorms!'

In the new age of terror public buildings grow more withdrawn and harder to read. Where a bank once looked like a temple to money and a cinema a palace of dreams, many buildings now are purely telecommunications centres, independent of location or geography. In *Terminal Architecture* (1998), Martin Pawley acknowledges a purity of design in this new style, very different from the grandiosity of conventional building, and the antithesis of heritage architecture. In the terminology of the immigration officer it is 'undocumented' construction, he notes, and no novelist or filmmaker has explored beneath its surface. The ultimate in anti-heritage is the concentration camp, a throwaway city which brings to mind its soft opposite, the contemporary shopping mall, in that camp and mall are all about the processing (and exclusion) of people and require similar minds for their design.

There is a bizarre, little-remarked footnote to Auschwitz. At the same time that the exterminations were in full swing, a plan was drawn up to turn the town into the equivalent of a yuppie settlement for young pioneers of the expanded Reich and a focal point for the new empire. The empire was mythologized in the same way that the Wild West had been in German popular fiction, with the Nazis romanticizing Poland as their version of the American frontier, a frontier to which they would bring the cultivated green of Germany, taming the landscape as well as subjugating the natives. There were degrees of pathos and self-pity, as with any myth, and the Germans were good at persuading themselves of the toughness of their task, but to speak of Indians in the context of the 'wild east' was already to contemplate extermination.

Planning permission for the redevelopment of Auschwitz was hurried through. Berlin committees channelled funds into the project. A civilian town planner and party member, Dr Hans Stosberg, was employed on site to execute drawings. His vision included 12 schools, 6 kindergartens, 20 playing fields and the removal of the Jewish cemetery to make way for a Nazi Party building with a hotel, cinema and restaurant. Stosberg's New Year's card for 1942 sent greetings from the birthplace of a new German town.

Stosberg's plans for the new Auschwitz are cautious and uninspired, perhaps in deference to Reichsführer Himmler's active interest. Nevertheless, one senses individual ambition, pride of purpose and a plum assignment, green-lit despite wartime restrictions. The I. G. Farben conglomerate, which was responsible for the labour plant in nearby Monowitz, paid for the urbanization of the residential town. This would form part of the Neue Heimat (New Homeland) and be designed to a high spec, with mod cons including central heating and hot water, gardens, garages, domestic gas and laundry rooms.

Also consulted was Heinrich Wiepking-Jürgensmann, a landscape designer from Berlin, who after the war became a conservationist of international repute. Civilian planners argued with the SS over the amount of sewage the camps were discharging into the local river because of Birkenau's inadequate latrine facilities. The ever green Himmler approved the construction of a sewage plant. The two sides clashed further over SS plans for family quarters to be built outside the camp. Their rustic look was deemed inappropriate to the larger design. The argument went all the way back to Berlin where committees decided in favour of the planners. But a proposal to relocate the camp, for reasons of landscape design, to a more appropriate setting where it would fit less 'inorganically' with its surroundings, was rejected.

Several hundred apartments, built as part of the IG staff estate, survive, but when it became clear the Auschwitz project was never going to happen, Stosberg was drafted into the army, survived, and returned home safely, his war work and party membership no hindrance to a distinguished later career. He and Wiepking-Jürgensmann ended up in Hanover where Stosberg was hired by another former party member, Rudolf Hillebrecht, who had been taken on by the British in 1946 to work on a reconstruction law. Stosberg was employed to help redesign Hanover as a modern garden city. By 1944 Bomber Command's 125 strikes had so levelled the city that the authorities briefly considered abandoning it and rebuilding elsewhere. Such was the destruction, notes *The Fire*, that Hanover before and Hanover after had nothing in common except a name and a location.

In *On the Natural History of Destruction* (2003), the Anglo-German writer W. G. Sebald claimed that ordinary Germans suppressed the trauma of the bombings, which went unmentioned except in the broadest clichés: 'The night Hell came to Dresden', etc. But he's wrong, as shown by the forensically accurate testimonies of the citizens of Darmstadt, which are reproduced in Max Hastings's *Bomber Command* (1979). Sebald ought to have known better because he included the Hastings book in his bibliography, but such direct accounts didn't fit his thesis of general amnesia. More accurate is

Virilio's contention that the twentieth century was one of disappearances, culminating in the demolition of the twin towers, an act that imploded capitalism, terrorism and, if Stockhausen's thesis is accepted, art: a perfect loop of endless repetition. And that trick was followed by the one of disappearing weapons of mass destruction.

Her first email
How wonderful to hear from you! A big surprise, really. The email address is totally correct. I still live in Berlin and do a lot of lectures. What about you?

Virilio's strangely gleeful *City of Panic*, provoked by the re-emergence of fundamentalism, marks a return of the biblical where the city is no longer the open metropolis of the *flâneur* but has reverted to the city-state of old, and the deserts of biblical history play host to the latest battle zones. In the last years of the prophecies of Nostradamus, it's hard not to be superstitious, hard too sometimes not to snigger at Virilio's doomsday-mongering, except that writing five years before the event he did note 'the anguished wait for the great accident, this GLOBAL CRASH that won't fail to occur one of these days'.

I watched Werner Herzog's semi-documentary *Fata Morgana* (1969) recently, another perfect, po-faced essay on the absurd: desert tracking shots, a sense of vanished cities, mirage, comic futility and the strangest couple, wearing sand goggles, hammering out tinny tunes on a piano and drum kit in an oasis brothel. A landscape in parallel to the crash: the crumbling sands that await all cities.

Second email
Did you know AC/DC only ever has number one hits in times of recession?

Dry stats, prosaic government, media consensus, technology and spin suggest Orwell and Huxley when a gothic reading better suits. For the English, twentieth-century gothic expressed itself in Hammer horror films and the renaissance of the romantic dandy in mass entertainment, while German twentieth-century history reads like a demented merger of the technological and the occult. The 'economic miracle' spawned German terrorism, whose revolt against bourgeois denial seemed motivated by the same underdog romanticism as Hitler's. Rainer Werner Fassbinder's middle-class satires *Chinese Roulette* (1976) and *The Bitter Tears of Petra von Kant* (1972), seem best read as gothic. (Poe, accused of plagiarism, replied: 'Terror is not of Germany but of the soul.') English gothic sadism didn't result in an equivalent to German genocide because the impulse was diluted by running an empire and by a robust democratic tradition that confined the perverse to art, architecture, public schools and the brothel.

But of course genocide was part of the English colonial equation (and others) as Lindqvist's *Exterminate All the Brutes* (1997) has shown, as was the concentration camp, whose invention is attributed to the British during the Boer War. The point was it all took place many miles from home: a pattern of land seizure and expulsion followed by the elimination of native races, a process endorsed by the latest intellectual thinking, which helped launder the whole business, as did the tyranny of distance.

Third email
In Germany we never suffered your belief in the never-ending value of property. I am rereading the greatest book by a Scottish writer about money, called *Frozen Desire*, which tells how the governor of the Bank of England had a vision in 1996, staring out of his office window. If the price level in London could be compared to the height of water in the Thames then this inflationary river, which was at 8 feet in 1800, and 10 feet in 1945, had risen to 200 feet by 1996.

The crash showed chaos as the underlying organizing principle of the modern world, with the US economy nearly as fucked as the old Soviet one, and the Chinese placed to take over, because of their enormous resources, their ability to graft previously irreconcilable systems, and because they tend to thrive in that domain of chaos where Western thinking fails.

Fourth email
I heard about a woman who does a lot of driving, alone and for her husband who doesn't drive. When on her own behind the wheel she finds she goes into a trance and loses all sense of direction and when she comes to her senses she is miles from home in places she doesn't recognize.

In an electronic 24-hour global market, previous regulations of time and space are replaced by instant states, instant panic and instant emergency, with the tactical emphasis on the pre-emptive strike. Virilio sees no distinction between the money market and the theatre of war. The same point was grasped by George Orwell in *1984* when he predicted a world of permanent wars fought elsewhere, served up as spectacles for a jaded populace:

> The audience [was] much amused by shots of a great huge fat man trying to swim away with a helicopter after him; first you saw him wallowing along in the water like a porpoise, then you saw him through the helicopter's gun sights, then he was full of holes and the sea around him turned pink and he sank as suddenly as though the holes had let in the water, [the] audience shouting with laughter when he sank.

Acceleration in time means there is no longer a messenger left to shoot.

Fifth email
I have to prepare a lecture on money and landscape, about the links between romanticism and money. Georg Simmel first noticed that romanticism was an extension of an urban sensibility as it required money, was a predecessor to tourism, involved going to another place, and was the discovery of townies, not a rural movement. The interesting thing about now is how to learn to be more imaginative with money, and I don't mean investing in art.

According to a survey, many Americans think they are living outside history (insufficient geography). Virilio's futurecity, a phantom one without limits and laws, can be seen in the US TV series on Los Angeles police corruption, *The Shield* (2002–8): lawless, gang-crazy, tribal, with drug wars and fabulous corruption, an invaded world gone loco, but remaining colonial in essence. It recalls Conrad: 'an inconceivable life of stress, of power, of endeavour, of unbelief—the strong life of white men, which rolls on irresistible and hard on the edge of outer darkness'.

Totalitarianism segues into globalization. Eco-politics is the psychology of the Cold War relocated. Foreclosure and exclusion become key words; Virilio identifies a 'panicky delinquency that is dragging the human race back to the original dance of death'. Hee-haw! Counter-movements exist between large blocs and neo-medieval pockets, technology versus superstition, consumption versus a need for terror. On the phenomenon of urban gangs, Virilio notes the replacing of solitary crime by social group crimes, what he calls 'camp crimes', that reproduce, on a smaller scale, those of the gulags and death camps, 'where the concentration of whole populations preceded their extermination'.

Sixth email

A lot of thought goes into the psychology of supermarkets, such as putting the fresh stuff first. US supermarkets have a fake new-bread smell (just as there's an aerosol new-car smell). Big supermarkets and malls are designed to eliminate conflict and make the shopper obedient. I am amazed at how well people behave, but in such a controlled environment it's almost impossible not to. I read that over 90% of food sold in the US is processed, which says a lot about the mess they are in.

After the cramped, scabby Safeway in the Kilburn High Road, what a treat to be able to drive out to the huge new parking aprons and luxurious aisles of Tesco, Brent Park. (This would have been in the mid-1980s.) Like a lot of the early giants it made an effort to present itself as part of a 'community', with a colonnaded walkway as an introduction to a diluted parody of the idea of a country estate, with shrubbery and drive, suggesting grocery shopping as an upmarket activity. A year or so later the big change came with the arrival of IKEA next door. Box. Big blue box. Very clever and unsentimental.

I have always preferred a good industrial estate to a landed one. Perhaps my liking for these boxes is nostalgia for a military childhood, where buildings did a job. Army barracks had a sense of exact narrative. It is interesting to note how the British army in Afghanistan has adopted the storage container as the basic unit of accommodation.

Seventh email
You hate supermarkets really. You are just looking for an original argument.

I hadn't realized until reading about it how supermarkets genetically modify vegetables to conform to size and how much they hate difference. How long before supermarkets genetically modify the shopper?

What irritates me about buying off the internet is being told: now you've bought that, you might like to buy this. It's depressing how often they get it right, enough to make me worry that I am entirely predictable.

Eighth email
In 1984 everything in the German press suggested England was still in recession when London was about to turn into a wide-open boom town. Berlin still had its wall, which many of us miss because, contrary to the image of somewhere besieged, it was a privileged and heavily subsidized enclave, given to congenial hedonism. In every other city there came a point when you got told to go home, in England earliest of all. Once we stayed up all night in some window-less Kreuzberg bar drinking black coffee and vodka, and when someone opened the door and walked in you thought the daylight outside was the nuclear flash.

Financial blitz, the market 'bombed'. Experts upbraided, world in denial. 'And so they all, each in his own way, reflecting or unreflecting, go on with their daily lives; everything seems to take its accustomed course, for indeed, even in these desperate situations where everything hangs in the balance, one goes on living as though nothing were wrong' (Goethe).

Ninth email
I am not convinced.

Driving as a double projection: flight from a past (life in the rear-view mirror), voyage into an unknown; a car full of disembodied voices: bad news, disappearances, tumbling markets, collapsed spending. Suicide cars, ghost bikes, roadside shrines, roadkill, greasy verges, light-spill of nocturnal traffic. Gas stations at twilight. Smokers' lungs. Night-time motorways like rivers of molten gold, a sight to lift the heart of an old conquistador. Driving in the dark, like all those economists were doing for years.

The headiness of recession.

Shopping malls are boredom's cathedral: boredom underpins consumerism; defines leisure (and desire), which collapses into shopping; boredom invites terror (as its only cure). In Lars Svendsen's *A Philosophy of Boredom* (2005): 'Boredom has to be accepted as unavoidable fact, as life's own gravity. There's no grand solution, because the problem of boredom has none.' Erich Fromm in the 1950s: the bored compensate for anxiety and depression by compulsive consumption.

Tenth email
Whatever you think of her, it took Mrs Thatcher to dismantle a wartime economy that had left the country with decades of debt. Germany by contrast got a clean slate in 1945, which resulted in the economic miracle, meaning that you all got to drive solid German machines instead of Minis that stopped every time you drove over a puddle. The example of British Leyland was important, bailed out against the wishes of Mrs Thatcher, who on that occasion was forced to bow to unions and party. What car do you drive now?

Driving triggers memories of other journeys: London, Berlin and the vast Düsseldorf conurbation to which we now all belong, along with the universal BMW/Mercedes/VW concession. Driving as argument between movement (refusal to commit to view) and static lock-off (refusal to narrate). Westway and the Berlin Wall: essays in concrete. London's outer orbital, going nowhere, versus Berlin's slick inner motorway circuit, a former race track. Le Corbusier: A city built for speed is a city built for modernity.

Eleventh email
Point proved.

The central dilemma of German Romanticism was home versus away, spiritual homesickness and the heart's restlessness. The present German craving for travel has been attributed to collective uprooting caused by wartime devastation. In *On the Natural History of Destruction* Sebald writes:

> In terms of social conditioning, this would make the ebb and flow of the population bombed out of their homes rather like a rehearsal for initiation into the mobile society that would form in the decades after the catastrophe. Under the auspices of that society, chronic restlessness became a cardinal virtue.

Twelfth email
On the changing inner London landscape of the 1980s—the gyms, fancy restaurants, mineral water, power dressing—that wasn't the English. It was the 1986 Financial Services Act which deregulated the City and opened it up to the Americans, Japanese and Germans. Everyone remembers the miners' strike but Mrs Thatcher also broke the union in the City, allowing for foreign influx and the big changes in money, attitude and opportunities that followed. These incomers started the mineral water craze and the lunchtime jogging because before that City boys got drunk for lunch.

Thomas Mann was first to note how life in the 1920s became increasingly manipulated and deceitful through a combination of economic inflation and the rise of mass communications. Fromm remarked of post-war US society that emotional necrophilia was a feature of a lifeless culture, as currently shown by the TV series *Mad Men* (2007–).

Thirteenth email
Disposable income, business expenses, restaurants, drugs and purchased sex.

The creation of the Groucho Club in 1985 changed the social landscape of London, marking the rise of the mediaocracy. Everything became more exclusive and synonymous with cocaine. Westminster Council allowing drinking on pavements changed Soho from indoor sleaze to café society. Old Compton Street became formally gay. The opening of the River Café in 1987 cemented the architecture/cuisine axis, marking the Rogerization of London and the start of celebrity TV chefs, of which there are now far too many, ditto comedians and architects.

Fourteenth email
A direct consequence of the first wave of capitalism in Eastern Europe after communism was a huge increase in sex trading. 1992 marked the first peak in the supply of Slavic women to Western Europe. Prostitution joined the boom when it was treated as an extension of the entertainment industry, as rich young City types (and some not so young) looked for novel ways to spend their inflated salaries. It became fashionable to pay for sex as though it was just another financial transaction.

Humans as intermediaries for technology, moving beyond the stage dramatized in Marc Augé's *Non-Places* (1995) ('On his way to his car Pierre Dupont stopped at the cash dispenser to draw some money'): built-in redundancy, abandoned narrative, the superfluous protagonist, coagulated consumerism, the last gasp of the petrol age, futility of movement. Spaces define us rather than the other way round. In the ubiquity of image overload, sound stays relatively private: eavesdropped conversations the aural equivalent of voyeurism.

In any financial scandal, there comes a point where the money doesn't exist.

Where is money now in art terms: cubism, post-impressionism or abstract expressionism? Did everything get dumbed down except money, which grew a mind of its own? Is the financial situation viral? Typewriters didn't catch colds. Funny how, just as we were supposed to get the big picture, it all fell apart and we moved from a world we thought we understood to one we didn't, except for the money bandits in Russia who went back to basics: land grab.

Fifteenth email
Student scientific clubs were allowed to organize beauty contests and pop concerts; many of those in the beauty contests found themselves sold into prostitution. Profits generated by currency exchange were used to fund the first computer revolution. Russia may have had no money but it was rich in natural resources and that made the oligarchs so rich.

Sixteenth email
An excess of speculative risk is characteristic of times of great change and uncertainty.

If law was the profession of the twentieth century, banking, as characterized by the deregulated market, succeeded it. The big change came in the recession of the early 1990s with the culling of the old-style bank manager, pillar of the community, symbol of caution and probity, who was succeeded by the advent of faceless, risky banking.

Words specific to now: 'security', away from the solid and reassuring towards control; 'container' without which there would have been no globalization. There are hotels now made of containers because container traffic is mainly east–west, with a surplus here because there's nothing to send back now the Chinese make everything. 'Traffic' is another of those words. When did fuck-you money first get called that?

Seventeenth email
English politicians have become more American, London a suburb of New York. UK tax breaks for foreigners make it the preferred residence of Russian oligarchs (cf. Loretta Napoleoni, *Rogue Economics*, 2008). New Labour was about enriching a small élite.

In a world of redrawn boundaries and mass migration, it's big business getting rid of deportees, a fee of two thousand pounds per head; an ex-copper, previously done for murder, ran a very lucrative business, sub-contracted by the Home Office, which was unaware of his record.

Sound of helicopters over the city: that's new.

Eighteenth email
You ask which came first, the giant supermarkets or the XXL people. The XXL people are a product of the giant supermarkets because they sell junk. Food becomes not about what you can carry but how much you can load in a car.

A German friend has embarked on an affair but talks fondly of his family in a way that suggests such betrayals are manageable. Niceness and absence of confrontation are how he ignores his marriage. Plus the distractions of music, films, exercise and a vigorous social life; sexual alertness softened by an unthreatening manner. He doesn't suffer anxiety. He is impractical, which is his way of not engaging with an adult world (though he is no longer young). Behind the adultery, a secret money life, the sly capitalist.

Nineteenth email
I'm not sure what the present state of guilt is in Germany. We had the DDR guilty/not guilty. So whoever is from the East doesn't feel guilty. We had Baader-Meinhof. Whoever was leftist, anti-Israel, anti-US doesn't feel guilty. Then we had the Hitler movie with Bruno Ganz and whoever saw that doesn't feel guilty anymore. Google German guilt.

Proposed TV channels: the madness channel, animal disease channel, overheated old-aged homes channel, death's waiting room channel, oxygen mask channel, struggle for breath channel, rebellious body channel, irritable bowel channel, rogue headache channel, aches and pains channel, bad back channel; next month they're sticking a camera up my arse channel; the shocking facts of sex slavery channel;

indigenous borders channel; lonely priests with wavering vocations channel; genocide channel; pointlessness of death channel; and channels devoted to denial, ritual and consumption compounding that denial (hang on, we've already got those).

Deregulation of television: an audio-visual Allied Carpets. New technology equals cost-cutting, assembly rather than editing, reduced from a fine art to keyboard skills, with executives able to stick their oar in more: can we see it this way now? Rhythm, as understood by those who had cut celluloid, went out of the window. Television became about shifting units and marketing. The BBC has become a commercial channel in all but name. The old model—Auntie—was generally understood: BBC1 entertainment, BBC2 more quality, with a sense of obligation on the part of the broadcaster. No one has the slightest interest in content now.

Twentieth email

There was a short film called the *The Pity Card* about a young American Jew who goes to the Holocaust museum with a blonde girl. She doesn't know about the Holocaust which is how he seduces her then feels guilty afterwards. If you look at *German Popstars*, you can see that we've arrived at a pretty multicultural society. I'm more worried that in this crisis former DDR politicians will become important again since they really believe in Marx. Yesterday I saw a TV documentary about the sperm and genetic labs in the US, which seems to be a number one export business (sperm from blond and blue-eyed Americans to South America, for instance) and the film had these recurring images of motorways, traffic and even concrete bridges, mostly shot at night. I don't know what association they wanted but it reminded me totally of your 30-year key word 'traffic'. The car lights had what are considered those bad video flares but it really was quite well done.

Rush-hour City faces, an echo of Robert Frank's photographs. Fainter echoes elsewhere of the first cinema: Islington canal and factory workers at the gate. But what factory now? In the maw of a trash culture: dead TV, rubbish, recycling. A society kept afloat by celebrity dirigibles and overheated economies. City tricksters. Magicians of the market. O and A. Oral and anal. Internet porn. Page Three Girls with native intelligence (knowing there's a gap but not sure what's in it). The mother in a supermarket who loses her child, found later in the toilet with two Dutch women, dyeing the kiddie's hair in a basin.

Things that fall from the sky: bombs, rain, stock-market crashes with those downward arrows on television news that look like critical weather fronts. Market as financial warfare: the City took another pasting today. After work, braying idiots the last customers in empty restaurants. White men dancing: tango classes, salsa! Never trust a man who doesn't dance. L. F. Céline wrote that most of us would put our hands in the till, given half a chance. Boom as licensed banditry. Soon we'll be as good as the Italians at corruption, as England becomes more Roman Catholic, in paraphernalia if not in belief: the idolatry of Diana contributing to the conquest of traditional reserve by tastelessness: 'Candle in the Wind'. Thirty years ago, I would have been amazed that anyone in the future might be interested in a film about the queen.

Twenty-first email
For me it was 80/81 with Boy George, Ronald Reagan and the rise of the ayatollahs. But since my view of history is cyclical we might just be on the other side of the cycle. Something just ended and something new is beginning. I liked your story of the woman having an email affair with a man, not realizing that the man's wife was answering the emails.

Spin was inseparable from New Labour, that most metropolitan of governments, ruled by Scots who, in the grip of the millennial twitch, brought their own brand of paranoia to the table and the self-devouring intrigue of Jacobean revenge drama. Spin was the negative of the growing addiction to positive thinking, itself a product of the depoliticization that turned the party system into a hall of mirrors. Blair copied Thatcher just as Cameron copies Blair, his leadership manifesto full of the same neat triangulations. With the coercion of government by management style, the methods of advertising and marketing become ubiquitous: Team fucking Britain, UK plc.

The London building boom of the 1980s was marked by an abandonment of brick for steel, glass and marble cladding. Postmodern playfulness is aging worse than most architectural fads. Canary Wharf was Michael Heseltine's baby, flogged in telly ads at reduced rates by actor/singer Adam Faith who had played TV's Budgie, strongly suggesting a dodgy provenance. In 1980 the vandal Heseltine had allowed the destruction of the art deco Firestone factory on the Great West Road, designed by Wallis Gilbert, responsible for the similar landmark Hoover factory on Western Avenue, which became a Tesco. The coming of Canary Wharf and stockmarket deregulation marked the liberation of capital and The Capital, as the city shifted east on its axis with the start of the moneygrab. Not long before, in the 1970s, there had been talk of an armybacked coup to overthrow the government, which is impossible to imagine now.

Twenty-second email
What do you propose? I am quite flexible.

Speaking of restlessness, I have moved something like 15 or 16 times since coming to London in 1971. In 1978 I sold Flat 4, 80 Gloucester Avenue, NW1 for £23,000, having bought it in 1975 for twelve, having just reached the salary scale of £3000 per annum required to be mortgage-eligible. The man who sold me Gloucester Avenue tripled his money, having bought for four, so figures were already climbing. In 1975 he bought a house in Hampstead (where he still lives) for £35,000. The house I bought in 1978 at 21 Streatley Road, Kilburn for £27,500 sold seven years later for over a hundred, a sum that seemed ridiculous then. Before the war it hadn't been unusual for houses to exchange hands for a few hundred pounds. In the 1970s Kilburn was Irish and republican; if you walked into Biddy Mulligan's with an English accent you were told to fuck off. At the height of the recent property boom houses in Streatley Road were worth three-quarters of a million quid (and you still wouldn't want to live there).

When I last looked, the Black Lion, where the IRA used to pass a money tin around, was a gastro pub run by middle Europeans.

Twenty-third email
That's a shame. Can you still come when the weather improves?

Reading

Augé, Marc, *Non-Places: An Introduction to Supermodernity*, (London: Verso, 2009).

Buchan, James, *Frozen Desire* (London: Picador, 1997).

Friedrich, Jörg, *The Fire: The Bombing of Germany 1940–1945* (New York: Columbia University Press, 2006).

Hastings, Max, *Bomber Command* (London: Pan Books, 1979).

Lindqvist, Sven, *Exterminate All the Brutes* (London: Granta Books, 1997).

Lindqvist, Sven, *A History of Bombing* (London: Granta Books, 2001).

Napoleoni, Loretta, *Rogue Economics* (London: Seven Stories Press, 2008).

Sebald, W. G., *On the Natural History of Destruction* (London: Hamish Hamilton, 2003).

Steinbacher, Sybille, *Auschwitz: A History* (Harmondsworth: Penguin, 2005).

Virilio, Paul, *City of Panic* (Oxford: Berg, 2005).

Commuting

Rachel Bowlby

In Tennyson's poem 'Tithonus', the beautiful dawn goddess Aurora is addressed by her ancient human husband, who never gets a proper chance to talk to her. When he is trying to get her to answer a crucial question, she rises and departs for her day. Later she comes home, 'returning on thy silver wheels', as the narrator puts it, in the final line of the poem. Aurora is the original and eternal commuter. She has been doing it forever and she will carry on doing it for the foreseeable. There was never a time when she was not already getting up early and returning late, on a daily basis, and without any weekends or holidays.

For transient human beings, though, commuting is quite a new mode of existence, one whose possibility was just beginning to appear during Tennyson's lifetime. In the mention of those 'silver wheels' on which Aurora returns, there may be already a flickering sense of this strange new way of daily life that the nineteenth century had begun to set in motion. It was the railways, along with the growth of suburbs around the new stations down the lines that led to the birth of the modern commuter.

By the next century, appointments diaries would be marking for each day the ever-changing times of sunrise and sunset: even Aurora's daily journey had been modernized in line with the new developments, appearing now with the printed precision and fixity of a train timetable. When you commute, you find that you have a sort of ticking consciousness at either end of the day. As it approaches, the exact time of each train is loomingly there in the sidings of your mind. Do you want to get this one? Go now! When you are still at work in the late afternoon, you can't help being aware when the last moment has passed for getting the 17.15, the 18.00, the 18.50 ... and you bear in mind the usefully short 25-minute space between the 18.50 and the 19.15, just before the full hour's gap that precedes the 20.15 (so you can risk missing the 18.50, but not the 19.15). Then there's the surprising reversion, just the once, to a convenient half-hour window, after which the evening settles down into three straight hours (20.45, 21.45, 22.45). Commuters are also, can't help it, computers, constantly counting the minutes. This can be boring. But then, a final flourish of seemingly random perversity, the last train at 23.37. (The last train is more like a party that's lost its energy. Most of the guests are half asleep and the ticket collector, a caring butler, politely asks you your station; he will come and wake you up.)

Commuting is partly marked by its rigid times but perhaps more fundamentally it is about the distance between two places, one work, one home. Aurora is not a classic commuter in this sense, because although she leaves home each morning to go to work, her work is en route, indeed her work *is* her route, and the only place she arrives is back home again. The separation of home and workplace, in symbolic as well as topographical ways, takes root with the industrial revolution: no one lives in a factory, or would want to, and the home to which the worker returns carries an emotional weight of comfort and sustenance in contrast to the fatiguing and soulless site of labour. From this it is only a small step to the identification of a divided or at least a twofold self, one that changes from one place to the other, from one time to the other: the very word 'commuting' appears to have mutation and even mutability at its heart. (In fact, its origin is in the nineteenth-century railroad 'commutation ticket', the American equivalent of a season ticket, in which one payment was substituted or changed for a number of individual payments for tickets.) In the nineteenth century it is the office worker who, more likely than the factory worker to live some way from the workplace, comes to epitomise a separation between domestic and professional personalities.

It might be thought that the home body is always experienced as the authentic one, as against the falseness of the working identity, but that is not quite the case. For the very fact that one is now two, even if one seems more real than the other, closer to home, has the effect of giving the real self its own form of artificiality: it is a real self, seen as such, only in so far as it is not the less real self that it might be or that it daily commutes itself into becoming. This is already clear in Dickens's novel *Great Expectations* (1861), which has a loving portrait of someone who may well be the first commuter in literature.

Mr Wemmick works as a clerk to Mr Jaggers, the criminal lawyer, and spends his days dealing with the numerous unsavoury clients who want to secure his boss's protection. An invitation to the novel's central character, Pip, to stay overnight at Wemmick's home—what he calls his Castle—provides the occasion for a full description of Wemmick's alternating and beautifully ordered double existence. 'The office is one thing, and private life is another', he explains, as if giving a capsule advance version of the ideology that would come to seem natural for twentieth-century urban and suburban man. He continues: 'When I go into the office, I leave the Castle behind me, and when I come into the Castle, I leave the office behind me.' Home consists of a mock castle, a 'crazy little box of a cottage', all fitted up with a miniature moat and drawbridge and a gun, the Stinger, which is fired at precisely nine o'clock every night, 'Greenwich time'. There is a water feature, also a vegetable patch and a number of small farm animals, so that in time of need the household could be self-sufficient. Indoors there is a 'collection of curiosities', a tiny 'museum', for Pip to examine, and there is also an 'aged parent', the much loved father who is full of admiration for the person addressed only here as John: 'This is a fine place of my son's.' There is 'a neat little girl in attendance' and also another regular female visitor, so that by the end of the novel there will be a wedding, and thus a wife to complete the picture of domestic perfection.

Halfway between Robinson Crusoe and B&Q Man, Wemmick has in effect constructed his castle and all its wealth of features himself: 'I am my own engineer, and my own carpenter, and my own plumber, and my own gardener, and my own Jack of all Trades.' Wemmick's home life as king of his castle, away from 'the office', is marked as the seat of his true affections and pleasures, but at the same time, and without any contradiction, it is an elaborate performance and display, complete with its own museum and its daily staging of a perfectly ordered pseudo-medieval life. The real identity is consciously invented and enjoyed as such; it is Wemmick himself who states, indeed insists upon, the difference of home and office, and also the dynamic role of home not just as a place on its own, a first place or starting point, but as a regular means of ridding oneself of the dirt that in his case arises both from the city and, metaphorically, from the job: 'It brushes the Newgate cobwebs away.'

With this radical contrast in mind, the journey to and from work takes on the role of a symbolic transition, bringing about the daily transformations, in each direction, of the commuting clerk. In the morning Wemmick is up early to clean the boots, do a spot of gardening, and enjoy his breakfast. But then,

> at half-past eight precisely we started for Little Britain. By degrees, Wemmick got dryer and harder as we went along, and his mouth tightened into a post-office again. At last, when we got to his place of business ... he looked as unconscious of his Walworth property as if the Castle and the drawbridge and the arbour and the lake and the fountain and the Aged, had all been blown into space together by the last discharge of the Stinger.

The commuting change is both gradual, 'by degrees', and absolute, so that by the time Wemmick enters the office it is as if the other life he has come from really was just a castle in the air, the figment of an imagination the professional Wemmick lacks. It is now the office which is, in that other sense, the real world, the daily grind, and the rest is fantasy—or rather the rest, as fantasy, must be put asunder, put at a proper mental and geographical distance, for the duration of the working day.

At home Wemmick is a self-made and self-making man; at work he takes orders. This aspect of the commuting alternation, between autonomy and servitude, is closely related to another contrast. Walworth is Wemmick's rural 'retreat' and the office is at the centre of urban crime and grime. The oppositions between the country and the city, and between work and retiring from it, are ancient ones, already enshrined in a long tradition of pastoral poetry. But before the late nineteenth century, its real-life embodiment is most often the privilege of wealth, with the slow, seasonal journeyings between the country place and the house in town. Modern commuting democratizes this division into a matter of commonplace everyday or weekly experience. Even if it is really in the suburbs, like Wemmick's castle, the domestic point of return is the place where a green tranquillity can be restored or created, the place where the office worker is master of his own hours and his own space.

With Dickens's Wemmick, the proto-commuter is a figure of affectionate comedy with his harmless and entirely successful achievement of domestic bliss, the perfect work–life balance. But as the train travels across the boundary into the twentieth century, the commuter seems to lose the possibility of eccentricity or any kind of difference from the next man. The conventional image of the commuter in his mid-twentieth-century heyday is that of conventionality itself: bowler-hatted, grey-suited, briefcase-carrying (even if, in an equally hackneyed joke, it only contains his packed lunch), he is part of a brainless and pointless 'rat race' in which he never arrives anywhere other than to and from the place of work. All commuters are the same, and the very idea of the rush hour with its swarm of men all moving in the same direction at the same time seems to suggest personal as well as temporal regularity, as if commuting and conforming were interchangeable. Almost by definition, the commuter lacks individuality; he is the type of the type, 'the man on the Clapham omnibus'. Writing in *Mental Efficiency* (part of *How to Live*) in 1918, Arnold Bennett refers to 'the average young man who arrives at Waterloo at 9.40 every morning with a cigarette in his mouth and a second-class season ticket over his heart and vague aspirations in his soul'. If he had been simply 'the young man' he would already have looked like all the others; to call him the *average* young man just makes him more of a sign or statistic. He is the same man (as every other young man in the station), taking the same train and smoking what is substantially the same cigarette each morning.

Perhaps it is the regularity of trains themselves that allows for human lives to be represented in such precisely repetitive terms (all the young men are the same, all the days are the same). In Saussure's *Course in General Linguistics*, which also goes back to the early 1900s, the primary illustration of how the world is lived through the medium of a network of repeatable signs, rather than through the separate naming of things, is a particular evening departure from Geneva to Paris: it is the 'same' train each day even though in terms of the rolling stock and the passengers any one day's train is completely different from the day before's. With Bennett's commuter, even the 'vague aspirations in his soul' come as standard—and Bennett's various *How To Live* self-help books are designed, in a half-chiding, half-avuncular way, to give this character some strong advice. *How to Live on Twenty-Four Hours a Day* is the fabulous title of one of them, the conceit being that time is the one resource that never varies, and that is distributed in equal measures to everyone, 'the daily miracle'. There are no differentials, there is no means of investment or increase in earnings; but what it is possible to do is to avoid waste, the waste of days and the cumulative sense of a wasted life that is a part of the picture for the readers that Bennett addresses. Making the most of that life after all is a matter not so much of grand hopes or 'vague aspirations' but of keeping to the minutiae of a daily timetable. The otherwise unused time of commuting is the period with which to begin: 'It is for this portion of the art and craft of living that I have reserved the time from the moment of quitting your door to the moment of arriving at your office.' The mental 'machine' must be taught to occupy itself during what would otherwise be the slack downtimes of the day: '"What? I am to cultivate my mind in the street, on the platform, in the train, and in the crowded street again?" Precisely.' Bennett recommends a little light Marcus Aurelius or Epictetus to get you started.

This self-making man whom Bennett admonishes and imagines is in one way—for all his private mental life and his classical reading —an extended version of the timed worker, his work and travel regulated according to specific hours. In Bennett's view the home and its hours must not be exempt from this regime; on the contrary, they are the part of the daily resource that remains to be properly utilized. You complain you don't have the time? Get up earlier. You say you need a cup of tea to get going? Amazingly, you can make it yourself:

> Rise an hour, an hour and a half, or even two hours earlier ... 'But,' you say, 'I couldn't begin without some food, and servants.' Surely, my dear sir, in an age when an excellent spirit-lamp (including a saucepan) can be bought for less than a shilling, you are not going to allow your highest welfare to depend upon the precarious immediate co-operation of a fellow creature! Instruct the fellow creature, whoever she may be, at night. Tell her to put a tray in a suitable position over night. On that tray two biscuits, a cup and saucer, a box of matches and a spirit-lamp.

The commuter is supposed to be programmed and predictable like his work schedule; unthinking in his daily A to B to A, up and down, round and round—the 'rat race' again. Of all the characters who populate the city, the commuter seems to have the function of representing this uninspired combination of the mechanical and the unimaginative. He never varies; he goes about his journeys and his business in a determined way; he does not see or smell or feel the city as a source of wonder or stimulation, but only as a means to an end, that of making a living and perhaps attaining a certain dull status. And while Bennett's study plan may be designed as a means of personal improvement, it is not meant to make its student stand out from the crowd. On the contrary, reading a small volume has the advantage that you will not look odd in the way that you would with more conspicuously different behaviour:

> The exercise is a very convenient one. If you got into your morning train with a pair of dumb-bells for your muscles or an encyclopaedia in ten volumes for your learning, you would probably excite remark. But as you walk in the street, or sit in the corner of the compartment behind a pipe, or 'strap-hang' on the Subterranean, who is to know

that you are engaged in the most important of daily acts? What asinine boor can laugh at you?

The insistence that studying on the way to work is unembarrassing touches on another aspect of commuterly conformity. It is not just that commuters are seen, from elsewhere, as being all the same, but that they are thought to resent any deviation from the norm on the part of one of their kind—or to dread some accidental manifestation of a difference of their own. Yet from this perspective it is just a small step to the emergence of another figure, the commuter who sees himself as differing from the rest not through some comical deviation from the compartmental code, but because of a secret certainty of superiority. In Richard Yates's novel *Revolutionary Road* (1961), it is early evening and Frank Wheeler, exceptionally, is taking the train after the one he normally takes from New York's Grand Central to a small town in Connecticut, where he lives with his wife and two children. He has spent the afternoon with a secretary from work called Maureen, and now after a culminating scene in her apartment, he feels 'like a man':

> Could a man ride home in the rear smoker, primly adjusting his pants at the knees to protect their crease and rattling his evening paper into a narrow panel to give his neighbor elbow room? Could a man sit meekly massaging his headache and allowing himself to be surrounded by the chatter of beaten, amiable husks of men who sat and swayed and played bridge in a stagnant smell of newsprint and tobacco and bad breath and overheated radiators?
> Hell, no. The way for a man to ride was erect and out in the open.

The contrast between the man and the non-men is cartoon-like in its divisions; Wheeler positively needs the emphatic rhetorical questions and the contrast of passively 'amiable', sedentary others within the carriage in order to set himself up as the one real man, on the outside.

Setting himself apart from the commuting crowd is not a new departure for Frank. Right from the start, he has seen his conventional office job—in the marketing section of a large company—as merely a means to pay the bills while his true self is put on hold. The company he works for manufactures office machines, like a parody of the self-perpetuating pointlessness of business. He imagines himself as the only one of his colleagues to hold himself aloof from a corporate identity, the only one who is simply going through the motions and holding on to a sense of another, rebellious self (the company is coincidentally the one for which his own father worked as a loyal small-town sales rep). His wife April is complicit in this fantasy of difference, in which the job and then the suburban home are to be experienced as only a pragmatic and temporary post-ponement of a creative, urban life. They are just playing at the inauthentic existence. The novel begins with an opening-night flop for the local amateur dramatics society, with April's own failure in the leading role. Frank and April's life then appears as a sequence of more or less successful performances, most distinctly in the scene set for Frank's return on the very night that he gets home a bit late. April—dressed in a special seductive outfit—proposes that they should all take off for Paris with the courage of their dreams. The plan to start a new life itself becomes, for a while, an energizing new project, a way of imagining themselves as exceptional. They are about to go on the big journey, the adventure that is thousands of miles away from the small-town commute. Both at home and at work—and on the train—the sense of identity, of really living, is generated through a repudiation of the stereotypical existence that everyone else is assumed to follow without irony.

Later on, there is a period when the Paris idea is fading, but at the same time Frank has unexpectedly been singled out at work as a result of a successful idea that happened half accidentally. He has taken to working late to complete a special assignment. At this point there is a shift in his relationship to commuting:

> He rather enjoyed having dinner alone in town and taking walks through the city at evening before catching the late train. It gave him a pleasant sense of independence, of freedom from the commuter's round; and besides, it seemed a suitable practice for the new, mature,

non-sentimental kind of marriage that was evidently going to be their way from now on.

Here, the 'freedom from the commuter's round' has lost the insistent edge of an absolute division between 'them' and 'me'; it is just a mild pleasure in doing something unusual within the daily cycle of a routine common to himself and others. In a similar way, Frank's months-ago one-afternoon stand with Maureen now becomes a regular affair, and he represents it to himself very differently from before:

> Each time, when he'd handed her into a taxi at last and turned alone toward Grand Central, he had wanted to laugh aloud at having so perfectly fulfilled the standard daydream of the married man. No fuss, no complications, everything left behind in a tumbled room under somebody else's name; and all of it wound up in time to catch the ten-seventeen.

Here there is both resignation and amusement at fulfilling a 'standard daydream' (and he wanted to laugh aloud, but didn't: nothing to embarrass himself or anyone else). Even the fantasies of the commuter, safely catching his 'ten-seventeen', come in a regulation form, and Frank can now smile (inwardly) at the picture of himself in his conventional transgressiveness, whereas previously he sought to place himself quite apart from the other men on the train.

Frank's commuterly dream, announced as itself a stereotype, plays on the assumption that commuters are regarded as almost the only category of city characters who see and do nothing beyond their 'daily round', their futureless and featureless *aller-retour*. The commuter is the city's antithesis to the *flâneur*: working not enjoying, conventional not bohemian, a traveller along straight, known lines, not an aimless, curious drifter. The commuter's minor affair can be as much a cliché as the regularly timetabled day that it simply extends. Everything is still conveniently compartmentalized. Something a bit out of the ordinary, a bit on the side, is going on, but not enough to derail the unsilver wheels and repetitive revolutions of Wheeler's daily journey.

Virginia Woolf's 1927 essay 'Street Haunting' also imagines the commuter's life as a combination of moderate distraction and dull return. Her alter-ego narrator is enjoying a leisurely, reflective city walk at dusk, and pauses to think about another kind of early evening journey:

> But the main stream of walkers at this hour sweeps too fast to let us ask such questions. They are wrapt, in this short passage from work to home, in some narcotic dream, now that they are free from the desk, and have the fresh air on their cheeks. They put on those bright clothes which they must hang up and lock the key upon all the rest of the day, and are great cricketers, famous actresses, soldiers who have saved their country at the hour of need. Dreaming, gesticulating, often muttering a few words aloud, they sweep over the Strand and across Waterloo Bridge whence they will be slung in long rattling trains, to some prim little villa in Barnes or Surbiton where the sight of the clock in the hall and the smell of the supper in the basement puncture the dream.

The commuters are granted an interval of childish fantasy as they escape from the office. Like the amateur actors of *Revolutionary Road*, they don the costumes for the dream roles that are ruled out the rest of the time and that have no bearing on their real lives. The train journey itself ('they will be slung into ...') is more an exercise in collective humiliation than an occasion for further fantasy, but something of private reverie still remains for 'puncture' by the time they arrive at the unsightly and internally malodorous 'prim little villa' that is home. This is Woolf's own peculiar view of a lower middle class who have little to look forward or backward to whether at work or at home. The brief moment of semi-freedom is in fact a 'narcotic dream' of mildly mad self-exposure: the people actually gesticulate and mutter aloud. It is the only time for useless imagination in a wearisome day that is not relieved or redeemed by any Wemmick-like establishment. Wemmick's domestic fantasy is both solidly grounded and playful; he takes private pride and pleasure in the home he loves and cares for. But Woolf does not go beyond the threshold to imagine various lives for her commuters even though her own vignette seems to point, in spite of itself, to other possibilities. Opening the door to the smell of a meal cooking and the sight of a familiar object is not self-evidently a depressing experience; but this, not someone's return to a cold and unpeopled dwelling, is the scene she comes up with to close the small story of the commuter's sad life.

Métro-boulot-dodo—tube, job, sleep—parodies the imagined tunnel of the commuter's mode of existence, seeing and doing nothing outside the usual parameters, and too exhausted for any new experience. If you step onto any commuter train in the early morning or early evening, you will see that in reality a lot of sleeping goes on in the travelling part of the day as well as before and after. But waiting for the 06.46 on Stonegate station, in the dark or the light depending on the time of year, you wouldn't imagine this. There will be two or three clutches of people all chatting away as if they've been up for hours. The conversation is domestic and familiar: spouses, dogs, children. Except for those who run it fine, risking a train-oblivious tractor in the early light of the summer months, there is normally a good five minutes of this platform sociability. (Set in the middle of the countryside, a mile from its village, Stonegate is a station to which almost all the passengers drive. It has a huge car park surreally surrounded by fields of sheep.) Then the train appears. But people do not sit with their platform acquaintances, and from now on an unspoken rule of compartmental silence is observed. A large number of the passengers already on the train are settled in sleep, and some of the Stonegate arrivals will join them: there is more than an hour before London in which to make up for the early rise.

Just now—late 2009—as the train waits outside the station for a platform at London Bridge, there are two big poster ads stuck up on facing walls of a new development of flats called Bermondsey Spa. One slogan reads, 'Staring out of the same train window every day? Change the view and enjoy living here.' And the other, 'Ditch the commute and enjoy living here.' The prospect of gazing out of your window enjoying the spectacle of the somnolent folk still stuck in the train was not a winning one to me, but like any commuter I do have my dreams of diversion, and once there was one that came true.

All stationmasters seem to know the ins and outs of every stop on their line, and they produce it when asked with rightful pride and confidence. But 'get off at Tonbridge and cross the bridge to platform three' had a magical ring to it the first Monday I took the Stonegate train to the Eurostar terminal at Ashford and began a few months of weekly commuting to Paris. 'Change!' Unlike the normal commute in which the same journey, tediously repeated day after day, seems to stretch ahead like some line to a featureless future, this period was marked by the wish that it need never come to an end (and the certainty that it would). I cannot, however hard I try, make London like Paris in my own particular Francophile imaginary, but the experience has taught me something I try still to carry with me as I continue to boringly go between Stonegate and London: that in reality no two journeys, even commutes, and no two days in the city, are ever the same—or not if you don't expect or want them to be. (I may write a self-help book on the subject.)

There are also the seasonal variations, the predictable ups and downs of summer and winter; these changes are at once entirely predictable and quite radical in the difference they make to the feel of commuting. Because it is so much extended at either end beyond the nine to five with which it is always associated, the commuter's day is in this one respect like the farmer's. In late spring and summer the sun is already up as you go to work, and your spirits rise with the morning light. But in the dark cold months, for me the months of most London days, commuting begins and continues long before dawn and long after sunset, and only the coffee, prepared these days all by yourself with a modern electric kettle, begins to set you on your unnatural way.

But aside from the differences, and the dreams, there can be a kind of comfort in commuting. The very dislocation of lengthily travelling between two places seems to lend the calm of an interlude to the period of the journey itself and its familiar spaces, inside and outside. This is 'your' train, your transitory home, and these are the sights from the window you know so well (at least in the summer). This is the space where you are mostly free just to read or think or do nothing ('I'm just going into a tunnel' is heard much more often than tunnels are actually entered). Years ago, in a world without mobiles when train passengers really were out of all possible contact, a friend used to rhapsodise about the privacy and pleasure of the commuting hour on her journeys to and from Brighton (she was an editor and it was the only part of the day, she said, when she could read her type-scripts in peace). When I first started commuting I didn't think I would ever be able to work on the train, but now I know what she means, and now I can probably concentrate better, if that's what I want to do, than at other times of the day or in other places. It is another commuterly adaptation, and it happens.

I left my fellow Stonegate commuters waking up a second time when their train reached the city, but when they come home the journey is not at all the same as the one at the start of the day. This time, of course, there is no pre-train platform camaraderie as every-one, with no distinction of destination, converges on Charing Cross together. And this time—at least until halfway through the evening —you have to be sure to arrive ten minutes before the train leaves if you want to be certain of a seat. Again, there is plenty of sleeping, but this is not, as it is in the early morning, the dominant activity. There are laptops out, mobiles, MP3 players. There is quite a lot of eating, quite a lot of reading. Unlike the early morning, there is a bit of con-versation. Once, on the 21.45, I learned a game called nine-card brag. For more than 30 years the two men sitting opposite had been playing this on the same train every Friday night on their way back to Orpington and Sevenoaks after an evening of cards at a pub near Victoria.

What else has ever happened? I have not seen anyone reading Marcus Aurelius but a while ago I twice found myself sitting near the same man—he got off at Tunbridge Wells—who both times (this is how I recognized him) was working his way through *The Interpreta-tion of Dreams*. The old Penguin Freud, but the smart light blue all the volumes had in the later printing, not the original bright orange. He'd read about another hundred pages, I'd say, by the time I noticed him the second time, so he was making progress or keeping at it, but I never saw him again. I wonder if he finished it.

Reading

Bennett, Arnold, *How to Live on Twenty-Four Hours a Day* (1910) and *Mental Efficiency* (1918), both reprinted as part of *How to Live* (New York: Garden City, 1925).

Dickens, Charles, *Great Expectations*, ed. Margaret Cardwell (Oxford: Oxford World's Classics, 1994).

Tennyson, Alfred, 'Tithonus', in *Selected Poems*, ed. Aidan Day (London: Penguin, 1991).

Woolf, Virginia, 'Street Haunting: A London Adventure' (1927), in *The Crowded Dance of Modern Life*, ed. Rachel Bowlby (London: Penguin, 1993).

Yates, Richard, *Revolutionary Road* (1961; London: Vintage, 2009).

Convalescing

Matthew Beaumont

Voluptuous Nerves

In his 'Meditations of a Painter', composed in 1912, the Italian painter Giorgio de Chirico narrated the enigmatic experience that inspired his famous sequence of metaphysical cityscapes, commencing with the 'Enigma of an Autumn Afternoon' (1910):

> One clear autumnal morning I was sitting on a bench in the middle of the Piazza Santa Croce in Florence. It was of course not the first time that I had seen this square. I had just come out of a long and painful intestinal illness, and I was in a nearly morbid state of sensitivity. The whole world, down to the marble of the buildings and the fountains, seemed to me to be convalescent ... Then I had the strange impression that I was looking at all these things for the first time, and the composition of my picture came to my mind's eye.

This is a classic modernist epiphany. Life itself, condemned to a state of deadening repetition, especially in the routine spaces of the city, is apprehended as if for the first time. In the 'Meditations' de Chirico cites Schopenhauer's dictum that, in order to have 'immortal' ideas, 'one has but to isolate oneself from the world for a few moments so completely that the most commonplace happenings appear to be new and unfamiliar, and in this way reveal their true essence'.

In the incident in the Piazza Santa Croce, the everyday is redeemed by 'the enigma of sudden revelation', as de Chirico calls it.

A number of his canvases from the 1910s revisit this scene. In 'The Mystery and Melancholy of a Street' (1914), to take one compelling example, a sudden silence seems to have descended on the city, softly flooding the most commonplace sights with some unidentifiable spiritual significance. The end of an ordinary day assumes the form of an ominous interruption. It is as if a mysterious curfew has been imposed on the city, less because of some specific threat of destruction than because of a generalized anxiety about death (though this abstract fear is, in 1914, no less historical than a more concrete one). This city, as Walter Benjamin might have put it, 'looks cleared out, like a lodging that has not yet found a new tenant'; or like one from which an old tenant has for nameless reasons been expelled. Its unsettling atmosphere is objectified in the sinister silhouette that falls across the piazza from the right-hand side of the composition, menacing the fragile, fairytale innocence of the child that skates up the street with a hoop.

'The Mystery and Melancholy of a Street', 1914 (oil on canvas) by Giorgio de Chirico (1888–1978). Private Collection/The Bridgeman Art Library. Copyright DACS.

In 'The Mystery and Melancholy of a Street', as in other paintings by de Chirico at this time, the city has become the implausible setting for what Marx once referred to, at least according to Benjamin, as 'socially empty space'. Looking at it, the spectator experiences a creeping sense of agoraphobic panic, one that mimics perhaps de Chirico's fear of fainting in the street, subsequently documented in his memoirs, and his neurotic habit, as a consequence, of sticking close to walls as he fumbled about in the city. 'In the noisy street,' he intones in the 'Meditations', 'catastrophe goes by.' So too, it seems, in the silent street. The dreamlike stasis of this painting evokes the unsettling sensation he apparently had in Florence, after his intestinal illness, of 'walking along on cotton wool'. The city he imagines in this composition is a physiological phenomenon, a tremulous physical extension of the painter's hesitantly, uncomfortably embodied consciousness. Its colonnades, streets and open spaces, in contrast to contemporary cities celebrated for their arterial freedom, themselves seem susceptible to a kind of intestinal inhibition that impedes uncomplicated movement, in spite of the absence of a mass of people. ('It is to be noted', states Henri Lefebvre, 'that a deserted street at four o'clock in the afternoon has as strong a significance as the swarming of a square at market or meeting times.') The city itself is in a state of preternatural sensitivity. So the painting depicts what Benjamin, discussing Baudelaire's relationship to Paris in the reflections he entitled 'Central Park', referred to as 'the infirmity and decrepitude of this great city'. But it also depicts the city's capacity to be regenerated or reborn through the contractions that gently convulse it.

The most striking aspect of de Chirico's autobiographical anecdote is, I think, its emphasis on his convalescent state; and on the concomitant fact that, suffused with what might be called a convalescent consciousness, the 'whole world' appears to be convalescent too. (The celebrated influence on de Chirico of Nietzsche, who devoted a section of *Thus Spoke Zarathustra* [1885] to 'The Convalescent', can no doubt be detected in this respect.) The child who dances a little desperately up the street with her hoop, either from fear or from a reckless happiness, is a displaced, perhaps idealized image of the convalescent painter's frail openness to re-experiencing the percussive rhythms of the city. In the literature on convalescence as an aesthetic, if I can put it like that, which dates back to the Romantics, and more specifically to Coleridge in a rural context and Baudelaire in an urban one, the convalescent's experience of his or her environment is often compared to that of the child. The convalescent's delicate receptiveness to life—a helpless openness to unexpected or half-forgotten sensations—has something of the brittle innocence of a child. It has, too, an innate poetic intensity. In the first volume of the *Biographia Literaria* (1817), Coleridge characterized genius as the capacity 'to combine the child's sense of wonder and novelty with the appearances which every day, for, perhaps, forty years, had rendered familiar'. The 'prime merit' of genius, he continued, and 'its most unequivocal mode of manifestation', is 'so to represent familiar objects as to awaken in the minds of others a kindred feeling concerning them, and that freshness of sensation which is the constant accompaniment of mental, no less than of bodily convalescence'. In convalescence, then, the whole world is made strange, made new. In a convalescent state even the most ordinary individual relates to life like a Romantic poet, or a modernist painter. Coleridge—at times an almost full-time convalescent himself, especially when living in Highgate, on the edge of London, in the final, drug-addicted decades of his life—captures precisely the state in which I am interested when he refers rhapsodically to 'the voluptuous and joy-trembling nerves of convalescence'.

'I had the strange impression that I was looking at all these things for the first time', de Chirico comments on his convalescence. In *Sons and Lovers* (1913), D. H. Lawrence also narrated an epiphanic moment in which everything seems convalescent. 'In convalescence,' the narrator comments, after describing an attack of bronchitis in his chapter on 'The Young Life of Paul', 'everything was wonderful.' As in de Chirico's roughly contemporaneous moment of revelation, the peculiar state of convalescence releases Paul Morel's sense of the pictorial qualities of everyday sights, albeit in a pastoral as opposed to an urban context. Seated in bed in his sick room, he abstractedly concentrates on the wintry view through the window, where snowflakes cling to the pane for a moment and are gone. In convalescence, as for the conception of spleen explored by Benjamin, 'time is reified: the minutes cover a man like snowflakes'. From Morel's convalescent perspective, the land suddenly comes to seem like a landscape; that is, detached from its instrumental functions, the countryside is spontaneously aestheticized. In this scene, the architrave effectively functions as a picture frame, and the deep snow outside acts as a blank canvas: 'Away across the valley the little black train crawled doubtfully over the great whiteness.' In de Chirico's paintings from this period, too, black trains that creep against the background are symbolic of an industriousness, indeed an industrialism, from which the convalescent feels gratefully exempt.

The 'nearly morbid state of sensitivity' evoked by de Chirico in his 'Meditations of a Painter', associated as it is with the aftermath of a sustained illness, situates the artist within a tradition that I want to characterize, in a deliberately Baudelairean formulation, as that of the convalescent as hero of modernity. As de Chirico's anecdote announces, the convalescent, and particularly the male convalescent, who is for social reasons less confined than the female convalescent, less domesticated, is in spite of his infirmity and decrepitude not necessarily confined to the sick room or to some bucolic retreat. I am especially interested in the moment when the urban convalescent, despite his nerves, takes his first reckless steps in the city from which he has been exiled by illness, and experiences a sense of freedom at once tentative and abrupt (in 'The Mystery and Melancholy of a Street' the open doors of that oddly disconsolate circus wagon are emblematic of this uncertain state of release). The streets, which he approaches cautiously, still a little feverishly, at first perhaps as an observer who must half-protect himself from the impact of the city, are the site of his groping re-engagement with everyday life. Edgar Allan Poe's 'The Man of the Crowd' (1840), to which I will eventually turn, is the archetypal myth of the convalescent, especially in so far as this is mediated by Baudelaire. The convalescent, who occupies some indeterminate space between health and illness, even reason and unreason, is at once acutely sensitive to his environment and oddly insulated from it. 'The body after long illness is languid, passive, receptive of sweetness, but too weak to contain it', wrote

Virginia Woolf in *Jacob's Room* (1922). He is both alive, painfully alive, to the life that continues around him, and dead to it, almost deliciously dead. He is at the same time calm and restless, contemplative and thoughtless. The aesthetics of the city and its anaesthetics are for the convalescent inseparable. The convalescent is thus an excellent instance of what Benjamin called 'the law of the dialectic at a standstill', a social being whose immobility itself incarnates the characteristic ambiguities of everyday life in a metropolitan city. As someone cautiously emerging from the state of isolation associated with sickness, and experiencing in consequence a process of more or less reluctant re-socialization, he is a graphic instance of the relationship between individual and society, private and public, in metropolitan modernity.

There are of course a number of other, superficially more plausible candidates, throughout the nineteenth and early twentieth centuries, for the role of hero of modernity. The most famous of these, and still the most popular, is no doubt the *flâneur* (whose affinities to the commodity, repeatedly emphasized by Benjamin, are all too often forgotten by those that celebrate him). As a social archetype, the convalescent has a certain amount in common with the *flâneur*: both of them, for example, tend to perambulate the city at a distinctly dilatory pace; and for both of them, as Benjamin puts it, 'the joy of watching is triumphant'. Like his cousin the *flâneur*, the convalescent inhabits what Fredric Jameson has called 'the bereft condition of the anti-hero who has no motivation at all'. The rough outline of the convalescent that I draft in this chapter, however, which sketches his scattered appearance in the streets and thoroughfares of the nineteenth-century city in particular, nonetheless constitutes an attempt to displace the *flâneur*'s importance in contemporary scholarship in the humanities. The convalescent—who does not patrol the marketplace; who, in Benjaminian terms, looks about but does not seek a buyer—is the *flâneur*'s poor relation. More precisely, he is his poorly relation. He is important, I think, not least because he has been oddly neglected in accounts of the metropolis and mental life. Even Benjamin, gazing past him at the *flâneur*'s coolly disappearing form, completely overlooks the symbolic significance of the convalescent.

The Ebb of Sickness

'It is strange that while so much has been written for the invalid in the time of sickness, there are but few books which deal with the special needs of Convalescence.' So argued the Rev. S. C. Lowry in *Convalescence: Its Blessings, Trials, Duties and Dangers: A Manual of Comfort and Help for Persons Recovering from Sickness* (1845), a book that explores convalescence as a spiritual, no less than physical, condition. The same statement might be made, *mutatis mutandis*, about contemporary scholarship, and this too has helped to make the convalescent almost invisible in the nineteenth and twentieth centuries. Sickness, and its role in nineteenth-century literature and culture, has been discussed *ad nauseam*. Athena Vrettos, for example, who has devised a 'poetics of illness', asserts convincingly enough that 'fictions of illness make their appearance in multiple and shifting areas of Victorian thought'. Symptomatically, though, her narrative of these 'somatic fictions' abruptly shifts 'from disease to health', and in so doing completely effaces the importance of convalescence. Susan Sontag is partly responsible for this state of affairs, since in her influential account of 'Illness as Metaphor' (1978) she effectively posited health and sickness as conditions that are, almost ontologically, absolutely distinct from one another, referring to them respectively as 'the kingdom of the well' and 'the kingdom of the sick'. The mention of Thomas Mann's *The Magic Mountain* (1924) alone should be enough to deconstruct this opposition. There is at present, then, no poetics of convalescence, though this indeterminate physical and psychological condition is of relevance both to individuals and to the collective imagination in the epoch of metropolitan modernity.

So how can convalescence be defined, if at all, in a technical sense? In the opening decades of the nineteenth century, when its impact on literature becomes apparent, a number of French medical students seem to have written dissertations on convalescence as part of their final examination. One of these, which I have chosen almost at random, can therefore function as an initial definition. In his thesis on convalescence presented at the Faculty of Medicine in Paris on 3 August 1837, Hyacinthe Dubranle makes this statement:

La convalescence ... est un état intermédiaire à la maladie à laquelle il succède et à la santé à laquelle il conduit. Elle commence à l'époque où les symptômes qui caractérisent la maladie ont disparu, et fini à l'époque où l'exercise libre et régulier des fonctions qui constituent la santé est pleinement rétabli.

This definition is manifestly not unproblematic, because like all definitions of convalescence it cannot make sharp distinctions between this transitional phase and the phases that precede and succeed it. Is it possible, it might be asked, to identify the moment when the symptoms of the disease disappear? Or when the free and regular exercise of those functions that constitute a condition of healthiness is fully restored (*pleinement rétabli*)? It is however useful enough; and not least because, in making obvious the difficulty of providing a precise definition at all, it implies that convalescence is a diffusive condition, one that spontaneously undoes an uncomplicated opposition between disease and health. If, on the one hand, convalescence simply occupies the neutral border territory through which the patient must travel in order to escape from disease; on the other hand, the convalescent state stealthily colonizes health itself, sometimes comprehensively. 'This flat swamp of convalescence, left by the ebb of sickness, yet far enough from the *terra firma* of established health', as Charles Lamb depicted it in 1825, has a habit of surreptitiously encroaching on *terra firma*.

The effects of an illness are often especially difficult to eradicate once the patient has resumed ordinary life, even if they manifest themselves mainly in the form of psychosomatic anxieties. In the capitalist marketplace, individuals frequently have to live with illness, accommodating it to everyday life, in order to sustain themselves. Prematurely forced by economic necessity to make regular if not necessarily free use of their physical and mental functions, to appropriate Dubranle's terms, many people are arrested in an almost perpetual state of transition from sickness to health, from health to sickness. These people, the proletarian equivalents of Mann's Hans Castorp perhaps, more or less forced to participate in an industrial capitalist society to which they do not feel properly fitted, a society in which they feel perpetually unfit, are at once hypochondriac and heroic. Convalescence is in this sense a chronic rather than an acute phenomenon, and it might even be identified as one of those almost existential conditions characteristic of the historical process of industrial modernization. Life in the metropolitan city is itself ineradicably febrile. 'The resistance that modernity offers to the natural productive élan of an individual is out of all proportion to his strength', Benjamin writes in 'The Paris of the Second Empire in Baudelaire'; and 'it is understandable if a person becomes exhausted and takes refuge in death'. For this reason, he argues, 'modernity must stand under the sign of death'. It can equally be said to stand under the sign of convalescence, or of some residual state of feverishness equivalent to it. Under capitalism, in its everyday forms, the individual permanently occupies a hinterland between what Benjamin's friend the philosopher Ernst Bloch might have called the utopian state of perfect health and the dystopian state of death.

If convalescence is a state of transition from sickness to health, then in narrative terms, so to speak, this process is not automatically a comic one. To the extent that sickness, at least in its less acute forms, offers temporary respite from the disciplinary demands of industrial capitalism, convalescence promises not so much the social reintegration that, like marriage, it signals in the plot of the nineteenth-century novel, as a form of disintegration instead. Reintegration and disintegration go together for the convalescent. So in his essay on 'The Convalescent', which dramatizes the narrative of convalescence as a tragicomic one, Lamb provocatively celebrates sickness. His mischievous claim is that in the 'regal solitude' of his sick bed the patient enjoys positively autocratic privileges that he should only reluctantly give up. In Sontag's kingdom of the sick, according to Lamb, all citizens are monarchs. 'How the patient lords it there! What caprices he acts without controul! How kinglike he sways his pillow', Lamb exclaims. The sick man is thus paradoxically disalienated (in Marx's phrase). 'How sickness enlarges the dimensions of a man's self to himself!' continues Lamb, in ecstasies of self-afflation. The convalescent, in contrast, is like a despot who has been violently deposed: 'from the bed of sickness (throne let me rather call it) to the elbow chair of convalescence, is a fall from dignity, amounting to a deposition'. He is abruptly reduced to the oppressed status of a *sans papiers* trapped on the border separating Sontag's kingdoms.

Specifically, Lamb complains that, as a convalescent, he has once again been made susceptible to the demands of labour. The convalescent therefore feels his or her body, after a delightful interval of enforced unproductivity, being more or less gradually instrumentalized and commodified again. Lamb insists that, because he must divest himself of 'the strong armour of sickness', robust health makes him vulnerable. Under capitalism our bodies are reified, although we are habitually forced to forget this fact. In the ambiguous state of convalescence, however, when we are uncomfortably poised between the health that qualifies us for the production process and the sickness that disqualifies us from it, we are briefly made conscious of the alienation of our physical lives from our mental or spiritual lives. The incontrovertible evidence for the relapse into a state of alienation decried by Lamb is of course the article on 'The Convalescent' itself, which he offers his editor (who has impatiently requested publishable copy from him) in the deliberately self-reflexive flourish of the final paragraph. Lamb's essay thus reinscribes his convalescence as an abrupt fall back into labour, which in a tone of satirical contempt he calls 'the business of the world'. It describes a brutal transition from a prelapsarian state, the domain of use value, to a postlapsarian state, the domain of exchange value. Ironically, however, it is the delicate nerviness of the convalescent, his euphoric sensitivity even, which has made it possible for Lamb to compose this clever, supremely self-conscious effusion for publication in the first place.

Lamb complains that convalescence 'shrinks a man back to his pristine stature', using 'pristine' in its strict sense to mean original, primitive, or ancient. He employs this adjective to evoke the almost primordial helplessness of the convalescent when, as if in some painfully mundane re-enactment of Adam's deposition from Eden, he is violently forced back into the everyday conditions of an advanced civilization. If human beings themselves, as Freud allegedly argued, are born prematurely, then the convalescent, once he inhabits the streets again, is in effect prematurely reborn as an urban subject. In

Lacan's allusion, in the essay on 'The Mirror Stage', to the 'real *specific prematurity of birth* in man', he discusses the 'relation between the organism and its reality' in the infant's initial development. This is a complicated process of mutual accommodation 'between the *Innenwelt* and the *Umwelt*', between individual consciousness and the environment. The infant's neo-natal months are characterized by what Lacan calls 'signs of uneasiness and motor unco-ordination'; and the 'mirror stage' itself is among other things the process by which these signs of 'foetalization' come to disappear and it assumes instead, as he puts it in rather Reichian terms, 'the armour of an alienating identity'. The convalescent, it might be said, is also 'foetalized', because he has not fully acquired the character armour that can equip him to cope once more with reality, especially the reality of the city. He must sit quietly on a bench, like de Chirico; observe the street from the protective safety of a café; or cautiously circumambulate the city at night. It is as if his battered carapace is still too soft to resist the countless shocks of urban life.

The trope that Lacan employs to summarize the infant's prematurity is that of 'dehiscence', a predominantly botanical term meaning to open up, to gape, to burst. The convalescent, whose pores have only recently opened up, rendering him painfully responsive to his environment, is dehiscent too, though in a potentially redemptive sense. His 'small hungry shivering self', to appropriate an image of George Eliot's from *Middlemarch* (1872), cannot completely insulate itself from the constant concussions, the perpetual compulsions and repulsions of metropolitan life in an industrial society. At the same time, however, it is exquisitely sensitive to the almost imperceptible aesthetics of the quotidian, so that consciousness, in Eliot's language again, is 'rapturously transformed into the vividness of a thought'.

The Rev. S. C. Lowry, whose tract from the mid-1840s I have already cited, is interested in convalescence as a spiritual condition, one that is specific to 'the transition period between the storm and tempest and the ordinary voyage of life'; and he too identifies it, potentially at least, as a state of dehiscence. He is conscious nonetheless of the individual's susceptibility, in this uncertain state, to what he calls 'the dangers of convalescence', namely indifference, shallowness and worldliness. Lowry worries in particular that, once the patient has returned from 'the cloistered seclusion' of the sick room to 'the busy duties of life', the repentant attitude he has acquired because of his illness will be fatally lost. 'We live at a fast rate these days,' he notes, 'and sometimes amid all the engrossing occupations and harassing competitions of life, our souls seem to stand a poor chance.' But if convalescence is susceptible to the spiritual perversion that is inseparable from 'worldliness', it is also, according to Lowry, 'a golden opportunity for *definite conversion* to God'. The former, it should be noted, is implicitly associated with urban life, and the latter with rural life. In this vision of convalescence, the extent to which it might redeem the patient can be measured by the aesthetic and hence spiritual intensity with which his relationship to nature is reinvented, and made transcendent:

> The flowers seem to glow with a lovelier radiance, the fields are clothed with a brighter green. The carol of the birds, the rustle of the leaves, the murmur of the stream, fall upon your ears with a fresh meaning.

The ideal convalescent, as Lowry's onomatopoeic diction no doubt unsuccessfully indicates, is as supremely sensitive, and as open to redemptive experience, as a pastoral poet.

A Poetics of Convalescence

For Charles Baudelaire, the most important proponent of convalescence as an aesthetic disposition in the nineteenth century, the convalescent is in contrast an urban poet, albeit one indebted to the Coleridgean tradition that can be detected in Lowry's book. Convalescence, as he argues, 'is like a return towards childhood', for 'the convalescent, like the child, is possessed in the highest degree of the faculty of keenly interesting himself in things, be they apparently of the most trivial'. Baudelaire primarily derives his interest in convalescence, which to him seems inseparable from a state of rapturous, febrile curiosity, from Edgar Allan Poe, and specifically from 'The

Man of the Crowd'. This is indeed the canonical instance of urban convalescence in literature, so I want to explore it in considerable detail.

In the second paragraph of Poe's celebrated short narrative, the narrator recalls the convalescent state he recently inhabited. For it was in the ambiguous condition of the convalescent that he obsessively pursued an enigmatic old man he happened to glimpse in the street; an old man that, in the end, mentally and physically defeated, the narrator identifies, in hopeless or triumphant tones, as 'the type and the genius of deep crime':

> Not long ago, about the closing in of an evening in autumn, I sat at the large bow window of the D– Coffee-House in London. For some months I had been ill in health, but was now convalescent, and, with returning strength, found myself in one of those happy moods which are so precisely the converse of *ennui*—moods of the keenest appetency, when the film from the mental vision departs ... and the intellect, electrified, surpasses as greatly its every-day condition, as does the vivid yet candid reason of Leibnitz, the mad and flimsy rhetoric of Gorgias. Merely to breathe was enjoyment; and I derived positive pleasure even from many of the legitimate sources of pain. I felt a calm but inquisitive interest in everything. With a cigar in my mouth and a newspaper in my lap, I had been amusing myself for the greater part of the afternoon, now in poring over advertisements, now in observing the promiscuous company in the room, and now in peering through the smoky panes into the street.

This is an exact description of convalescence as an aesthetic, a state of unpredictable, half-repressed euphoria in which, because he is temporarily exempt from the routine demands of everyday life in an industrial capitalist city, the individual's 'electrified' senses are preternaturally attuned to experience. The convalescent is painfully sensitive to his environment and at the same time feels oddly distanced from it (as in de Chirico's account of walking on cotton wool). The film has departed from his mental vision but he nonetheless peers at the life of the city through 'smoky panes'. His empty, appetitive mood is at once both the opposite of boredom and oddly characteristic of its restless calm: it is 'the converse of *ennui*'; or its obverse. His consciousness processes the shocks of urban life, the traffic on the roads and pavements, as concussions that seem exquisite because he can remain detached and half-insulated from them.

Poe's urban fable might, like de Chirico's painting, have been called 'The Mystery and Melancholy of a Street', but Poe locates these atmospheric qualities in the presence rather than the absence of masses of people. Detached from the 'dense and continuous tides of population' that rush past the café as the evening closes in, and from the rhythms of routine production they collectively embody, his convalescent describes his fascination in the people he sees commuting home. He is soon lost in contemplation of them: 'At this particular period of the evening I had never before been in a similar situation, and the tumultuous sea of human heads filled me, therefore, with a delicious novelty of emotion.' Initially he examines the mass of human forms that pass him in the abstract. He is particularly interested in those that seem unconfident on the street, those that 'were restless in their movements, had flushed faces, and talked and gesticulated to themselves, as if feeling in solitude on account of the very denseness of the company around'. These are the people for whom everyday life in the city is itself a kind of sickness or fever (in contrast to Lamb, who boasted in 'The Londoner' [1802] that, although inclined to hypochondria, 'in London it vanishes, like all other ills'). Then Poe's convalescent examines the passers-by in more concrete detail, as if they inhabit some grimy aquarium. Sliding down 'the scale of what is termed gentility', as the light thickens, he classifies their physiognomies, their clothes and their step, carefully sifting through the aristocrats, the businessmen, the clerks, the artisans, the 'exhausted labourers', the pie-men, the dandies, the con-men, the pickpockets, the beggars and the prostitutes. The innumerable drunkards he sees from the café, their countenances pale, their eyes a livid red, clutch at passing objects 'with quivering fingers' as they stride though the crowd.

It is 'thus occupied in scrutinizing the mob', his forehead pressed against the glass beside his seat, that the convalescent glimpses the 'decrepid old man' whose *physiologie*, he finds, he is completely unable to taxonomize. He stumbles into the street, his curiosity heightened by the snatched sight of a diamond and a dagger beneath his cloak, and resolves in a moment of heated decision to follow the old man. 'For my own part I did not much regard the rain,' he notes, 'the lurking of an old fever in my system rendering the moisture somewhat too dangerously pleasant.' He traces the man's mysterious movements, throughout the night and into the day, as he roams the city in an apparently futile attempt to understand what motivates him; but he finally only tracks him back, on the evening of the second day, to the coffee house from which he had first set out. The old man, who appears completely unconscious of the narrator, seems to be more than human—as if his labyrinthine path through the streets had traced not the arbitrary trajectory of an individual but the secret form or logic of the corrupt, decrepit metropolitan city itself. So the convalescent abandons his pursuit: '*He is the man of the crowd*. It will be in vain to follow; for I shall learn no more of him, nor of his deeds.'

The old man incarnates the industrial capitalist city in its antiheroic rather than heroic form. In 'On Some Motifs in Baudelaire', composed exactly one hundred years after this short story was first published, Benjamin decides that he cannot ultimately identify Poe's 'man of the crowd' as a *flâneur*, mainly because in him 'composure has given way to manic behavior'. Instead, according to Benjamin, he exemplifies the destiny of the *flâneur* once this intrinsically urbane figure has been 'deprived of the milieu to which he belonged' (a milieu, he implies, that London probably never provided). The same might be said of Poe's convalescent, in whom composure must compete with a positively monomaniacal mood. Indeed, it might be argued that 'The Man of the Crowd' allegorizes the process by which, in the hectic conditions of a metropolis like London in the mid-nineteenth century, the *flâneur* splits apart and produces two further metropolitan archetypes, one almost pathologically peripatetic, the other static to the point of being a sort of cripple. The former is the nightwalker, a disreputable, indeterminately criminal type who hypostasizes that half of the *flâneur* characterized by a state of restless mobility; the latter is the convalescent, who hypostasizes the half of him characterized by a state of immobile curiosity. For Poe, these characters are spectral doubles.

Baudelaire's discussion of 'The Man of the Crowd' is contained in the opening chapter of 'The Painter of Modern Life' (1863), his encomium to the artist Constantin Guys, 'a passionate lover of crowds and incognitos'. He portrays Guys there as someone whose genius resides in a childlike curiosity, which he characterizes in terms of 'the fixed and animally ecstatic gaze of a child confronted with something new, whatever it be'. Like the child, who actually 'sees everything in a state of newness', and who is consequently 'always drunk', Guys is exquisitely susceptible to impressions. For him, 'sensibility is almost the whole being'. Ordinarily, Baudelaire emphasizes, adults can only recover this spontaneously poetic disposition when they are in a state of convalescence. Guys, however, positively personifies this disposition, because he is 'an eternal convalescent'. 'Imagine an artist who was always, spiritually, in the condition of that convalescent', Baudelaire concludes, 'and you will have the key to the nature of Monsieur G.'

Baudelaire identifies Poe's convalescent as his inspiration for this claim:

> Do you remember a picture (it really is a picture!), painted—or rather written—by the most powerful pen of our age, and entitled *The Man of the Crowd*? In the window of a coffee house there sits a convalescent, pleasurably absorbed in gazing at the crowd, and mingling, through the medium of thought, in the turmoil of thought that surrounds him. But lately returned from the valley of the shadow of death, he is rapturously breathing all the odours and essences of life; as he has been on the brink of total oblivion, he remembers, and fervently desires to remember, everything. Finally he hurls himself headlong into the midst of the throng, in pursuit of an unknown, half-glimpsed countenance, that has, on an instant, bewitched him. Curiosity had become a fatal, irresistible passion!

It is immediately apparent from this paragraph that Baudelaire's principal interest does not lie in the drama described by Poe's narrative, that is, the convalescent's pursuit, through the tortuous, sometimes tedious streets of London at night, of the abstracted, evil old man about whom he has become obsessed. Instead, he seems more interested in the scene in which the story is initially set. He insists on representing Poe's narrative, in fact, as a relatively static picture, as if he is himself examining the convalescent through a frame. Perhaps it is most accurate to state that he reconstructs the story as a diptych. In the first panel, the convalescent is passively seated in the coffee house. As he observes the street life through the pane of glass, he simultaneously introjects the scenes outside, assimilating them to his consciousness, and projects his consciousness onto the scenes outside, assimilating his consciousness to them. He is 'pleasurably absorbed in gazing at the crowd, and mingling, through the medium of thought, in the turmoil of thought that surrounds him'. *Innenwelt* and *Umwelt* are therefore one. The convalescent 'rapturously breath[es] in all the odours and essences of life', making the surface of his body seem absolutely porous, even as the solid pane of glass that he sits beside has apparently been rendered completely permeable. In the second panel, Baudelaire's description captures Poe's protagonist, as if in a photograph, in the act of flinging himself into the street —like the Baudelairean protagonist who, according to Benjamin, 'plunges into the crowd as into a reservoir of energy'. He is freeze-framed, so to speak, as he 'hurls himself headlong into the middle of the throng'. The convalescent thus metamorphoses into a noctambulist.

The second of these portraits is in effect an image of the convalescent as hero, actively seeking to satisfy his feverish curiosity, even if it is finally fatal to do so (as if Baudelaire had resolved to stalk the seductive widow he wistfully describes in 'À une passante'). Baudelaire's convalescent is thus saved from the humiliating defeat that Poe visits on his convalescent at the end of 'The Man of the Crowd', when he is forced to admit that he has failed to identify the man he has so assiduously pursued through the metropolis, at least as an individual. Poe's spectral convalescent, more spiritually decrepit than Baudelaire's, and less rapturous, is not so deeply indebted to the Coleridgean tradition, in spite of the fact that Baudelaire probably encountered this tradition through the mediation of Poe. But, like Poe's convalescent, Baudelaire's convalescent remains terminally peripheral to the life of the street, in contrast to the *flâneur*. The *flâneur*, according to Baudelaire, in the same section of 'The Painter of Modern Life', is situated 'at the centre of the world' even though he also 'remain[s] hidden from the world'. In this respect, as in others, he is like the commodity, which is so pervasive as to be invisible. The convalescent, Baudelaire implies, by contrast resists the performative aspect of the *flâneur*'s life in the streets and refuses the spectacular logic of the marketplace.

It is implicitly Poe himself, however, and not Constantin Guys, who ultimately embodies the spirit of convalescence for Baudelaire. Baudelaire had first referred to what he so evocatively describes as 'convalescence, with its fevers of curiosity' in 'Edgar Poe, sa vie et ses ouvrages' (1853). In this piece, which subsequently reappeared as the introduction to his translations in the *Histoires extraordinaires* (1856), Baudelaire locates the 'single character' that populates Poe's numerous narratives as 'the man of razor-sharp perceptions and slackened nerves'. He concludes that 'this man is Poe himself'. This description, I want to contend in conclusion, perfectly captures the constitution of the convalescent, who is acutely sensitive to the life of the streets but at the same time oddly anaesthetized to it. The poetics of convalescence that is perceptible in Poe, and that Baudelaire elaborated, make him absolutely central to the process by which Romanticism, in nineteenth- and twentieth-century literature, became urbanized. Poe is for Baudelaire one of the patron saints of metropolitan modernity because, as 'the writer of the nerves', he too is a perpetual convalescent. In the urban sensorium described by Poe, Baudelaire and Benjamin, the sick are too sensitive to cope with the shocks of everyday life, and the healthy are constitutionally insensitive to its secret aesthetics. To be absolutely modern, as Rimbaud demanded, one must be convalescent.

Reading

Baudelaire, Charles, *The Painter of Modern Life and Other Essays*, trans. Jonathan Mayne (London: Phaidon Press, 1995).

Benjamin, Walter, 'A Small History of Photography', in *One-Way Street and Other Writings*, trans. Edmund Jephcott and Kingsley Shorter (London: Verso, 1979): 240–57.

Benjamin, Walter, *The Writer of Modern Life: Essays on Charles Baudelaire*, ed. Michael W. Jennings (Cambridge, MA: Belknap Press, 2006).

de Chirico, Giorgio, 'Meditations of a Painter', trans. Louise Bourgeois and Robert Goldwater, in *Theories of Modern Art: A Source Book by Artists and Critics*, ed. Herschel B. Chipp (Berkeley: University of California Press, 1969): 397–401.

de Chirico, Giorgio, *The Memoirs of Giorgio de Chirico*, trans. Margaret Crosland (New York: Da Capo Press, 1994).

Dubranle, Hyacinthe, *Essai sur la convalescence: Thèse* (Paris: Rignoux, 1837).

Jameson, Fredric, *The Modernist Papers* (London: Verso, 2007).

Lacan, Jacques, 'The Mirror Stage as Function of the I as Revealed in Psychoanalytic Experience', in *Écrits: A Selection*, trans. Alan Sheridan (London: Routledge, 1977): 1–8.

Lamb, Charles, 'The Convalescent', in *Essays of Elia*, ed. Jonathan Bate (Oxford: Oxford University Press, 1987): 208–12.

Lefebvre, Henri, *Rhythmanalysis: Space, Time and Everyday Life*, trans. Stuart Elden and Gerald Moore (London: Continuum, 2004).

Lowry, S. C., *Convalescence: Its Blessings, Trials, Duties and Dangers: A Manual of Comfort and Help for Persons Recovering from Sickness* (London: Skeffington, 1845).

Poe, Edgar Allan, 'The Man of the Crowd', in *Selected Tales*, ed. David Van Leer (Oxford: Oxford University Press, 1998): 84–91.

Sontag, Susan, *Illness as Metaphor and AIDS and Its Metaphors* (Harmondsworth: Penguin, 1991).

Vrettos, Athena, *Somatic Fictions: Imagining Illness in Victorian Culture* (Stanford: Stanford University Press, 1995).

Daydreaming

Gregory Dart

Daydreaming is inescapable in the metropolis. Whatever the direction in which our typical day takes us, whatever our time-worn trajectory, the city barlines are always there to give pitch and shape to our reveries. An emporium of endless delights, the big city is also the home of sheer functionality and the notion that time is money. Not since we were children have we been shown so many things and then told not to touch them. Sitting on the top deck of the bus in the early morning we see our route to work mapped out before us. So to steal a glimpse of other people getting on or off at various stops, crossing the street, or simply standing on the pavement, is to imagine for ourselves (every day) many different ways of being, alternative rhythms as well as alternative directions. Regardless of what these people are actually thinking and seeing, and of where they are going, to the man on the top of the Clapham omnibus they are all just so many tempting side-streets to his own avenue of inevitability, an eager spray of possibilities around his narrow isthmus of self. Nor is the accuracy of such imaginings ever an issue, for in such moods other people are only there to act as surrogates or ideals. That is why we should never talk about the big city as if it were a fundamentally rational or irrational place, but rather, as a space in which the highly systematic nature of late capitalist work-discipline is always, however inadvertently, giving birth to its opposite—fantasy, reverie, daydream—as a form of resistance.

The city-dweller, as Georg Simmel knew, is the most hard-headed of creatures. Transport maps, social topographies, market values, codes of dress—one must master all these systems in order to survive. But as hard knowledge about the city increases, so too does a sense of its infinite pliancy. As an everyday revolt against the working life of the city—its infinite demands, and the innumerable anxieties that they engender—daydreaming is an instinctive means of escape, in spite or perhaps because of the fact that it always leaves us in exactly the same place when it is over, looking out of the same café, or sitting in the same seat on the bus. Daydream is that special kind of holiday where you don't need to take out travel insurance; it is the traceless transgression, the victimless crime. Sometimes we don't even know we are doing it, with a whole train of thoughts having been pursued, toyed with, and then laid aside before we are belatedly returned to ourselves. Like Addison's man of polite imagination, the urban daydreamer can 'assume a kind of property in everything he sees'. Streets, squares, hotels and cafés—he can frequent them all with his eyes, effortlessly, and without any of the inevitable disappointment that real encounters bring.

The status of daydream as a modern metropolitan pastime was well established in the 1820s; the Romantic essayists were already familiar with its dear, distracting pleasures. In 1823 William Hazlitt wrote a piece caricaturing the London Cockney—by which he meant anybody who had lived all his life in the big city and got all his ideas from it—as a creature addicted to fantasy and false consciousness. 'A real Cockney', Hazlitt wrote, 'is the poorest creature in the world, the most literal, the most mechanical, and yet he too lives in a world of romance—a fairy land of his own.'

> He is a shopman, and nailed all day behind the counter: but he sees hundreds of thousands of gay, well-dressed people pass—an endless phantasmagoria—and enjoys their liberty and gaudy fluttering pride. He is a footman—but he rides behind beauty, through a crowd of carriages, and visits a thousand shops.

The Cockney, Hazlitt considered, is a kind of great man 'by proxy' who simply by virtue of living in a big city and coming so often in contact with fine persons and things gradually becomes surcharged with 'a sort of second-hand, vapid, tingling, troublesome self-importance'. 'He meets the Lord Mayor's coach, and without ceremony treats himself to an imaginary ride in it. He notices the people going to court, or to a city-feast, and is quite satisfied with the show.'

Hazlitt's great friend Charles Lamb, who spent his working life as a clerk in the City of London, made metropolitan daydream the prime impulse of his writing, considering himself 'in some sort a speculative Lord Mayor of London'. Lamb is a master of the ironically cultivated urban fantasy. In the middle of one essay, 'A Complaint of the Decay of Beggars in the Metropolis' (1822), he tells a story—clearly apocryphal—about a blind beggar and a clerk:

> A clerk in the Bank was surprised with the announcement of a five hundred pound legacy left him by a person whose name he was a stranger to. It seems that in his daily morning walks from Peckham (or some village thereabouts) where he lived, to his office, it had been his practice for the last twenty years to drop his halfpenny duly into the hat of some blind Bartimeus, that sate begging alms by the wayside in the Borough. The good old beggar recognised his daily benefactor by the voice only; and, when he died, left all the amassings of his alms (that had been half a century perhaps in the accumulating) to his old Bank friend. Was this a story to purse up people's hearts, and pennies, against giving an alms to the blind? or not rather a beautiful moral of well-directed charity on the one part, and noble gratitude upon the other? I sometimes wish I had been that Bank clerk … Reader, do not be frightened at the hard words, imposition, imposture—give, and ask no questions. Cast thy bread upon the waters. Some have unawares (like this Bank clerk) entertained angels.

A beautiful moral of well-directed charity and noble gratitude? This story is an outrageous imposition on Lamb's part, and his gloriously subinsinuating tone confesses it. But it is also, one feels, an allegory of some personal significance, in spite of the airiness of its presentation. Essentially it is the daydream of a modern commuter, someone ensnared in the new time-and-money matrix of the early nineteenth century. The life of a clerk, as Lamb knew, was all prudence and punctuality, buffed shoes and book-keeping, and in giving his daily halfpenny to the Borough beggar, the office-worker is, in some small way, rebelling against this straitjacket. He is paying a small tribute to the time-freedom of the wayside and the mysterious usury of the streets. The irony is, of course, that far from being a disorderly figure, the beggar is, in his way, as regular and prudent as the commuter. He acts all along as the Bank clerk's banker, and is at his station—and his office—every morning. The beggar has come, as it were, not to destroy accounting but to transfigure it, first recommending heedless charity (by inviting us to 'give and ask no questions') and then, quite unexpectedly, redeeming it, through his own Christ-like book-keeping.

An indulgent comedy surrounds Hazlitt and Lamb's exploration of daydream; it is only in the work of Thomas De Quincey that its hypocrisies are exposed. In 'The Pleasures of Opium' section of the *Confessions of an English Opium-Eater* (1821) De Quincey detailed his two favourite ways of spending Saturday night in London. After taking laudanum he would either go to Covent Garden to hear Grassini the famous opera singer, or he would stroll alone among the night markets of the poor. And in the latter case, it seems, the Opium-Eater loved nothing better than to join their parties, involving himself sympathetically in their household concerns:

> If wages were a little higher or expected to be so, or the quartern loaf a little lower, or it was reported that onions and butter were expected to fall, I was glad; yet, if the contrary were true, I drew from opium some means of consoling myself. For opium (like the bee, that extracts its materials indiscriminately from roses and from the soot of chimneys) can overrule all feelings into compliance with the master-key.

Laudanum acts like a kind of bottled daydream, throwing a rich, gauzy film over the world outside. Everything is harmonized by its soundtrack, its happiness montage. Like Lamb's tale of the beggar, De Quincey's drug-addled reminiscence is a fantasy of class connection without confrontation, of bourgeois sympathy, as it were, without any baggage. What turns this situation on its head, however, is the account the Opium-Eater then gives of how these excursions came back to haunt him in later years:

> Some of these rambles led me to great distances, for an opium-eater is too happy to observe the motion of time; and sometimes in my attempts to steer homewards, upon nautical principles, by fixing my eye on the polestar, and seeking ambitiously for a northwest passage, instead of circumnavigating all the capes and headlands I had doubled in my outward voyage, I came suddenly upon such knotty problems of alleys, such enigmatical entries, and such sphynx's riddles of streets without thoroughfares, as must, I conceive, baffle the audacity of porters and confound the intellects of hackneycoachmen. I could almost have believed at times that I must be the first discoverer of some of these *terrae incognitae*, and doubted whether they had yet been laid down in the modern charts of London. For all this, however, I paid a heavy price in distant years, when the human face tyrannised over my dreams, and the perplexities of my steps in London came back and haunted my sleep, with the feeling of perplexities, moral and intellectual, that brought confusion to the reason, or anguish and remorse to the conscience.

The repressed returns, as it always does, with a vengeance. Where before there was Oedipus the detective-hero, the first explorer of 'sphinx's riddles of streets without thoroughfares', now there is only Oedipus the retrospective criminal, perplexed by his own steps. Everything that was skated over in the Opium-Eater's original day-dream is painfully revisited in the new realm of night, with the dreamer now paying a 'heavy price'—a healthy chunk of interest, one might say—on his unpaid debt to the past. The guilt is, in this case, both personal and social, incorporating all the faces that he took in so casually when 'slumming it' on opium, but with a special glance towards his former friend and protector Ann, the Soho prostitute, whose face he had lost in the London crowd several years before.

Baudelaire was heavily indebted to De Quincey, reproducing extensive chunks of the Opium confessions in his *Paradis Artificiels* of 1860. And in 'The Double Room', one of the *Spleen de Paris* prose poems (1869), the Frenchman tears through narcotic daydream with a similar intensity. 'The Double Room' opens with a room 'that resembles a reverie', an elegant Parisian apartment where 'the atmosphere is tinted rosy-blue', where 'muslin showers down abundantly in front of the windows and the bed', and where the furniture itself 'has the appearance of sleepwalking'. 'There is no artistic abomination on the walls. Relative to pure dream, to simple impression, definite art, concrete art is a blasphemy. Here, everything has the just-sufficient clarity and delicious obscurity of harmony.' On the bed lies 'The Idol', the sovereign queen of one's dreams, whose eyes flame imperiously in the twilight. It is an evocative fantasy—evocative but vague. 'No! there are no more minutes,' the narrator says, 'no more seconds! Time has disappeared, it is Eternity who reigns—an eternity of delights!' Suddenly there is a knock at the door, which 'as in infernal dreams' strikes the narrator 'like a pickaxe'. A Spectre enters: it's a bailiff, he thinks, or an unhappy mistress, or a messenger boy from an editor demanding copy, and no sooner do these anxieties return to haunt him than his fantasy-room evaporates:

> O Horror! I remember! I remember! Yes! This slum, this eternal resting-place of boredom, is where I live. Here is the stupid furniture, dusty and dog-eared; the chimney cold and without coal, all smeared over with spittle ... and this perfume from another world, with which I had intoxicated my sophisticated sensibility, alas! it is replaced by a fetid odour of tobacco and some kind of nauseating mould. Now all one can breathe here is the rancid smell of desolation.

Time returns, and a whole circus of allegorical Fears and Nightmares, and each second that shakes the pendulum says 'I am Life, insufferable, implacable Life!' The overall movement, as in De Quincey, is from daydream to nightmare, but it is also, if seen in more positive, literary terms, a shift from fashionable stasis back into vulgar action, with empty form being superseded by messy, multifarious content.

In 'Creative Writers and Daydreaming' (1908) Sigmund Freud argued that whereas dreams tend to be highly personal, formally experimental and gothic, daydreams are much more derivative and conventional. He made a clear connection between daydreaming and popular fiction in this respect. In our daydreams, Freud says, we are always inheriting a fortune or marrying the boss's daughter; we are always the triumphant hero of the tale. Daydreams, like night-dreams, have the remnants of infantile wishes contained within them, he argued, repressed desires that are unpalatable to the conscious ego. But whereas a night-dream only ever undergoes a kind of incomplete 'secondary revision' as the waking sleeper struggles belatedly to pull it into acceptable shape, the latent content of daydream is much more thoroughly polished and revised. For as Freud himself described it in *The Interpretation of Dreams* (1900): '[Daydreams] stand in much the same relation to the childhood memories from which they are derived as do some of the Baroque palaces of Rome to the ancient ruins whose pavements and columns have provided the material for the recent structures.' Daydreams are extrovert façades trying to cover up illicit foundations. Theirs is the rosy blue mask of unconscious desire. That is one reason, perhaps, for their characteristic flatness, and the partic-ular kind of impersonality that they tend to exude. What writers of popular fiction do, Freud suggested, is re-present infantile wishes— their own, and those of their audience—in a carefully disguised, self-consciously fashionable form, somewhat akin to daydream, with the broad appeal of these fictions only being enhanced by their off-the-peg nature.

Freud saw something limited and two-dimensional about day-dreaming. D. W. Winnicott, his English follower, took the critique even further. In a famous essay on 'Dreaming, Fantasying and Living' (1971) Winnicott distinguished between playing, dreaming and living —all of which he considered as different ways of grappling with real objects—and daydreaming, which he considered as mere dissocia-tion, a meaningless form of escape. He illustrated this theory with a case study, the story of a woman who, in the course of a seemingly normal but in fact excessively compliant childhood, had gradually developed the habit of going elsewhere in her mind. 'Fantasying possesses her', Winnicott wrote, 'like an evil spirit':

As my patient grew so she managed to construct a life in which nothing that was really happening was fully significant to her. Gradually she became one of the many who do not feel that they exist in their own right as human beings.

She became addicted to solitaire, and to 'doing everything while doing nothing'. She became, in short, like a woman trapped on a bus, whose mind is everywhere but on her own journey. The only way out of this condition, Winnicott considered, was for his patient to learn to discriminate between her dreaming—which was productive, and significant, and had to do with real wishes—and her daydreaming, which was none of those things. The problem was that this distinction proved very hard for the patient herself to recognise, and for her analyst it was all but impossible. No matter how intently he listened to her testimony there was no easy way for him to tell, purely from a verbal description, what had really being going on in her mind. On waking, a daydream about 'hectically cutting out, planning, working on a pattern for a dress' would typically take over from a 'real' dream on the same subject, revising it, normalizing it, and emptying it of personal meaning. And it was this daydream, in all its tidy literalness, that the patient would remember and take to the analyst. Gradually, Winnicott turned the very uninterpretability of daydream, its radical lack of suggestiveness, into a defining symptom: 'The fantasying is simply about making a dress. The dress has no symbolic value. A dog is a dog is a dog. In the dream, by contrast, the same thing would indeed have had symbolic meaning.' 'The key word to be carried back into the dream', Winnicott told her, 'was *formlessness*, which is what the material is like before it is patterned and cut and shaped and put together … her childhood environment seemed unable to allow her to be formless but must, as she felt, pattern her and cut her out into shapes conceived by other people.' Formlessness, here, is associated with creative playing as well as dreaming, whereas daydreaming, as Freud himself had already suggested many years earlier, is what adults do when they no longer know how to play.

Pitched as it is somewhere between lyric poetry and popular fiction, the Baudelairean prose poem is a flirtation with formlessness, pitting dream against daydream, imaginative freedom against conventional narrative. So it's not surprising that when the Surrealists strove to give dreaming a political valency in the 1920s the example of the *Spleen de Paris* was at least as important to them as the more recent writings of Freud. The Surrealists' main antagonist, in politico-aesthetic terms, was functionalist modernism, and the highly rational metropolis that it sought to bring into being. Special loathing was reserved for Le Corbusier and his *Ville Contemporaine* plan of 1922, a forest of rectangular apartment blocks interspersed by square parks and highways. For Michel Colle, writing in 1948 in the first issue of the journal of the avant-garde art movement COBRA, 'poetry and dreaming' was a useful shorthand for everything Le Corbusier and his followers had set out to destroy: 'We have been given the machine for living in, where very often nothing is given over to the only truly human parts of life, to poetry and to dream.'

So it was as a tool to beat back modernist fantasies of rationality, and of the utterly streamlined city, that André Breton and the Surrealists started campaigning on the dream ticket in the 1920s. And what did they have to oppose to the *Ville Contemporaine*? They had the arcades, the old covered walkways, lined with cafés, shops, restaurants and brothels, which had been installed in central Paris (and London, and other major European cities) in the first part of the nineteenth century. What the arcades offered, especially in their much-decayed twentieth-century state, was a murky, disorderly, irrational space, a space full of outmoded objects and unexpected encounters, a space, in short, which was very much like the realm of dream that had been so brilliantly invoked in Freud's recent writings. Here was a landscape in which—as Louis Aragon declared brazenly in the 'Passage de l'Opera' section of *Le paysan de Paris* (1926)—the unconscious could discover its objective:

> The whole fauna of human fantasies, their marine vegetation, drifts and luxuriates in the dimly lit zones of human activity, as though plaiting thick tresses of darkness. Here, too, appear the great light-houses of the mind, with their outward resemblance to less pure symbols. The gateway to mystery swings open at the touch of human

weakness and we have entered the realm of darkness. One false step, one slurred syllable together reveals a man's thoughts. The disquieting atmosphere of places contains similar locks that cannot be bolted fast against infinity. Wherever the living pursue particularly ambiguous activities, the inanimate may sometimes assume the reflection of their most secret motives: and thus our cities are peopled with unrecognised sphinxes which will never stop the passing dreamer and ask him mortal questions unless he first projects his meditation, his absence of mind, towards them. But if this wise man has the power to guess their secret, and interrogates them in his turn, all that these faceless monsters will grant is that he shall once again plumb his own depths. Henceforth, it is the modern light radiating from the unusual that will rivet his attention.

De Quincey's London had brimmed over with *terrae incognitae* and 'sphinx's riddles of streets without thoroughfares', highly diverting in the opium-soaked present, increasingly menacing in the dreams of later years. In Aragon's Paris, however, the sphinx is a helpful monster, and the realm of darkness repeatedly illuminated by 'great [phallic] lighthouses of the mind'. Come into the hall of mirrors, says Aragon, and give yourself up to the 'magique circonstentielle'! In recommending this total immersal in the psychopathology of urban life, the Surrealists hoped that a liberation of the unconscious would help post-war Europe out of its contemporary *impasse*. What is more, they saw the city, in so far as it was capable of nurturing man's creative irrationality, as the main agent of this change. And it was for this reason, Aragon insisted, that the arcades of Paris had to be preserved, not as museums of past consumption, but as blueprints for the future.

An avid reader of Aragon, Walter Benjamin had seen a similar revolutionary potential in dream-regression. To him it was helpful to think of nineteenth-century bourgeois society as having descended into a kind of 'dream-sleep', an unreal fantasy of the material happiness that was going to be brought about by mass commodities. And this 'dream-sleep', in Benjamin's evocative formulation, had a lot in common with Freudian 'daydream', constituting one vast, shared realm of standardized desire. The only way to wake up from this sleep, Benjamin reasoned, was to return to its infantile sources, and to recover all that was most utopian—and unfulfilled—about the bourgeois ideal.

Like the Surrealists, Walter Benjamin saw the Parisian arcade as a dream space. 'In the arcades,' he said, in his enormous, unfinished *Arcades Project* (1927–40), 'we, as in a dream, once again live the life of our parents and grandparents.' A product of capitalism's first childhood, the arcade was the neglected toy cupboard of bourgeois society, with the products it contained being so quaint and out-of-date, so completely lacking in the glamour of the new commodity, that they had a curious effect upon the twentieth-century observer. Children's books and toys, gentlemen and ladies' fashions, luxury foodstuffs, accessories, ornaments, maps: the effect of many of these images, Benjamin argued, was dialectical: one was struck by two thoughts at once. One saw, with new sympathy, the utopian aspirations of the nineteenth-century, and one also saw, with new understanding, how unrealized they had been. So the message one received from the arcades, those treasure troves of discarded fantasies, was powerful but complex. The viewer was imbued all over again with something of the naive idealism of early bourgeois society, but also, at the same time, with an increased suspicion of the commodity form. He was subjected, in short, to a revolutionary awakening of extraordinary immediacy, a process that Benjamin described—in one of those highly arresting phrases of his—as 'dialectics at a standstill'.

'Children can redeem the daydreams of their parents', Benjamin wrote, referring to the twentieth century's relationship to its predecessor, and inviting us to think of the commodity itself as a kind of daydream, containing all the hopes of humanity, but in fetishized, inaccessible form. Nor was the metaphor of childhood taken up lightly, for it was Benjamin's opinion that, in order to fulfil a truly revolutionary role, the people of the future would, in truth, have to act like children, re-engaging, through play, with the concrete world of things. 'The fading of the nineteenth century', he wrote, 'is the historical condition for the setting free of its relics as elements of a dream world and a children's world.' Children took nothing for granted, getting to know objects by laying hands on them, and by playing with them creatively were able to release new kinds of meaning. And it was precisely in terms of the spirit of subversive play secretly embedded in the midst of commodity fetishism that Benjamin imagined the germ of revolution: 'The imminent awakening is poised,' he wrote, in 'Konvolut K' of the *Arcades Project*, 'like the wooden horse of the Greeks, in the Troy of dreams.'

After the Second World War, the Situationists took over from the Surrealists in the battle against urban functionalism, and they too recommended a form of awakening through dream. 'The sleeping creator [in everyone] must be awakened,' declared Asger Jorn in the first issue of the *Situationist International* (1958) 'and his waking state can be termed "situationist".' The Situationists built upon Surrealism's privileging of the unconscious in their movements about the city, but they also succeeded in democratizing it through the notion of the *dérive*. The *dérive*, or drift, was an embracing of the disorderly in both subject and object, and, what is more, it was open to everyone. Essentially, it involved free-associating around the city in search of 'ambient spaces', that is, spaces with a special character borne of peculiar, heterogeneous and often accidental elements. One such space, as discovered by Guy Debord and a friend in his 'Two Accounts of the Dérive' (1958), was the Ledoux Rotunda, an old customs gate, at the meeting point of the canal de l'Ourcq and the place de Stalingrad in north-east Paris:

> [Next they came across] the admirable rotunda of Claude-Nicolas Ledoux, almost ruined, left in unbelievable neglect, the charm of which was singularly increased by the passage, very nearby, of the overhead metro. One thinks here of the happy prediction of Mikhail Toukhachevsky, cited formerly in *La Révolution Surréaliste*, on the beauty that Versailles would gain when a factory had been built between the lake and the château.

A busy confluence of road and rail, air and water, the place de Stalingrad could be linked with geographical illustrations in children's text books, 'where one finds collected in a single image a port, a mountain, an isthmus, a forest, a river, a dyke, a cape, a bridge, a ship and an archipelago'. Debord was particularly struck by the view from the rotunda looking north-east down the canal de l'Ourcq, which reminded him of a couple of harbour paintings by the seventeenth-century painter Claude. But it was not, as he was at pains to point out, the picturesque beauty of these views that had drawn his admiration, but rather their sense of playfulness and potentiality:

> It will be understood that in speaking here of beauty I don't have in mind plastic beauty—the new beauty can only be a beauty of situations—but simply the particularly moving presentation, in both cases—of a *sum of possibilities*.

While the streets and suburbs of post-war Paris were being reconfigured to improve circulation, Guy Debord championed the claims of the entangled and the eclectic, of little squares, streets and corners with their own intricacies and interconnections. There was no Romantic nostalgia in this, he insisted, but rather a profound conviction that such ambient spaces could provide a model for the future. 'The mark of the city', as Lewis Mumford had written, with tragic optimism, in 1938, 'is its purposive social complexity. It represents the maximum possibility of humanising the natural environment and of naturalising the human heritage ... as life becomes insurgent once more in our civilisation, conquering the reckless thrust of barbarism, the culture of cities will be both instrument and goal.' As for Mumford, so too for Debord, the ideal city was one in which all human creativity would be maximized. It would be an imaginatively suggestive space, not a streamlined or spectacular one. Such a city would be to some degree structured like the unconscious, a realm in which all elements would exist in an open relationship with one another. It would be a multi-layered space, difficult to control, impossible to plan, the ultimate success of which would be gauged by the 'situational possibilities' it made available. What is more, the Situationist dream city would be inimical to daydream to the degree that it would do away with the need for it, re-dissolving spectacle back into situation, and fantasy back into play. How the city looked would be less important than how it could be used: it would be the final transcendence of art by everyday life.

Benjamin, the Surrealists and the Situationists had all imagined political awakening to be irrevocable; Freud and Baudelaire suspected otherwise. In *The Interpretation of Dreams* Freud had written extensively of 'secondary revision' as the process by which, during the latter stages of a dream and indeed while just on the point of waking, the dreamer will already be hard at work trying to bury some of its more troubling implications. It's as if, even in our sleep, we can't help reworking our dreams into daydreams—making something more conventional, more palatable, less real.

Forty years earlier Baudelaire had already anticipated how secondary revision might work upon the social imagination. In 'The Eyes of the Poor', another one of his *Spleen de Paris* prose poems, the narrator describes an evening with his lover on one of Baron Haussmann's new boulevards. The couple are ensconced in a glittering new café, having spent the entire day in pursuit of a daydream. Their fantasy was that from that moment on they would share all their thoughts with one another, so that 'their two souls would be one', an idea that, as the narrator admits, 'had nothing original about it', even if 'having been dreamt by all men, it has been realised by none'.

Outside, the splendours of the new boulevard shine through the half-cleared-away rubble; inside, the café is bathed in shimmering light. On the walls there is a golden mural depicting page-boys with plump cheeks being pulled along by dogs, laughing ladies with falcons perched on their wrists, nymphs and goddesses carrying on their heads fruit, pies and game. There are also Hebes and Ganymedes offering with outstretched arms whole amphoras of mousse and veritable obelisks of ice cream. It was, in short, as the narrator says, 'all history and mythology put in the service of piggery' (*goinfrerie*).

Right in front of them, on the pavement, stands a poor family in rags. There is a man of forty, tired-looking and greying, a boy holding his father's hand, and in the man's arms, a baby, too weak to walk. All are staring intently at the café, and the narrator thinks he can discriminate their thoughts:

The eyes of the father said: 'How beautiful it is! How beautiful! One would say that all of the gold of the poor world has gone into the decoration of those walls!'—The eyes of the small boy: 'How beautiful it is! How beautiful! But it is a house where only people who are not like us can go.'—As to the eyes of the little one, they were too fascinated to express anything other than a stupid and profound joy.

Not only does the narrator feel softened by this 'family of eyes', he is also made to feel a little ashamed by them—ashamed, as he says, 'of our glasses and our carafes, which were much bigger than our thirst'. He turns his eyes towards those of his companion, hoping to see these self-same thoughts reflected there, and as he plunges deeply into her beautiful soft green orbs, 'inhabited by Caprice and by the spirit of the moon' she suddenly bursts out: 'I find these people unbearable, with their eyes as wide as coach-gates [*portes cochères*]! Can't you ask the *maître du café* to get rid of them?'

The prose poem—or short story—concludes with the narrator speaking directly to his beloved: 'How difficult it is to understand one another,' he says, 'and how incommunicable is thought, even between lovers!' In fact, the story had begun with the same thought, only expressed more angrily, a bitter reflection, as it were, from the morning after: 'Ah! You would like to know why I hate you today. It will no doubt be easier for me to explain than for you to comprehend, because you are, I believe, the best example of feminine impermeability that one could ever meet.'

A masterpiece of concision at just over a page in length, 'The Eyes of the Poor' is a dream trapped inside a daydream; a revolutionary bomb that has been defused. Considered solely from the narrator's point of view, the piece has all the hallmarks of a daydream wish-fulfilment. However disgruntled he pretends to be at the beginning, he is still (if only in his own mind) the little hero of the tale. He is the one who feels sympathetic towards the poor family on the pavement, the only one who really understands them. It is his lover—a kept mistress probably—who supplies the impediment.

But there is a flaw in the narrator's argument. In the first flush of pity for the poor family he turns to the soft, green eyes of his mistress, fully expecting to see his own sympathetic feelings sweetly mirrored therein. The problem is that the gentle eyes he encounters give absolutely no warning of the anger and frustration that their owner is about to express. And if the gap between his mistress's look and her inner thoughts is so enormous, how then can he be so confident in reading the eyes of the poor?

The narrator's day had begun with a daydream of transparency—between himself and his beloved—and it ends in the same way, but with that fantasy now directed towards the poor. And the key note of his ventriloquizations, as he moves from the father to his son and then to the young baby, is one of humble awe. All hunger and anger have been removed from the picture; there is nothing to trouble the police. What is more, the succession of voices exactly mimics the process of infantilization that bourgeois culture has always tried to foist upon mass society, encouraging it to dissolve all difficult questions of money and class into a 'stupid, profound joy' in modern spectacle.

Is the narrator angry at his mistress's class prejudice? Or is he simply angry that her thoughts don't mirror his own? She wants the poor family taken out of the urban picture (and sent back to the suburban margins, presumably, where Haussmann thought they belonged). But in the framing of the story the narrator could be accused of doing the same thing—that is, of displacing the poor from the centre of the picture, and placing the prime focus on the argument between himself and his beloved. This, we might suggest, is secondary revision in action—the reworking of a troubling social encounter into a story of domestic disagreement.

The message of the story from the narrator's point of view is simply that he was the one pursuing sympathy and transparency while his mistress, regrettably, remained *imperméable*. He could read into the eyes of the poor; all she could see was *portes-cochères*. An unexpected not to say surreal image, *portes-cochères* are the kind of gates, vast, wooden and double-doored, that guard the old aristocratic mansions of Paris. Some readers have speculated that the mistress in Baudelaire's story might herself be of working-class origin, a reasonable assumption given the sexual mores of the time.

She might even, at a stretch, be the mother of the children on the pavement, although there is no evidence for this in the text. So there might be Malthusian anxiety in her reading of this avid 'family of eyes'—and possibly a painful recollection of her own similarly avid childhood. But why does she describe them as having eyes as wide as *portes-cochères?* Coach-gates are the kind of gates one can drive a coach through—they're wide, they allow traffic, but they also demarcate and even objectify class boundaries. To a Frenchman the phrase might recall 1789 and the Paris mob's storming of Versailles—but even that doesn't quite exhaust its sum of possibilities. Placed where it is in the text it functions as a dialectical image, simultaneously conjuring up naivety and avidity, openness and hollowness; it is like one of those unrecognized sphinxes in the arcades of Aragon.

It is plausible that behind the eyes of *portes-cochères* the narrator's mistress might be seeing *portes-cochons,* fantastical dream-gates preventing or permitting the flow of piggery (*la goinfrerie,* mentioned earlier by the narrator) and/or the flow of trash (*la cochonnerie* in French). A further way of thinking about the *portes-cochères* would be to link them with the Ledoux Rotunda in 'Two Accounts of the Dérive'. There Guy Debord had taken an old customs-gate, a former place of taxation and restriction, and re-imagined it as a new kind of playground for adults. In Baudelaire's story it is the narrator who, for all his apparent sympathy, subdivides and subdues the poor family's gaze. It is his mistress, by contrast, who dares to look deeper into its openness (its *formlessness,* one might almost say, following Winnicott), and is appalled by its hungry potential.

The professed shame of the narrator when confronted by the 'have nots' on the pavement has its repressed corollary in the pleasurable surprise he feels at seeing himself as one of the 'haves', looking out from his café table with a large carafe by his side. But what this particular daydreamer fails to acknowledge is the extent to which, as Guy Debord put it in *The Society of the Spectacle* (1967), 'Spectacular Oppositions conceal the *unity of poverty'*: 'If different forms of the same alienation struggle against each other in the guise of irreconcilable antagonisms, this is because they are all based on real contradictions that are repressed.' The narrator believes in the opposition between café and pavement. However, the new café, dazzling as it is, is still only a café, a place where aristocratic fantasies can be freely indulged, but only until night (and the bill) comes. And the rubble that litters the new boulevard continues to tell of a society in process, in which there is still a huge gap between the spectacle—the lavish mural, with its promise of universal plenty—and the surrounding reality. The narrator is closer to the family than he thinks in this respect, indeed what he sees in their eyes ('What a beautiful place! But it is not for the likes of me') is what is already in his own.

The striking thing about 'The Eyes of the Poor' is the way it encourages us to think of dream and daydream, those two different forms of utopian imagining, as gazing out from the same café table, indeed as being very nearly inseparable. Dream is terrifyingly open; it is the state in which the unconscious meets its objective; daydream is self-conscious and self-consoling, and seeks to 'frame' dream's vision. But they are like a warring couple in that there can never be one without the other, with the one always seeking to distract from what the other has already seen.

Reading

Aragon, Louis, *Paris Peasant*, ed. Simon Watson-Taylor (New York: Exact Change, 1999).

Baudelaire, Charles, *Paris Spleen* (Prose Poems), trans. Louise Varèse (New Directions: New York, 1947).

Benjamin, Walter, *The Arcades Project*, ed. Rolf Tiedemann (Cambridge, MA, and London: Belknap Press, 1999).

Debord, Guy, *The Society of the Spectacle* (London: Rebel Press, 1992).

Freud, Sigmund, *The Interpretation of Dreams*, ed. Angela Richards (Harmondsworth: Penguin, 1991).

Hazlitt, William, *Metropolitan Writings*, ed. Gregory Dart (Manchester: Carcanet Press, 2005).

Lamb, Charles, *Essays of Elia*, ed. Jonathan Bate (Oxford: Oxford University Press, 1987).

De Quincey, Thomas, *Confessions of an English Opium-Eater*, ed. Grevel Lindop (Oxford: Oxford University Press, 2008).

Winnicott, D. W., *Playing and Reality*, ed. Robert Rodnam (London: Routledge, 2005).

Driving

Iain Borden

Material conditions in architecture and cities such as glass, concrete or tarmac, texture, transparency and sound, can be engaged with through different activities, like walking, looking, skateboarding and cycling. From these kinds of engagement, different cultural meanings result, such as those to do with ownership, control, identity, pleasure and humour. Here rests the full social potential of architectural and urban materiality, where it becomes a true machine of possibilities.

So what of driving and the experience of architecture and cities from the car? Firstly, and perhaps most obviously, there is the sheer quantitative presence of the automobile. Some 1 billion cars were manufactured in the twentieth century, and currently over 700 million are still operating—quite possibly 1 billion will be operating by 2030. And geographically, massive new economies and developing countries—notably China—are now developing a new car culture.

Driving is, however, not just a simple function of the quantitative amount of cars on the road and the number of car journeys undertaken. Driving is of course a gigantic ensemble, of cars and roads, but also of all kinds of different architectures derived from driving, from petrol stations to billboards, and of people, the thoughts we have, the actions we make, the images we consume and imagine, the meanings we make, the codes and regulations we negotiate. It is also the speeds at which we drive, the spatial conditions we encounter, the ways in which we look at and listen to the landscape, the very emotions and

attitudes we have towards driving and the city. As A. B. Filson Young—author of the *Complete Motorist* of 1905, which provides many illuminating insights into driving—stated: 'The true home of the motor-car is not in garage or workshop, showroom or factory, but on the open road. There it comes into its own, there it justifies itself, there it fulfils its true and appointed destiny.'

Given such comments, and given the vast literature available on cars and automobiles, it is curious how little thought has been given to the actual experience and pleasures of driving. There is a multitude of writings on car design, car production, on marketing, racing, and maintaining cars, on highway and road design, on traffic management, on the economics of cars and on their representation in art; but there is comparatively little on the actual activity of driving itself. So what are the various pleasures involved in different kinds of driving, at different speeds and in different kinds of spatial landscape? And how do these pleasures relate to distinct encounters with cities and architecture, so producing similarly distinct political and cultural experiences? I want to look in turn at four distinct intersections of motoring speeds and landscapes.

City Driving: 0–30 mph

The impact of automobiles and car driving on cities and architecture is, of course, immense. Apart from the visible impact of the cars themselves—whether moving or parked—there is also the whole range of roads, signs and street furniture, car parks and general urban form which we see everywhere in cities worldwide. This is a truly global and everyday architecture, one which scarcely existed a hundred years ago but which today occupies, for example, 50 per cent of all land in Los Angeles and 25 per cent in London.

So what are the cultural connotations of driving in this urban form? Most powerful of all is the notion that driving is the true harbinger of democracy, creating a world where all men and women are equal, where they can do anything, go anywhere, meet anyone.

In architectural and urban design, this is the promise of projects like Frank Lloyd Wright's 'Broadacre City', a decentred utopia where mobility, and in particular the mobility offered by the car, enables the American dream to come true. This is the same promise of dense metropolitan cities, where cars like the Mini have helped people to cross class and gender boundaries and to express their individuality and sense of liberation in the metropolis. For example, one

famous 1968 publicity shot of the English television presenter Cathy McGowan shows this youthful and highly fashionable media figure smiling in the driving seat of her new Mini while a building is under construction in the background—an image clearly intended to demonstrate strong connections between McGowan, the city, the car and the act of driving as a symbol of 1960s female independence and cultural innovation.

In particular, it is not just the owning but the driving of cars like the Mini which helped to create this kind of everyday democracy: driving as a kind of exuberance, a playful darting around city streets. This can be clearly seen in the original version of the film *The Italian Job* (1969), directed by Peter Collinson, where the bullion-robbers use three Minis (in red, white and blue, the colours of the UK Union Jack) to escape through the alleys and inner courtyards of Turin in a celebratory and adventurous form of town driving. In 2007, Fiat, whose cars were used by the mafia and in traffic-jam sequences in the original film, showed a series of television adverts entitled *The Italian Job Revisited*, in which their new Punto cars (now in red, white and green, the colours of the Italian flag) replicated the exhilarating driving through Turin that had been performed some 40 years earlier. In a similar vein, BMW, marketing its version of the Mini in the summer of 2001, launched an advertising campaign with the strap-line, 'It's A Mini Adventure!' This campaign used devices such as dramatic cartoon-style stories, movie-placement in the Austin Powers film *Goldmember* (2002), and interactive internet-based videogames. In addition, huge billboards were constructed on 13 sites in city centres around the UK, using full-size cars apparently driving up and over urban buildings, accompanied by texts such as 'New Mini Attempts To Drive Up Building. Succeeds. The End.' Directed by the advertising and brand-developing agency WRCS, this was clearly intended to extend the original Mini's exuberant character and notions of exhilaration, speed, independence and surprise.

Although many of these cultural representations of driving occur in the formats of film and television, it is nonetheless very much within normal people's everyday lives that the city car operates, allowing them to negotiate the conflicts they may feel in their lives.

For example, driving cars such as the Fiat Punto and the BMW Mini—partly through their sporty performance, and partly through the cultural associations constructed through the media campaigns—encourages young parents to reconcile the drudgery of childcare and family life with exciting ideas of leisure and outdoor adventure. City driving and car usage is, then, not just a dynamic act, nor just a representation, but a way people constitute themselves in relation to their metropolitan context through a complex intersection of cultural associations and actual driving experiences.

But what does this experience of town driving entail? What particular visual and spatial experiences are involved? Perhaps the most obvious aspect of urban car driving is the reduction of city form to a series of signs, billboards and lights. That is, car driving offers a reading of the city that focuses on the abstract, the visual, and on the surface. Most famous here is the analysis offered by Robert Venturi, Denise Scott Brown and Steven Izenour in *Learning From Las Vegas* (2007), which posits an architecture of decoration, symbolism, repetition and communication. The experience of the city here is highly semiotic, based on a reading of signs and signals as much as on a plastic, sensuous experience of actually driving through space.

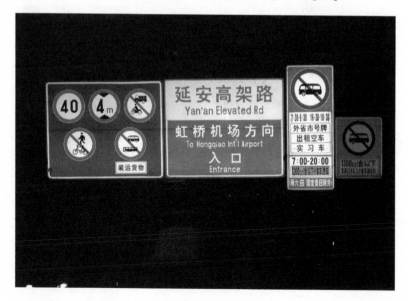

This kind of semiotic experience is not as culturally reductive as many would have us believe, for signs are capable of speaking to us in a multitude of different ways. For example, a single car journey will provide signs for traffic management, traffic direction, communication networks, entertainment, retail and historical traces of all kinds. All of this is contained within people's everyday lives and routines, such that although this system of signs may not be consciously thought about, it is undoubtedly an immensely complicated and variable communication system.

There is also a condition of temporality in the urban driving experience. In city driving, this means a temporality of the nippy, fast and short-lived. Driving here creates a sense of quick communication, a kind of physical email. But these journeys are of course also held within a highly individualistic timetabling of instants and fragments of time—individual journeys to work, our social life, and so on. Thus the fast pace of urban life is matched by the stop-start, perpetually impatient nature of urban driving.

What urban driving produces, therefore, is an experience of visual signs and signals, but also of time, hearing, smelling, judging space and size, danger and safety, impatience and frustration and an overall sense of every-ready alertness—qualities which counter the views of Henri Lefebvre and others who see such activity as a purely sensationless, culture-free zone. For it is in the very dynamic of urban driving that we find its cultural meanings—meanings both as metaphor for, and constituent element of, modern urban life. Indeed, the situation is even more complicated in that while the urban driving sensibility is certainly dulled—given that we do it many times and often routinely—it is also hyperactive, always aware of the changing state of the city around us, always restless. It is, therefore, an experience that represents the dual character of the city, that which is simultaneously anonymous, repetitive and flat, and personal, rhythmical and variegated.

To negotiate this complex condition, urban drivers have to generate a strong sense of control. Primarily, this is achieved by cognitive mapping—that is, of knowing where one is driving not only in the abstract terms of the street map but also in the specific terms of the

Photograph: Chris Underwood.

local and personal map. Given the mass of information and precise actions involved in remembering and implementing such mapping processes, it is no accident that the London cab drivers' test is referred to as 'The Knowledge', implying that this understanding involves a complete comprehension of the capital. But the London cab driver's experience is far from being just about abstract maps and locations; urban driving is about a whole range of related spatial tactics, such as taking short-cuts, merging, doubling back, overtaking, pulling out, speeding, and so on—a technique of spatial vectors. All of this enables the driver not just to get around the city but to produce themselves as a metropolitan resident—as someone who not only knows the city, but knows how to live in an urban manner. The culture here is the challenge of the city to the self, and hence the ability of the driver not simply to survive but to thrive.

Countryside Driving: 30–55 mph

From the start of the twentieth century, automobiles were far more than purely work-oriented machines—Henry Ford, the British car manufacturer William Morris, and Adolf Hitler all saw the car as a means for families to go on gentle drives in the countryside. Principal among these motoring delights was simply seeing new parts of the country. As Filson Young declared, 'the road sets us free [and] allows us to follow our own choice as to how fast and how far we shall go, permits us to tarry where and when we will'. When they stopped, as they frequently did, inter-war motorists took photographs of their spouse on their new Kodak camera, went camping in motor camps, or visited wildernesses like Yellowstone Park.

So when we become concerned about our over-use of the car in the countryside, and discuss ways of preserving nature, it is important to realize that our very experience of nature has often been produced from the car and its journeys through landscapes. Of course, this is exactly what car manufacturers play on when they include depictions of nature and the environment in their advertisements, typically showing 4x4s rushing through deserts and other wildernesses, dramatically throwing up sand and dirt from over-sized and deep-treaded wheels.

There are also other pleasures to the tourist drive, ones that are less dependent on travelling into new landscapes and more on the sensual pleasures of mobile experience. This is quite a complicated argument, which has been rehearsed by Sara Danius and others in artistic and literary debates, and it is worth summarizing its main features here under three categories: how objects appear differently; ways of seeing; and the effects of speed.

Firstly, driving heightens the Ruskinian distinction between 'numbing habit' and 'unmediated sensory experience', which is to say that driving can shock us out of our normal, unthinking and disconnected relationship with the world, and instead make us aware of the pure sensory experience of encountering the world around us. As a result, *objects appear differently*, so that which once was familiar now becomes strange. Trees, buildings and other vehicles all look

different from the car than they do from the roadside. In particular, they often take on the appearance of a 'purposeless beauty', whereby objects are divorced from their original context or function, and so appear as items of non-contextual contemplation. Objects also appear differently in other ways. For example, one of the main effects of driving is that the mobile becomes immobile—for the driver, the car and other cars around it appear to be stationary.

Conversely, the immobile becomes mobile—i.e. cars animate land-scapes, such that stationary objects appear to be moving. As Filson Young wrote of telegraph posts in Hertfordshire:

> As you pass ... they begin to crowd together, by twos and fours, coming, you would think, from nowhere, flying in all directions over the ancient roofs of the town and past the chimneys and weather-vanes like gathering rumours or like flurried passengers making haste to be in time.

Secondly, the *way we see* when driving is different. By releasing objects from their context, the process of seeing these objects is in turn released from contextual knowledge, and, as a result, this seeing process becomes a form of seeing 'in the first person', allowing the driver to see what he or she directly sees rather than what he or she knows. This process is particularly attractive to artists and writers,

allowing them to see things as pure seeing, and so to provide appropriate metaphors for modern life, rather than relying on seeing via the intellect. Other forms of seeing are also implicated in the driving experience, notably the way in which the windscreen acts as a frame, limiting the landscape within a carefully prescribed boundary and hence converting it into an object of pleasure. Through this frame, landscapes become fragmented by driving, rendered into a series of discrete objects, vistas, markings and so on, but also then reconnected and resynthesized as a sequence—a specific narration, if you like, constructed by the particular driver.

Thirdly, *increased speed intensifies these kinds of experience*, exacerbating the sense of strangeness, newness and disconnectedness. In particular, the landscape appears in cinematic terms—notably those

of framing, sequencing, editing, unusual juxtapositions and montage, changing pace, unexplained events and sights and so on, all of which is induced by the speeding, kinematic nature of driving. Furthermore, it is not just the landscape that is altered in this process, for the driver's body is also animated by speed and the sense that one is somewhere in between being in control and being out of it. Indeed, the driver's body is no longer theirs alone, with many drivers often commenting on how the car comes alive, merging with their own physical self to make one seamless, living whole.

In short, the kinaesthetics of driving involves a substantial reorientation of the experience of time and space, where sight, senses, intellect, landscape, meaning, artistic creativity and the human body are all potentially reconfigured. As Filson Young wrote of driving:

> It flattens out the world, enlarges the horizon, loosens a little the bonds of time, sets back a little the barriers of space. And man, who created and endowed it, who sits and rides upon it as upon a whirlwind, moving a lever here, turning a wheel there, receives in his person the revenues of the vast kingdom it has conquered. He lives more quickly, drawing virtue and energy from its ardent heart.

Driving kinaesthetics changes the viewer, the viewed, and the process of viewing.

This, then, constitutes the experiential mechanics of the driving experience. But what are the new meanings or qualities of human life that can be explored through driving at speed? As already noted, the driver's body is in part reconfigured by the driving experience, but what is involved in this process? As Merleau-Ponty noted, perception is oriented to the kinaesthetic awareness of body so that the body is 'geared' to the world around it. In short, the driver's body is not just processing information from the road and car in the manner of a machine, but experiencing the process through body memory. And what that body experiences are sensations and qualities of the world largely unique to the state of motion and mobility. For example, via the car, the driver experiences such things as grip, friction, sliding, undulation, curvature, inclination, acceleration, deceleration, wind, noise, vibration, direction, vector, ripples, proximity and distance.

These are not qualities easily found when sitting still, walking, or even travelling in a train or airplane—they come from the direct relationship between driver, car and road. Primary here is the sense of adrenalin-fuelled exhilaration that often accompanies driving at speed, the exhilaration which comes from truly sensing oneself in motion, and of feeling wind, air and noise as part of the movement. A feeling of recklessness, of being out-of-control, may of course heighten such an experience, but it is not essential. Rather what matters is the simple *possibility* of being out-of-control—a sense of nearing the limits of control, even if these limits are never transgressed. What matters, then, is the self, and placing the self in a realm where it is challenged and, consequently, reasserted.

So here we arrive at one of the most important aspects of automobile experience: driving as an existential condition whereby the driver seeks to express, confront, explore and produce the self through encountering the world outside of the self. This, of course, has been obviously explored in film, perhaps most famously in Stephen Spielberg's *Duel* (1971), where David Mann, played by Dennis Weaver, is constantly attacked by a truck. Although the film ends with nothing being explained, the true meaning lies in Mann's own resoluteness and determination: if he has learned anything, it is about himself.

In a similar vein, yet even more extreme, is *Vanishing Point* (1971), directed by Richard C. Sarafian, where driver Kowalski (Barry Newman) drives a white Dodge Charger in an amphetamine-fuelled police-pursued sprint from Denver to San Francisco. A former policeman and Vietnam veteran, Kowalski epitomizes—according to 'Super Soul', the blind DJ who guides Kowalski via radio broadcasts—'the last great American hero to whom speed means freedom of the soul'. In the end, rather than give himself up, Kowalski chooses to kill himself by plunging headlong into a blockade of bulldozers. Nihilistic and desolate rather than triumphalist, *Vanishing Point* portrays a degeneration of the human condition. This is driving as the ultimate existentialist experience, a test for the driver's sense of who they are, and who they choose not to be. This is not, of course, to suggest that we should all swallow a bag full of blues, drive across the countryside at high speed, and meet our end in an explosive fireball, but it does point out something common to many driving experiences: namely, that many drivers prefer to drive alone, using the experience of control, power, discovery and potential danger to think about themselves, the world around them, and their place within it. Driving is not just an action, it is also a mirror.

But if driving is often the practice of a solitary driver, the car can also be a space of conversations and relationships. Again, movies provide innumerable examples, from Rossellini's *Voyage in Italy* (1953) to Peckinpah's *The Getaway* (1972), to Ridley Scott's *Thelma and Louise* (1991), wherein it is the juxtaposition of the unfolding journey against the car interior that comes to the fore. As stories are told over the course of the journey, thoughts and feelings are intensified. Here, driving can be a form of emotional nurturing, creating a space where intimacies grow and unravel.

Motorway Driving: 55–100 mph

So what does happen when we drive along a particular kind of road? I take here the example of the motorway—freeway, *autobahn*—which more than any other kind of road represents a globally repeated, almost uniform, driving experience.

Many architects have, of course, been obsessed with urban constructions based around motorway-type roads—whether Le Corbusier in his plans for the *Ville Contemporaine*, where the centre of the city is given over to a vast transport interchange; or the British architect and landscape designer Geoffrey Jellicoe and his designs for the new town of 'Motopia', constructed around a grid of elevated motorways and roundabouts; or the American Norman Bel Geddes, and the 'Futurama' city vision constructed for the 1939 New York World's Fair. Nor, of course, were such visions confined to the drawing board. Germany began construction of its autobahns in the 1930s—from 1933 to 1935 road construction consumed 60 per cent of all public investment in work projects, and by September 1939 some 2,400 miles of autobahn had been constructed. In the USA, the first Californian freeway was the Arroyo Seco Parkway (later the Pasadena Freeway), opened in 1940, while in the UK, the first long-distance motorway, the M1 from London to Birmingham, began construction in the late 1950s.

So what are the qualities associated with driving on these kinds of road? From the start, contemporary commentators were quick to identify the fact that motorways provided a whole new kind of space and construction, and that they raised questions about how to drive, in what cars, and with what kind of attitude. Other commentators noted the way in which the surrounding landscapes were designed to be free of visual distractions, or how service and petrol stations seemed to offer a new kind of foreign, youthful and modern lifestyle. For example, the first M1 service stations were a favourite destination for teenagers, while London's computer-controlled elevated freeway, the Westway, opened on 28 July 1970, was viewed as a place of progressive modernity, and was even favourably compared with the continental lifestyle offered by Paris's Boulevard Périphérique.

If these were some of the initial reactions to motorways and freeways, what have decades of actually driving on these highly distinct roads given to us by way of urban experience? Perhaps most commonly of all, the motorway has been described by theorists such as Lefebvre as being placeless, a terrain that is abstract, flattened, destination-focused, devoid of consciousness and bodily senses. But although undoubtedly true in part, such descriptions are also highly reductive, and are often based largely on a comparison with public space conceived as people walking through a busy urban square.

But surely public life is not purely pedestrian? For example, different kinds of driving behaviour communicate different kinds of social connection, such as kindness through letting someone else filter or change lanes in motorway traffic, or aggression through tailgating, or social risk and adventure through overtaking. As Peter Schindler has noted in *On the Road* (2005), it was actually driving on the urban streets of Shanghai, the countryside roads of Italy and the autobahns of Germany that allowed him fully to encounter and comprehend some of the most significant cultural characteristic of these countries' residents. For example, Schindler describes making a right-hand turn in Shanghai, across a seemingly impenetrable stream of bicycles, in the following terms:

> I almost closed my eyes as I turned. The ocean parted and I was in the promised land, on Mao Ming South Road. In the brief interval of time from moving east on Huai Hai Zhong Road to moving south on its perpendicular, what took place was remarkable. All the moving bicyclists, presumably alerted by my blinker, made room for me with consummate bicycling skill, the instant they saw my turn beginning … It was a miracle. There was no cursing, no hand-waving, no mean looks, nothing except a shared stoic acceptance on the part of the bicyclists that, in these circumstances, it was alright for might to turn right. That was a revelation. Might, I had learned, should not make right. Before driving in Shanghai, I was inclined to dismiss anything else as stupid. Yet here and then, it worked beautifully well. That was an unforgettable lesson that I could not have learned by taking the train or the tram, staying at home or meeting my neighbour on a deserted island. Plus, I think I could get to like such tolerant people.

As Virilio states, speed 'is not a phenomenon, but rather the relationship between phenomena'. This much is already clear to intelligent drivers like Schindler who understand speed both implicitly and explicitly, comprehending subtle social relations from the movement of traffic and the behavioural patterns such movement involves. There are, therefore, cultural conditions and meanings at work in car traffic, but to be fully disclosed they have to be encountered through the actual act of driving.

Besides these kinds of sociability, motorway driving also offers different ways of seeing. In contrast to the kind of placeless nowhere described by Lefebvre and others, motorways in fact offer all kinds of images and associations, including scenes of landscape, flora and fauna, power networks and other transport systems, as well as clues as to such things as accidents (the inevitable roadside emergency scene) forms of protest (bumper stickers), people and their everyday lives (views into fellow drivers' cars), and international connections (the numerous overseas trucks which pound up and down the UK's motorways). In particular, the visual regime of motorway driving involves a constant oscillation from the detail to the territorial, from the local to the global—one sees here a burst tyre, there an international transport system; here a fuel gauge, there a global energy supply. This, as Young wrote, 'is the supreme charm of this kind of travel; that it takes us from one world to another ... open to and conscious of the things that connect those worlds with each other, so that we see the change coming and know how it has come'. Undertaken and viewed in an appropriate manner, motorway driving allows the driver to contemplate that which is out there as well as that which is close to hand.

Most notably, motorway driving, perhaps more than any other kind of driving, produces a cinematic view through the windscreen, a place where high speeds mean that foregrounds are blurred and the distant view is privileged. The British architect Gordon Cullen and, after him, Appleyard, Myer and Lynch in the US, were particularly keen on this kind of driving experience; the latter proposing, in *View from the Road* (1964), a series of events along a highway, including transitions and other such cinematic devices.

In more everyday experiences, however, the result is not so much the kinds of notational and analytical codes proposed by Appleyard et al., as that the driver creates what Virilio calls a series of 'speed pictures' on the windscreen. Images that are lined up with the

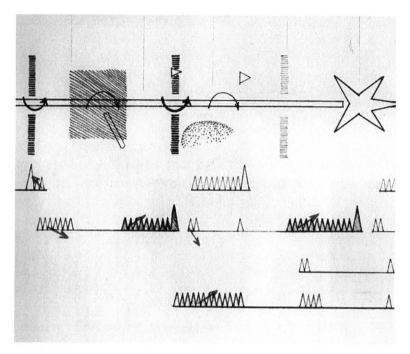

Cinematic Coding of the Highway. Appleyard, Lynch and Myer (1964).

windscreen seem to accelerate towards it as they get nearer, and then, at the last instant, flee down the side windows. Indeed, the visuality of motorway driving is even more dynamic than Virilio realizes, for driving vision is not confined to the panoramic view through the windscreen. Driving vision is a new kind of spatiality, involving looking ahead, yes, but into the distance, mid- and close distance, as well as through side windows, side mirrors and rear-view mirror. A driver's vision is not straight-ahead and steady, but fractured, simultaneously shuttling between different viewpoints and distances.

Besides vision, the motorway also offers a new kind of temporality. So a short section of road is measured by the time it takes to journey along it—in the case of London's Westway, for example, this is about three minutes. More commonly, as anyone who has been to LA will testify, motorway and freeway distances are often judged in terms of time, not miles. 'How far are you from the UCLA campus?' 'Oh, about twenty five minutes.' Freeway driving makes cities a matter not of miles but of minutes. In addition, of course, motorway driving produces a sense of endless time, a time without beginning and end, whose occasional stops serve only to reinforce their relentless character. Most extreme are motorways such as the M25 and the M60, loop motorways which literally never stop. As Chris Petit and Iain Sinclair note in their film of the M25, *London Orbital* (2002), the best depiction of the M25 is produced by surveillance and speed cameras—cameras that are never turned off. And this is why disruptions to motorways are reported so dramatically on the news. When the UK Buncefield oil depot fire occurred in December 2005 the media reporting centred almost as much on the closure of the nearby M1 motorway as on the fire itself.

The apparent endlessness of motorways does not, however, necessarily produce the kind of pure boredom that many would have us believe is endemic to this kind of driving. Several studies have shown that a great deal of work is done journeying along motorways— meeting at service stations and travel inns, making phone calls, reading, smoking, eating, drinking, putting on make-up, and other such actions. But, more importantly, motorway driving is often used as a space for contemplation, where the very neutrality and supposedly boring nature of driving is reinvigorated by thoughts and memories. Indeed, the motorway offers a very distinct simultaneity, at once alert and focused on immediate traffic and speeds, and, at the same time, half-dreaming, half-distant, half-removed from the specificity of driving. Yet another cultural layer is also frequently in play here, for music is one of the most powerful ways of achieving the interrelation between dreams and attentiveness, providing at once the catalyst for thoughts and, importantly, the rhythms and mental alertness that keep the driver connected with the road ahead. From radios to cassette decks, CD-players to iPods, music is a constant presence for many drivers, a continual cultural mediation of driving experience.

This raises the question as to how a driver keeps in control of this demanding modern condition. How does he or she know where they are going, and how do they undertake such a complex set of visions, sounds and actions? To do this, the driver must become a different kind of person, someone who is—and though this is something of a cliché it remains true—partly human and partly machine, a hybrid constructed from the driver's own actions and also, increasingly, from software control over engine, brakes, lighting and so on, as well as from sophisticated ergonomics and instrumentation systems. The car-human machine-body is in fact the single most sophisticated space that most of us routinely encounter. No other space is as intensively conceived, designed and experienced as that of being the driver of a car. Compared to driving, being at home or at work is like being in a stone-age cave—the car and its interior in motion is by far the most intensively interactive space with which we now engage. Consider the sat-nav systems now fitted into many cars. Such systems allow cars to be located almost anywhere in the world within a few feet; they let the driver know where they are going, while also providing warnings of speed camera sites, congestion zones and accident black spots; and simultaneously, through all manner of additional forms of connectivity, they enable telephone, email, fax and internet connections to take place. All of this takes place not despite of but in integration with the driver moving across the country at relative high speed. This is what Virilio calls 'accelerated temporality', a way of knowing not only where one is physically and geographically but also informationally.

Driving at 100+ mph

This brings me to the final section of this schema for the experience of driving: the altered states that are the consequence of driving at speeds of approximately 100 mph or more. These states produce driving experiences which are relatively devoid of site specificity, and which also carry with them particular dangers and associated psychological conditions.

Since the eighteenth century and the arrival of new kinds of horse-drawn carriage, speed has been celebrated as a form of exhilaration where the driver engages with the world around them through their mobility. In particular, speed has been associated with the transcendental, that is, with moving not just from one place to another but from one state of being to another. Speed means flight, intoxication, rapture, horror, hallucination—a kind of modern-day sublime. This is why the Futurists placed so much importance on speed, and why high-speed journeys must be considered in transcendental as well as quantitative terms. Driving at high speed seems to produce another kind of space and time, a condition that is at once tumultuous and calm.

In many cases this involves actions that are illegal, as with the night-time racing that occasionally breaks out on Tokyo's streets and freeways, which is disseminated via the internet and through DVDs such as *Midnight Racer: the Ultimate Japanese Street Racing Video* (2004). Most notorious of all is the film *C'était un Rendezvous* (1976), directed by Claude Lelouch, which shows a nine-minute high-speed journey through Paris in the small hours of the morning. In this film, a camera is gyroscopically mounted low down on the front of a car, thus creating a hyper-accelerated view as the unidentified driver hurtles past fellow motorists, through red lights, and along both wide boulevards and narrow back streets. Such depictions show something of the addictive, perilous, undoubtedly reprehensible but also curiously compelling nature of high-speed driving. Such experiences, as Filson Young wrote, offer 'the exaltation of the dreamer':

> The ineffable thrill and exhilaration of such a flight none but they who have experienced it in their own bodies can ever conceive. It is beyond everything else in our physical existence. It is the exaltation of the dreamer, the drunkard, a thousand times purified and magnified … And to your exalted, expanded senses the noise of the movement is heavenly music, the wind like wine of the gods.

Such exaltations help to explain why many have tried to emulate this kind of high-speed driving, either passively, through watching car chases on films, or actively, either through virtual reality games such as *Gran Turismo*, *Need for Speed* and *Grand Theft Auto*, or the burgeoning market in trackday driving at race circuits. For example, the Nürburgring Nordschleife facility in Germany—originally constructed in the 1920s for vehicle testing and club racing, and as a showcase of German engineering—has now reached almost iconic status as a place for drivers to encounter 13 miles of unforgiving, mountainous and tree-lined corners and straights.

This raises a final point about driving, which is that such high-speed experiences cannot be separated from crashes, injury and even death. For example, at a recent track day at the Nürburgring the morning briefing session started with an instructor telling the 50 or so assembled drivers to, 'look around the room—by lunchtime, five of you will have hit the barrier'. This was not, of course, an instruction to crash, but conversely that those present should, while driving at speed, try hard not to damage themselves or their vehicles. And what such a statement implies, therefore, is that the ability to control and *avoid* such accidents is part of the demanding pleasure of driving.

This is one of the reasons why driving is often seen as more satisfying than train journeys, for it brings the driver to the edge of herself or himself. Like skiing, skateboarding, surfing or other kinds of highly mobile sporting activity, in high-speed driving danger is neither denied nor celebrated, and is instead acknowledged and confronted. Some, of course, have actively sought accidents. J. G. Ballard and Andy Warhol, for instance, both explored car crashes as events of eroticism, mediation and repetition. But more generally it is the transcendental or cyclical nature of speed and the crash which appears within driving culture. It is worth recalling that the seminal moment of the *Futurist Manifesto* (1909), in which both life and death are signified, is Marinetti's account of his roadside recovery from the car crash he experienced in 1908:

> With patient, loving care those people rigged a tall derrick and iron grapnels to fish out my car, like a big beached shark. Up it came from the ditch, slowly, leaving in the bottom, like scales, its heavy frame-work of good sense and its soft upholstery of comfort.
>
> They thought it was dead, my beautiful shark, but a caress from me was enough to revive it; and there it was, alive again, running on its powerful fins!
>
> And so, faces smeared with good factory muck—plastered with metallic waste, with senseless sweat, with celestial soot—we, bruised,

our arms in slings, but unafraid, declared our high intentions to all the living of the earth:

Manifesto of Futurism
1. We intend to sing the love of danger, the habit of energy and fearlessness.

Through driving—a continual and restless mobile interaction with cities, architecture and landscape—the human subject emerges as someone who has experienced one of the most distinctive and ubiquitous conditions of the modern world, and who has become, as a result, a different kind of person.

Reading

Appleyard, Donald, Kevin Lynch and Jon R. Myer, *The View from the Road* (Cambridge, MA: MIT Press, 1964).

Brandon, Ruth, *Automobile: How the Car Changed Life* (London: Macmillan, 2002).

Danius, Sara, 'The Aesthetics of the Windshield: Proust and the Modernist Rhetoric of Speed', *Modernism/Modernity* 8 (2001): 99–126.

Edensor, Tim, 'Defamiliarizing the Mundane Roadscape', *Space & Culture* 6 (2003): 151–68.

Marinetti, Filippo, 'Futurist Manifesto', trans. R. W. Flint, in *Documents of 20th Century Art: Futurist Manifestos*, ed. Umbro Apollonio (New York: Viking Press, 1973): 19–24.

Merriman, Peter, *Driving Spaces: A Cultural-Historical Geography of England's M1 Motorway* (Oxford: Blackwell, 2007).

Schindler, Peter, *On the Road: Driving Adventures, Pleasures and Discoveries* (Hong Kong: On The Road Editions, 2005).

Schnapp, Jeffrey T., 'Crash (Speed as Engine of Individuation)', *Modernism/Modernity* 6 (1999): 1–49.

Taylor, John, *A Dream of England: Landscape, Photography and the Tourist's Imagination* (Manchester: Manchester University Press, 1994).

Venturi, Robert, Denise Scott Brown and Steven Izenour, *Learning from Las Vegas* (Cambridge, MA: MIT Press, 1972).

Virilio, Paul, 'Dromoscopy, or the Ecstasy of Enormities', *Wide Angle* 20 (1998): 11–22.

Young, A. B. Filson, *The Complete Motorist: Being an Account of the Evolution and Construction of the Modern Motor-Car* (London: Methuen, 1905).

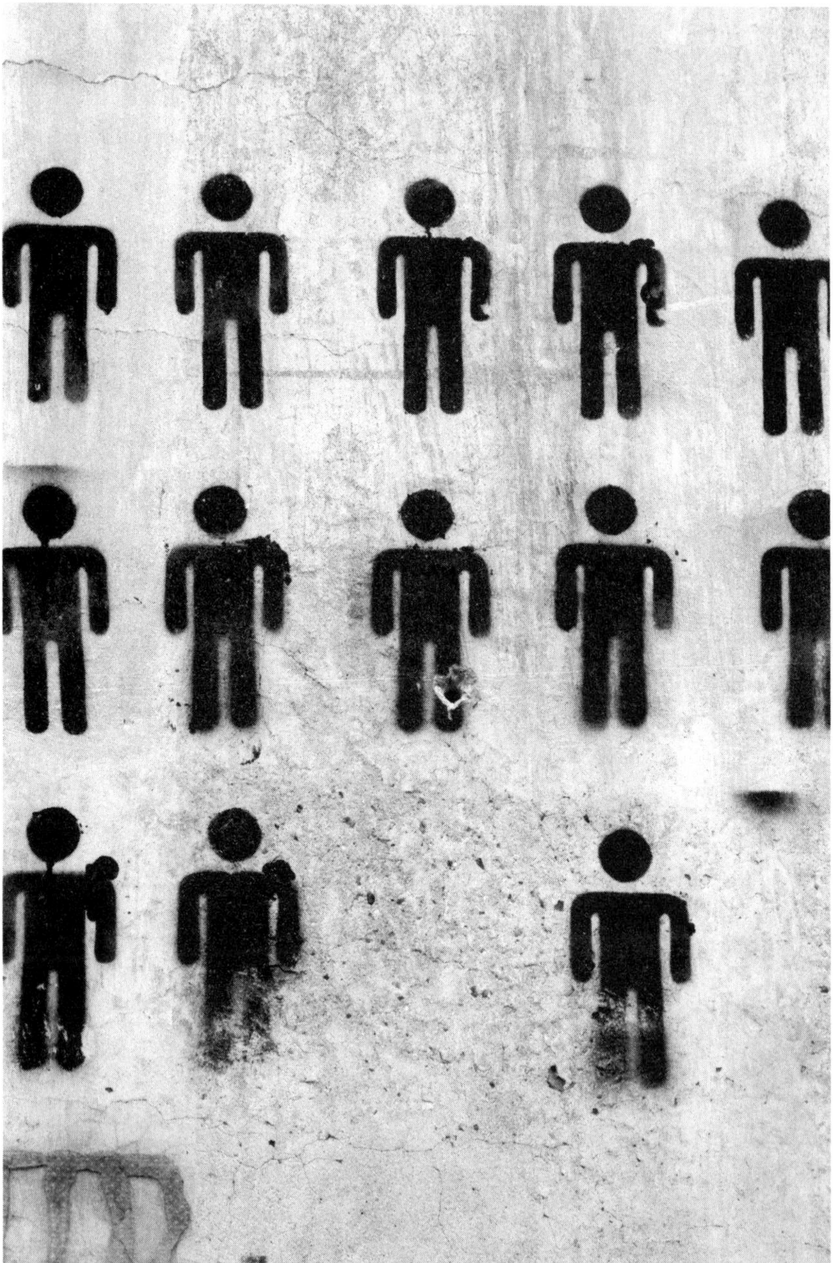

Falling

Marshall Berman

What is the city over the mountains
Cracks and reforms and bursts in the violet air
Falling towers
Jerusalem Athens Alexandria
Vienna London
Unreal
> T. S. Eliot, *The Waste Land*

What are the roots that clutch, what branches grow
Out of this stony rubbish?
> T. S. Eliot, *The Waste Land*

My city's in ruins
My city's in ruins
Come on rise up
Come on rise up
Rise up
> Bruce Springsteen, 'My City in Ruins'

When I talk about ruins, I'm an interested party. In the 1970s, the South Bronx, where I grew up, became one of the greatest aggregations of ruins in the world. It went back to the late 1950s and early '60s, when Robert Moses, State Commissioner of Highways (and of many other things), blasted an expressway through a dozen neighbourhoods, including some of the densest in the city, and displaced 50,000 people, maybe even more. (Our family was part of what the next generation of urban planners called 'secondary displacement'.) Blight spread gradually southward from this highway. In the late 1960s and through the '70s, the pace and scope of disintegration became spectacular, devouring house after house and block after block, driving hundreds of thousands of people from their homes like some inexorable plague. Those were the years when, after decades of peaceful anonymity, the Bronx finally made it into the mass media, as a symbol of all that could go wrong in a city. 'The Bronx is Burning!' resonated all over the world. British, Swedish, Italian, Polish and Japanese camera crews poked through the rubble, along with the makers of Hollywood's *Fort Apache the Bronx* (1981) and *Wolfen* (1981), and of independent films like *Wild Style* (1983). My family had moved when the Cross-Bronx Expressway was being built, but all we had to do was to turn on the news and we could see our old neighbourhood in close-up, in real living color—urban fires make great visuals—as it went up in flames. Or we could consult the little boxes in each morning's *New York Times* that itemized buildings that had burnt down or collapsed the day or the night before. Every time I saw or heard about the destruction of another landmark of my life—streets I had played in, friends' and relatives' houses, shops, schools, synagogues—I felt like a piece of my flesh was being ripped away.

Whenever our family got together in the mid or late 1970s, we would talk about 'our house', the apartment building where we had lived for 20 years. Was it still standing? Were people living in it? No one had heard anything since the fires, collapses and abandonments had begun. Maybe no news was good news, but in those plague years none of us could bear to go back and take a look. However, I was writing a book on the meanings of modernity, *All That Is Solid Melts Into Air* (1982), and I realized the Bronx had to be included. So finally, on a lovely spring day in 1980, I took the D train, got off at my old stop, East 170th Street, and hoped for the best. As I came up the subway stairs I saw a dreadful sight: a row of splendid red brick apartment houses with beautifully detailed façades—houses that had signified 'class', way beyond our reach, not so long ago—transformed into an enormous mass of ruins. The façades were charred black, some of the upper walls had collapsed, the windows were shattered (probably by firemen: this must have been one hell of a fire), a whole block, cordoned off, was still strewn with debris. I walked downhill about half a mile to where we once had lived, and an immense panorama of ruins unfolded before me. Some had been sealed up with cement blocks. This might mean that their owner (almost certainly the city) was planning to leave them standing in the hope they could be made liveable once more someday. Or it might mean that the city simply hadn't found the time or money to tear them down. (New York was just starting to emerge from a fiscal crisis in which it had nearly gone bankrupt.) Others, in various stages of demolition or decomposition, presented jagged expressionist forms that were far more arresting than they had been when they were people's homes. Some had two wings, one sealed off, the other inhabited. But the ongoing life was precarious: the ragged APARTMENT FOR RENT signs hanging from fire escapes suggested that services and maintenance had been cut to the bone, that scared tenants were moving out as fast as they could find places to go before winter began. I saw a couple of blocks that I remembered as close and dense and noisy, with sidewalks too narrow for their crowds; but now, in this space, there was no place. The rubble from the buildings had been carted away, and it was as open and empty as a desert.

As I got closer to our old house I began to sweat. A few small houses were, as ever, shabby but intact. The synagogue where I had had my *bar mitzvah* was recently burned, cordoned off, close to collapse. A block from our house, I found myself abruptly alone; the buildings were still standing, but sealed up. What if, when I got to the spot, there was nothing there? At last I turned the corner—and there it was. And there were people living in it, names on the buzzer, kids jumping rope in the courtyard. I thought, *Thank God!* (Then I thought, *Idiot!* The idea of a God who would burn up 1455 and 1457 and 1459 and 1461 and 1463 College Avenue, but leave 1460 intact, was pretty silly; the Bronx needed this theology like a hole in the head.) I relaxed, metaphysically relieved; I felt my roots were still alive. Now I could take the D train downtown and go on with my adult life.

And yet, I found, I couldn't just go on. I kept going back. I spent many afternoons wandering through the ruins. They went on and on, block after block, mile after mile. For years, the ruins were the most impressive spectacle in New York, a city of spectacles. (And New York's most famous spectacles—Times Square, Brooklyn Bridge, Central Park, Coney Island—seemed to be wearing out all through the 1970s; only the ruins grew and grew.) It wasn't just blocks that were empty, it was the wild, expressionist fragments of buildings. It was the streets where the buildings were still intact—mostly tenements from the 1880s and 1890s—but everything was abandoned, all sealed up, and all the people were gone. This was the scene portrayed on the cover of the world's first rap music hit, 'The Message', by Grandmaster Flash and the Furious Five: emptiness in a place designed for overfullness. 'The Message' was thrilling, a great rap, authentically creative. (It still swings.) But it could have been called 'The Lower Lower Depths'.

My family took it all personally, as if the ruins were meant for us and us alone. In our sense of loss, we had plenty of company. The South Bronx lost over 300,000 people in the 1970s; thousands more fled the Lower East Side, Harlem, Brownsville, East New York, Bedford-Stuyvesant, Bushwick, and other neighbourhoods I'm forgetting. (New York City as a whole lost population for the first time in its history; other American cities had been losing people for decades.) The fires often afflicted people more than once: they would flee, but the blight would catch up with them. Many of my students at CCNY went through this. In fact, it was happening in working-class neighbourhoods and industrial towns all over the USA. In the 1980s, urban ruin hit the pop charts. Songs like The Specials' 'Ghost Town', Bruce Springsteen's 'My Hometown', and The Pretenders' 'My City Was Gone', were simple realism. In 'My City', Chryssie Hynde returns to Akron, Ohio, where she grew up:

> I went back to Ohio
> But my city was gone.

There was no train station,
There was no downtown.
Everything had disappeared,
All my favorite places.
My city had been pulled down,
Reduced to open spaces ...

How many people did these sad songs speak for? It's hard to know. The most elaborate study of housing displacement, conducted in 1981 by Richard LeGates and Chester Hartman, suggests that in a 'normal' year around 2.5 million Americans are forced to leave their homes. This estimate tried to include various forms of 'indirect displacement': people whose landlords stopped maintaining their buildings and who could not live without heat or water; people whose neighbourhoods were burning up, and who left in fear that they would be next. But these numbers did not include people like us, who no longer lived in the fire zones, but who felt emotional bonds with them, and who felt devastated to see their roots torn up. In their grief for their lost world, the people of the South Bronx had plenty of company.

It is important not to get carried away. On the scale of twentieth-century violence, these ruins do not loom large. For years the South Bronx looked like a giant bombsite, but far fewer died. If we could keep track of untimely dead, from the 1970s to the 1990s the Bronx's number would be somewhere in the high four figures, or maybe in the low five. Now, in an age when bombs have killed 150,000 people in a few minutes, this is not such a big deal. Still, the assault on the South Bronx may be our civil society's closest encounter with what Goya called 'the disasters of war'. Some people will probably ask, *But what about 9/11?* Maybe we need to distinguish between different modes of disaster. If the attacks on 9/11 were a civilian Pearl Harbor, the attacks on the South Bronx, much smaller but drawn out for years, were our very own London Blitz.

There may well be a kinship shared by the survivors of these protracted assaults, civilians who have spent years under fire. These are people who know what it is like to take the most elaborate care to protect themselves, and to see it all come to nothing. They have lost not only their homes, their jobs and their loved ones, but their whole world; they feel like they have to create the world again, just to get through the day. These stricken people belong to one of the most important shadow communities in the world today, victims of a crime without a name. Writing in 1984, I gave it a name: URBICIDE. The murder of a city. I later discovered that the name had been used already, in the early 1960s, by people whose neighbourhood, known for decades as Radio Row, was being torn down to create the architectural 'footprint' for the World Trade Center.

The Oldest Story in the World

If there is a shadow community of people whose communities have been destroyed, this fellowship extends not only outward in space, but backward in time. As long as people have lived in cities, they have been haunted by fears of urban ruin. It isn't hard to see why. Any city is a work of human construction and cooperation, but anything that is constructed can be destroyed, and any bunch of human beings who can work together can also turn against each other and destroy everything they have made. A city is one of the earliest and most enduring expressions of collective pride, but every language contains proverbs to remind people that pride comes before a fall. A city is an attempt at a kind of collective immortality—we die, but we hope our city's forms and structures will live on. Ironically, our attachment to these forms makes us more vulnerable than ever: now there are more ways than ever for our lives to be destroyed. In fact, myths of urban ruin grow at our culture's roots. Here, in one of the greatest Greek tragedies, Euripides' *The Trojan Women*, an Athenian man imagines himself a Trojan and a woman: 'O Troy, once so huge over all Asia in the drawn wind of pride, your very name of glory shall be stripped away. They are burning you, and they drag us forth from our land, enslaved ...' And, in Lamentations, from roughly the same period, a Jew laments the destruction of Jerusalem:

> How lonely sits the city that was full of people!
> How like a widow she has become,

She that was a princess among the cities ...
She weeps in the night, tears on her cheeks,
Among all her lovers, she has none to comfort her ...
The roads to Zion mourn,
None comes to the appointed feasts.
All her gates are desolate ...
All the people groan and they stretch for bread;
They trade their treasures for food ...
Is it nothing to you, all who pass by?

From ancient times to our own times, the experience of seeing one's city in ruins has been one of the primal traumas. And urbicide has been one of the primal crimes.

After my visits to the South Bronx in 1980, I read widely in the literature of urbicide. It was heartbreaking, but also luminous and profound. It was as if people had to learn to see and to speak all over again: to learn to communicate by signalling through the flames. It seems that this ordeal often enlarged the people who could survive it. They were forced to concentrate and reorganize their minds, just to get the picture straight: the destruction of all the places, all the things, all the sights and sounds, all the activities and institutions through which they built up and understood their lives; their inability to take care of themselves in the most basic ways—to get food, clothing and shelter; the suffering of their children (a persistent, obsessive theme in the literature of urbicide), whose dependence on their parents becomes urgently acute just when their parents become unable to help them; the total inability of traditional leaders and traditional forms to deal with life in ruins. Then they have had to stretch all their faculties to find new ways to define themselves, to connect with each other and relate to the world, just to survive every day. Finally, they have had to reach into the depths of their inner lives, and to drill for new depths, to deal with overwhelming questions: What is the meaning of these ruins, where our city used to be? How can this have happened to me, to you? What kind of world is this where things like this can happen? Some of their answers over the ages can show us what our lives are made of, and how in the midst of death we can make life anew. Again and again, all through human history, some of our most dreadful experiences have inspired our capacity for renewal. This is one of those dialectical ironies that our species has mobilized to keep itself alive.

Some of the earliest literature of urbicide is still just about the best: for instance, the Old Testament books of Jeremiah and Lamentations, along with associated psalms and prophetic fragments, from the time of the first destruction of Jerusalem by the Babylonian army in 583 BCE; and Euripides' tragedy, *The Trojan Women*, written and presented in Athens in 415 BCE near the climax of the 30-year Peloponnesian War, one of the most brutally urbicidal wars in history. Virgil's *Aeneid* tells the Trojan myth in much fuller detail, but Euripides gets closer to the bone. These ancient works give us most of the images and structures of feeling that we still use in our attempts to come to terms with the ruins in our lives today.

So: what is the meaning of our city's destruction? One conclusion often drawn by victims of urbicide is that it has no meaning, and that there is no meaning to be had. Euripides puts this cry of cosmic despair into the mouth of Hecuba, who used to be queen of what used to be Troy. 'Can it be, my lord, from your throne in heaven's bright air,' the chorus of crushed women asks, 'that you have forgotten [our] city, which is ruined?' Her comment on this invocation is caustic: 'O gods—what wretched things to call on—gods—for help.' She says: 'That mortal is a fool who, prospering, thinks his life has any strong foundation; for our fortune's course is the reeling way a madman takes.' In lines like these, we come close to the existential abyss faced by Shakespeare's tragic heroes: Lear ('As flies to wanton boys are we to the gods, They kill us for their sport'); and Macbeth ('a tale Told by an idiot, full of sound and fury, Signifying nothing'). In our time, this abyss, like everywhere else, is more densely populated than it used to be. But it is worth remembering that, as long as cities have been torn down, existential despair has grown out of their ruins.

Hecuba, as she is about to be taken into slavery, tries to perform one last act that she thinks will mean something: to throw herself into her city's flames and die with it. Alas, she fails. The Greeks pull her out of the fire and take her away. Still, Euripides suggests, this would be a worthy way to go. Even though the universe means nothing, the bond between a city and its citizens means something—especially where the bond is frail, where both cities and citizens are endangered species.

Ancient Jewish responses to urban ruin are more twisted and neurotic than the Greek; but maybe, in their twisted way, more profound. The prophets agree with Euripides: when their city was destroyed—Jerusalem was destroyed by Babylon in 583 BCE—they agree that GOD DID IT. Only they think God was right. They say the city's horrible fate was just punishment for horrible sinfulness. They offer searing indictments of life before the fall. The generals, the rich merchants, the high priests, the official prophets, all ran after wealth, conquest, success; and stained themselves with the people's blood. The rich laid house to house and field to field, so there was no place for the poor in their own land. Meanwhile, these poor people seemed to want only to change places with their oppressors. People of every rank and class made war on each other, devoured each other's flesh. The covenant between Israel and God, the calling of a holy people, were forgotten by everyone ... When the prophets shouted—and ancient Israel had some great shouters—people laughed. So, says the Lamenter, even as we recoil in horror to see our city in ruins, we have to recognize how much we ourselves are to blame. The Babylonian army finished the job, but only after we had rotted the foundations and destroyed Jerusalem from within.

What are we supposed to make of this 2,500 years later? If we remember that these are victims speaking to victims—survivors grubbing for food and shelter, captives weeping for their lost loved ones—there seems to be something morbid in this passion for collective guilt and blame. Haven't the people of Jerusalem suffered enough? And isn't it self-delusory to think that little Israel could have held off the gigantic empires that surrounded it, if only the people were good? In some ways the prophetic faith is a dangerous flight from reality. But in other ways, the prophets penetrate more deeply into reality. Like Socrates a century later, they entice their people to know themselves, to leap into collective self-awareness. In centuries to come, as Jews learn to take the vow, 'If I forget thee, O Jerusalem, may my right hand wither' (Psalm 137), one of the things they will need to remember is how fragile and vulnerable cities are, especially when their citizens do not take care of them.

This knowledge is cruel and painful. The prophets are so determined to inflict it because they think the Jews are going to get a second chance. They see urbicide not as the Greeks did, as an inevitable cosmic fate, but as an intermediate stage in a spiral, part of an ongoing historical process that will eventually lead to renewal and progress. They see how the bitterness of exile can be transformed into collective learning. 'Seek the welfare of the city where I have sent you,' God tells Jeremiah, 'and pray to the Lord on its behalf, for in its welfare you will find your welfare.' The prophetic hope is that in exile, 'in a strange land', in their enemy's city, the Jews will learn what they could not learn in their own city: how to be citizens.

The climax of the prophetic dialectic is a triumphant vision of rebuilding. This is proclaimed near the end of *Yom Kippur*, the Day of Atonement, one of the high points of the Jewish liturgical year. The text is the book of Isaiah, Chapter 58. If Jews can learn to pour themselves out to all the afflicted, to share their bread with the hungry, to clothe the naked, to bring homeless poor people into their houses—which means, to recognize that they are surrounded by people even more homeless than themselves—then, but only then, 'your ancient ruins will be rebuilt; you will raise up the foundations of many generations; you will be called the repairer of walls, the restorer of streets to dwell in'. In this dialectical vision, the destruction of Jerusalem appears as a sort of Fortunate Fall. It is only through losing our city that we can find the right way to live in a city. The prophets' searing indictment of the city's past is meant to empower the people to transform the city's future. If we can learn why we were overcome yesterday, we will overcome tomorrow.

In the 580s BCE, when Babylon overwhelms Israel, that empire seems invulnerable. But in less than two generations, in the 530s BCE, it will be crushed by an even greater empire, the Persian. Will the Jews cheer to see their captor destroyed? Not if they have learned anything from their prophets; if they have learned, they will feel a sense of connection with Babylon, a mix of joy and tears, a new form of ambivalence. Jeremiah urges his fellow-Jews to identify with a city that is going through exactly what they went through:

> Suddenly Babylon has fallen and been broken.
> Wail for her!
> Take balm for her pain; she may be healed ...
> But Israel is small, its support is not much help:
> We would have healed Babylon,
> But she was not healed.

Babylon is not healed, it loses its political identity; and the Jews, along with many other captive peoples, get a chance to 'go home'. Many of them will. (Their story is told, or imagined, in the Book of Nehemiah.) But in fact—and this is a world-historical fact—most of them will not. They will remain in the captors' city—more precisely, the ex-captors' city, a city that has been 'broken' itself—and seek their identities there. Or rather they will *transform* their identities there. They will become the first known urban *diaspora*. They will ask themselves one of the deepest questions in the history of culture: 'How can we sing the Lord's song in a strange land?' (Psalm 137). They will answer their question by JUST DOING IT, and they will go on doing it. They will do it in many ways. They will become citizens of Babylon, yet they will face towards Jerusalem when they pray. (Devout Jews still do this today.) Their descendants will create the Babylonian Talmud, which will be far richer and fuller than the Jerusalem Talmud. They will spend centuries singing the Lord's song in places they experience as 'strange lands', in many strange lands around the world. And they will enrich the world by creating many cultures that grow out of their self-division, their inner dualism, their split personality. They will be spiritual ancestors of the twentieth and twenty-first century Jews and Blacks and Latins who have inhabited the Bronx and who give it meaning.

Back to Modern Times

A little earlier I mentioned 'The Message', the first international rap hit, by Grandmaster Flash and the Furious Five, which put hip-hop on the world map in 1982. 'The Message' dramatizes a nightmarish vision of life in the Bronx. You'll remember the refrain:

> Don't push me 'cause
> I'm close to the edge
> Trying not to lose my head (huh)
> It's like a jungle sometimes
> It makes me wonder
> How I keep from going under
> (Huh-hu-huh-huh)
> It's like a jungle sometimes
> It makes me wonder
> How I keep from going under

The song goes on to tell a story about horrific everyday life and death in the Bronx. It ends with everybody getting arrested and taken away. Police presence defines the song's climax. It reaches a dramatic crescendo ... Then it stops—as if there's nobody left to police, as if the last one to leave has turned out the light, or turned off the sound.

One of the early clichés about 'The Message' was that it proclaimed 'The Bronx Is Dead'. According to the US Census, the Bronx had lost 300,000 people in the 1970s. So these guys were saying that it was only a matter of time before the remaining 1.3 million got the idea and hit the road (and the Bronx was full of excellent roads). I found this idea both offensive and ridiculous. And I couldn't believe that a song I loved could have such a hateful message. Around the tenth or twentieth time I heard it, I noticed some lyrics that seemed to point another way:

> They pushed a girl in front of a train
> Took her to the doctor sewed her arm on again
> Stabbed a man right through the heart
> Gave him a transplant and a brand new start

Here, I came to believe—I still believe—was the real message: social disintegration and existential desperation can be sources of life and energy. A generation of kids, from ruined neighbourhoods that the policy of 'Planned Shrinkage' would have destroyed forever, broke out of poverty and isolation and became sophisticated New Yorkers with horizons as wide as the world. They had been through great losses without losing themselves. Not only had their suffering not destroyed their idealism: in some mysterious way, their suffering had *created* idealism. These kids could tell the world, 'We come from ruins, but we are not ruined.' Their capacity for soul-making in the midst of horror gave New York as a whole a brand new aura, a weird but marvellous bank of bright lights.

In the early 1980s, I went to the ruins a lot. Some of you will remember, they went on for miles. Sometimes they looked and felt like a whole new planet. But after a while I had to stop. The images of destruction, so alive, got to be too much for me to bear. All my life I have loved the Bronx Zoo; but for years I stopped going there, because I couldn't bear to take the trip—from the Upper West Side, where I live now, it was the #2—through those miles and miles of ruins. Finally, in 2005, I bit the bullet. My younger son Danny's class at PS 75 was making a class trip to the zoo. They desperately needed parents, it was a lovely day, and I had the day off, so I felt there was no way I could decently say No. As we came into the Bronx and the subway came out into the open, I dreaded the worst. The kids would be sitting down, and they would miss the worst of it. I stood up, craned my neck, braced myself, and—THE RUINS WERE GONE! In their place there were ordinary buildings, kids on bikes, trucks unloading, mothers with babies, old people on folding chairs watching the world go by—the whole *schmeer* of modern city life. 'Look!' I said to the teachers who were on the train with me, 'It looks like an ordinary city!' They said, 'Well, isn't the Bronx an ordinary city?' I suddenly realized that these teachers were young, still in their twenties. When 'The Bronx [was] Burning!' they weren't even born. Now, it looked like nothing much—and yet, a miracle. The transformation of the Bronx into an ordinary city from an apocalyptic ruin: this is a remarkable story, and a tremendous achievement. I don't think the story has been properly told. Two important factors in it are Edward Koch and the transformation of urban housing. Koch, mayor in the late 1980s and early '90s, got a $4 billion bond issue through the State Legislature, marked explicitly for housing renewal. That is where most of the money for those new buildings comes from. It is a perfect example of the liberal Welfare State at its best. But since leaving office, after being defeated by David Dinkins in 1989, Koch has moved so far to the Right that he is embarrassed to be associated with the population of the Bronx, the neighbourhood in which he was himself born.

The other thing I want to highlight here is the achievement of a great deal of the new South Bronx housing: to look like far less than it is. Much of it was built by the New York City Housing Authority, but the new buildings don't have the dread 'project look' at all. They are integrated into the street system; they look like colourful, accessible versions of the thousands of ordinary, vernacular apartment houses that served for generations as symbols of New York—and especially of the Bronx—until they were burned down. (They look like my old house on College Ave.) They also look like some of the 'social housing' in Western and Central Europe, where post-war Left governments built millions of housing units to replace the Second World War's immense urban ruins.

The new South Bronx is a fine instance of the *resiliency* of modern cities, and of modern men and women, the people we are: people who have the capacity both to commit urbicide and to overcome it; to reduce their whole civilization to ruins, but also to rebuild the ruins; to turn apocalyptic surreality into ordinary nice reality where we can feel at home; to sing the Lord's song in a world full of strange lands.

Reading

Berman, Marshall, *All That Is Solid Melts Into Air: The Experience of Modernity* (London: Verso, 1983).

Berman, Marshall, 'Falling Towers: City Life after Urbicide', in *Geography and Identity: Exploring and Living Geopolitics of Identity*, ed. Dennis Crow (Washington: Maisonneuve Press, 1996): 172–92.

Berman, Marshall, 'Views from the Burning Bridge', in *Urban Mythologies: The Bronx Represented since the 1960s*, ed. Lydia Yee and Betty-Sue Hertz (Bronx, NY: Bronx Museum of the Arts, 1999): 70–83.

Berman, Marshall and Brian Berger (eds), *New York Calling: From Blackout to Bloomberg* (London: Reaktion, 2007).

Davis, Mike, *Dead Cities: A Natural History* (New York: New Press, 2004).

Graham, Stephen, 'Lessons in Urbicide', *New Left Review* 19 (January–February 2003): 63–77.

Jensen, Robert (ed.), *Devastation/Resurrection: The South Bronx* (Bronx, NY: Bronx Museum of the Arts, 1978).

Jonnes, Jill, *South Bronx Rising: The Rise, Fall and Resurrection of an American City* (New York: Fordham University Press, 2002).

Kahane, Lisa, *Do Not Give Way to Evil: Photographs of the South Bronx, 1979–1987*, (New York: powerHouse Books, 2008),

LeGates, Richard and Chester Hartman, 'Displacement', *The Clearinghouse Review* (July 1981): 207–49.

Milosz, Czeslaw, 'Ruins and Poetry', in *Writers of Poetry*, (Harvard: Harvard University Press, 1984).

Rosenblum, Constance, *Boulevard of Dreams: Heady Times, Heartbreak and Hope along the Grand Concourse in the Bronx* (New York: New York University Press, 2009).

Rosenthal, Mel, *In the South Bronx of America* (Willimantic, CT: Curbstone Press, 2000).

Vergara, José Camilo, *The New American Ghetto* (New Brunswick, NJ: Rutgers University Press, 1997).

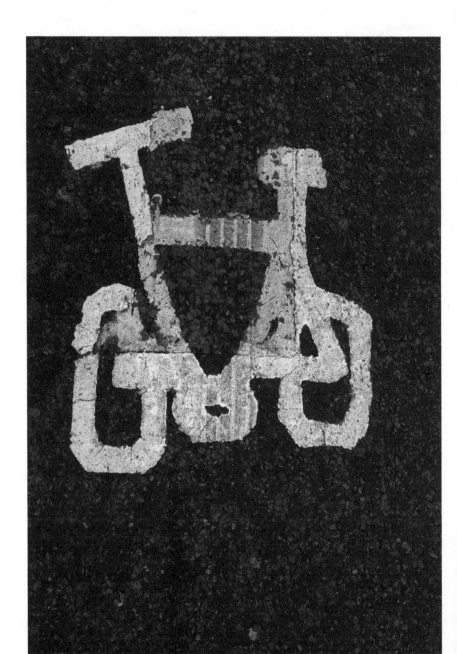

Imaging

Patrick Keiller

On an overcast afternoon at the end of August 2008, I was cycling along Harrow Road, in north-west London, towards Harlesden. Passing Kensal Green Cemetery, I saw that a section of its high wall had collapsed, apparently not long before, so that passers-by could see in from the street for the first time, perhaps, since the wall was built in 1832 and the cemetery opened in January the following year. According to the newsletter of the Greater London Industrial Archaeology Society, a 100-metre section of the half-mile-long wall collapsed at around midnight on 30 August 2006. Most of the bricks fell into the cemetery, so that although many monuments were damaged, no one was injured. The wall varies between ten and twelve feet in height, and is a grade II listed structure, with stone copings and foundations five feet deep. It was built to keep out bodysnatchers.

I had not seen inside the cemetery since the early 1980s, when I visited a few times as an architectural tourist and would-be photographer, and I was reminded of that on this occasion. I also remembered cycling along the same route on a Sunday afternoon in December 1980, when I had set out to look for a place I had seen from a passing train a few days earlier. It was a north-facing hillside of allotments behind the corner of two streets of suburban houses, beyond the railway's bridge above the North Circular Road. I'm not sure why I went to look for the place on a bicycle, as it was quite a long way: I think it was probably because the vehicle I then owned was out of

action. The view had seemed to me a curiously northern-looking landscape to find in outer London, and I had thought it might be a subject for a photograph, which it was; but it led me to another, more compelling spatial subject for both a photograph and, a few months later, a first film, so that this earlier bicycle journey had been, for me, a significant, perhaps even life-changing, event.

It was not the first time that I had been to Harrow Road with a camera during that year. In May, I had resorted to going out very early to various parts of inner London in the hope of producing photographs of the urban landscape. One of these locations was Harrow Road, between the north end of Ladbroke Grove and Harlesden, the stretch that passes Kensal Green Cemetery. None of the resulting photographs, which included some of the cemetery, were very successful, although there is one of the Harley Gospel Hall, at a bend of Harley Road alongside the railway, of which the subject, at least, recalls some of O. G. S. Crawford's photographs of Southampton in the 1930s. It was not a very original photograph. In the view of this street in Google Earth, someone has posted what looks like a found colour transparency of the same subject, seen from almost the same angle, at what looks like about the same date.

As far as I know, the literature of urban cycling is not very extensive. The bicycle is better established in a rural context. One of Alain Resnais's short films, *Châteaux de France* (1948), was made on a journey or series of journeys by bicycle. I am not much of a cyclist, but over the last decade I have cycled as a means of getting around London. My bicycle dates from the early 1970s, or perhaps even earlier. I don't know exactly how old it is, but it is light, fast, and still has its original Weinmann centre-pull brakes, which were once considered glamorous. In my experience, if the journey is long enough and the road not too busy, the slightly detached condition of cycling can encourage lengthy associations of ideas or recollections. Walking, driving and looking out of the windows of trains, buses and aeroplanes offer similar possibilities, but there seems to be something about the experience of riding a bicycle, the way in which one is both connected to and moving above the ground, that promotes a particular state of mind.

In August 2008, I was about two-thirds through a ten-month period of intermittent cinematography for another film, not yet complete as I write. Apart from the collapsed state of the cemetery wall, and the memory of the previous journey, the ride did not lead to any

very significant discovery. But it took place in a curious atmosphere of expectation, exacerbated by the weather, which recalled that described in the opening paragraphs of Edgar Allan Poe's 'The Fall of the House of Usher' (1839); an atmosphere in which it was becoming clear that the 'worst' of the collapse of the financial sector was still to come, an apprehension confirmed by the failure of Lehman Brothers two weeks later, and by subsequent events, all of which felt at the time as if they might constitute a historic *moment*. Any sense of justification or satisfaction that accompanied this long-predicted turn of events was tempered for me by fear of financial shipwreck, following a misunderstanding with my employer, and especially since I was riding to what advertisements describe as Europe's largest car supermarket, in Harlesden, where I had identified a possible replacement for my car. I had bought the car in 1995, when making a film called *Robinson in Space* (1997), which had involved journeys all over England; but I did not believe I could realistically expect it to survive another annual test, due very shortly. It was an absurd destination for a bicycle ride, and an absurd time to be contemplating any major purchase, especially something as questionable as a car, but it would have been very difficult to continue the project without one. I had ridden across Kensington Gardens, up Ladbroke Grove, past the junction with Portobello Road, the setting for some of the final moments of *The Lavender Hill Mob* (1951) and parts of the film of Harold Pinter's *Betrayal* (1983), over the railway and the canal into Harrow Road—a place which, along with Harlesden, is a part of London I have come to associate with creative anxieties of one kind or another, some of them dating from the years immediately before and after 1979, when I was migrating unsteadily between careers, others from earlier. A few days later I decided to have the old car repaired, so that the journey, and much of the accompanying anxiety, were for nothing.

I arrived in London in September 1967 to become an architecture student, a few weeks after my seventeenth birthday. From around this time, I remember a view of the backs of houses, seen from a train as it passed through what I later identified as Willesden Junction station, and which I came to recognise as an indication of imminent arrival at Euston. Willesden Junction station is in Harlesden, not Willesden (as a former borough, Willesden, like Hornsey and West Ham, is difficult to place), and is very close to Harrow Road, which continues, crossing the North Circular Road, to Wembley and beyond. I am not sure when I first travelled by the route to Euston, but the journey would probably have been from Coventry, and was either just before or not long after starting university. I remember thinking what an endless undertaking it would be to rebuild the vast area of London's worn-out Victorian suburbs. I had travelled to London many times before, but usually either by car, when one mostly passes the fronts of houses, or by train to Paddington, and for some reason the house-backs of Ealing and Notting Hill had failed to prompt this sub-Orwellian response to urban dilapidation.

About 18 months later, by then an unsettled and not very successful second-year student, not long after the occupation of the University of London Union building in Malet Street by locked-out LSE students and others, into which I had wandered from what then seemed an unfashionably technocratic Bartlett School of Architecture, I first visited Willesden Junction. I was living in surprisingly alienated circumstances with a friend with first-hand experience of student radicalism in Germany, in a small flat not far from Finchley Road and Frognal station, from which we sometimes travelled to Kew Gardens by the North London Line. At Willesden Junction the line is elevated as it crosses the Bakerloo line and the main lines running out of Euston, so the platforms are high up, with long views over the surrounding landscape. The North London Line crosses other radial main lines at several points as it circumnavigates the city, one of which can be seen from Copenhagen Fields, to the north of St Pancras station, in Alexander Mackendrick's film *The Ladykillers* (1955); but at Willesden Junction the crossing coincides with a station, so that one can get off and properly explore the view. Beyond it, the line passes through a landscape of railway lines and other marginal territory, its longest stretch between stations. Attracted by the station and its surroundings, we set out on a day, I think, in February. I was reminded of this visit on reading, recently, that George Soros worked at Willesden Junction as a porter when a student at LSE in the 1950s.

It was a time when I was managing on very little sleep, which no doubt exacerbated a euphoric experience of the landscape that might have produced photographs, worthwhile or not, had it occurred to me to take a camera. A few years later, this would have been the primary aim of such a trip, but I did not then have any idea of a future making images, so that this first excursion was perhaps closer than any since to a *dérive*, although there were only two of us, and my clearest memory of it now is that it ended in the Galway Bay Restaurant, a celebrated café of which, sadly, I can find no trace. I think it was in Station Road. The meals were served on oval pictorial plates.

A few months later we moved to an unfurnished flat in Kentish Town, a miserable post-war construction in a one-house gap made in a terrace by a bomb, near Kentish Town West station, also on the North London Line. I had found the flat advertised on a shop-window notice board. The rent was £7 a week. Six years later, in 1975, by which time I was in full-time professional employment, we moved again, to a flat overlooking Parliament Hill, where I stayed until January 1981, so that I lived on the North London Line for a total of about 12 years. From the flat in Hampstead, we could see the trains, both passenger and freight. Among the latter there were and still are shipments of nuclear waste from the power stations at Bradwell, now being decommissioned, and Sizewell, which join the main west coast route at Willesden Junction, en route to Sellafield.

In the late 1960s, the North London Line ran from Richmond to Broad Street, in the City. The trains were never very busy except, perhaps, on Saturday afternoons and other occasions when Arsenal were playing at home. They had three carriages, the central one of which had a Victorian no-corridor layout, with nine separate ten-seat compartments in any of which a person might find him- or herself isolated with several possibly ill-disposed fellow-passengers. These carriages were eventually modified in about 1980 in an attempt to reduce vandalism. In the mid-1970s, a style of large-scale multi-colour calligraphic graffiti appeared on walls and other surfaces along the line, in which the two leading tags were 'Colonel Cav' and 'Columbo'. Not much of a television viewer, I didn't find out who

Columbo was until later. I wondered if Colonel Cav was a character in a comic. Cav was, I thought, short for Cavendish, but it seems more likely that it was an abbreviation of cavalry. The trains ran every 20 minutes.

During the 1970s, I sometimes travelled on the line as a commuter from Highbury and Islington to Hampstead Heath, returning from the North East London Polytechnic's school of architecture in Walthamstow, where I taught one afternoon a week. Until then I had encountered it mainly in connection with pleasure, sometimes just the pleasure of riding on the trains. I think this arises partly from the possibility the route offers to circumnavigate the city, and hence, perhaps, to become more familiar with something that is convention-ally unknowable, inadequately experienced in a journey towards or away from the centre. In an essay entitled 'Benjamin's Paris, Freud's Rome: Whose London?' (1999), in which he argues that London is 'an essentially unsatisfactory and even frustrating lin-guistic structure'—assigning it, in the end, to Mrs Wilberforce, the leading character of *The Ladykillers*—Adrian Rifkin discusses the similar character of the 253 bus route, which then ran between Aldgate and Euston station, via Hackney. These routes recall the ancient practice of circumambulation, which has been carried out in many cultures, over many centuries, for a variety of purposes; recently, for example, by Iain Sinclair for *London Orbital* (2002).

Despite a succession of post-privatization operators, the North London Line still seems to be known by its old name, and has been recognized as the prototype for and already-existing fragment of what one day might be a London orbital railway. In the 1980s it was added to the underground map, since when it has no longer seemed so exclusively the preserve of people who live and work along it. When Broad Street station was demolished, the route was extended east from Dalston to North Woolwich (via West Ham, where it crossed the northern outfall sewer, along the top of which is a path that leads to Beckton). With this modification, the extraordinary industrial architecture of Silvertown and Beckton, and the Woolwich Ferry, became more easily accessible by train from other parts of London (at the time of writing, the line beyond Stratford is closed, to reopen as part of the Docklands Light Railway). Crossing the ferry, a tourist could return to the centre through south London.

In 1979, I embarked on a postgraduate project in Peter Kardia's Department of Environmental Media at the Royal College of Art, where I began to make films and identified a canon of relevant texts, including Walter Benjamin's essay 'Surrealism' (1929), in which I read that 'the true creative overcoming of religious illumination ... resides in a profane illumination, a materialistic, anthropological inspiration'; and that:

> No one before these visionaries and augurs perceived how destitution—not only social but architectonic, the poverty of interiors, enslaved and enslaving objects—can be suddenly transformed into revolutionary nihilism. Leaving aside Aragon's *Passage de l'Opera*, Breton and Nadja are the lovers who convert everything we have experienced on mournful railway journeys (railways are beginning to age), on Godforsaken Sunday afternoons in the proletarian quarters of the great cities, in the first glance through the rain-blurred window of a new apartment, into revolutionary experience, if not action. They bring the immense forces of 'atmosphere' concealed in these things to the point of explosion. What form do you suppose a life would take that was determined at a decisive moment precisely by the street song last on everyone's lips?

The Surrealist *frisson*, as a phenomenon, is described in literature (most explicitly in Louis Aragon's *Le Paysan de Paris*), but is experienced primarily as a subjective transformation of appearances. It is easy to associate it with the impulse to take a photograph, with *photogenie*, which Christopher Phillips refers to as 'the mysterious transformation that occurs when everyday objects are revealed, as if anew, in a photograph or on the motion picture screen'. While Surrealism, especially after the Second World War, may not have lived up to Benjamin's appreciation of its revolutionary potential—Henri Lefebvre, writing in 1945, was particularly scathing—the Surrealist preoccupation with transfiguration, and hence the sacred, endures for us in the now-commonplace presence of everyday objects in art, and

in the subjective transformation, radical or otherwise, of everyday surroundings, the most familiar manifestations of which are the various practices of urban exploration that have become so widely established, especially in London, since the early 1990s.

My image-making developed over several years. In 1977, I began assembling a collection of colour slides documenting 'found' architecture, and discovered a precedent for this in the Surrealists' adoption of particular locations and structures in Paris. The buildings I found were certainly interesting, but the pictures were not always very successful. I had embarked on the project with the intention of extending it with moving-image media, either video or film, but had been discouraged by their poor definition compared to that of photographs, and by the limits of the camera's frame. I spent several months trying to develop a technique of architectural photography, and eventually, on a trip to France, made a series of photographs which became the basis of an installation combining monochrome slides and spoken narration, which was followed by another made with photographs of a high wall behind the prison on Wormwood Scrubs. These two works were fairly well received—they were later included in an exhibition at the Tate Gallery—and I recovered the

project's initiative, which led me, a few weeks later, to cycle along Harrow Road.

When I arrived at the place I had seen from the train, I found that it was overlooked by an extraordinary structure, a metal footbridge I had not noticed as the train passed beneath it. About 200 metres long, it carries pedestrians over both the main line and a branch that passes underneath it, at an angle, in a tunnel. The longer of the bridge's two spans is oriented so that Wembley Stadium is framed between its parapets. The bridge's architecture suggested a renewed attempt at moving pictures: its long, narrow walkway resembled the linearity of a film; its parapets framed the view in a ratio similar to the 4 x 3 of the camera, and its elaborate articulation, with several flights of steps, half-landings and changes of direction, offered a structure for a moving-camera choreography which might include occasional panoramas.

The resulting film had two parts, the second of which was photographed a few weeks after the initial visit to the bridge, by walking a hand-held camera across it during a continuous ten-minute take. By this time, I think I had already decided to write fictional narration to accompany the picture. I discovered another footbridge, a square of walkways above the nearby junction of Harrow Road and the North Circular, with a spiral ramp at each corner, and photographed another ten-minute moving-camera walk, which became the first half of the film. This bridge was demolished in about 1992, when an underpass was built at the junction. The film was called *Stonebridge Park* (1981). Its narrative, such as it was, recalled the context, in the first part, and the immediate aftermath, in the second, of a theft committed by the narrator.

This rudimentary film was neither made nor conceived in a *moment*, but it originated in the unusual, unexpected experience that produced the photograph from which it evolved. Becoming more experienced in making images, I came to rely less on anything resembling the experiential phenomena of Surrealism, and became increasingly uncertain about their political significance. Exceptional moments of natural light seemed to offer similar conceptual transformations, and produced better pictures; for many who work with photographic media, the weather is not merely analogous with a state of mind. I have sometimes wondered whether I might have addressed these questions better if more of Henri Lefebvre's writing had been translated into English sooner than it was. *La Production de l'espace* was first published in 1974, but did not appear in English until Blackwell published Donald Nicholson-Smith's translation in 1991. I first encountered the book in 1994, before which I knew of Lefebvre and his relationship with the Situationists only from a brief mention in *Leaving the Twentieth Century* (1974), Christopher Gray's anthology of Situationist writing, an essential text for any would-be-literate punk-rocker in the 1970s. There I had found Gray's translation of part of Raoul Vaneigem's *Traité de savoir-vivre à l'usage des jeunes générations* (1967), known in English as *The Revolution of Everyday Life*, from which I often quoted:

> although I can always see how beautiful anything could be if only I could change it, in practically every case there is nothing I can really do. Everything is changed into something else in my imagination, then the dead weight of things changes it back into what it was in the first place.

(Nicholson-Smith's 1983 translation is closer to the original: 'though not everything affects me with equal force, I am always faced with the same paradox: no sooner do I become aware of the alchemy worked by my imagination upon reality than I see that reality reclaimed and borne away by the uncontrollable river of things'.)

In *The Production of Space*, Lefebvre writes: 'the fact is that the space that contains the realized preconditions of another life is the same one as prohibits what those preconditions make possible'—a thought not unlike that in Vaneigem's paragraph. I wondered if the prohibition that Lefebvre identifies is sometimes suspended within the spaces of a film, and, if so, whether this might explain some of the attraction, and the seemingly utopian quality, of so much film space, and why some people are willing to devote so much time and effort to making films.

In the third volume of his *Critique of Everyday Life* (1981), translated into English in 2005, Lefebvre wrote of:

> Intense instants—or, rather, moments—it is as if they are seeking to shatter the everydayness trapped in generalized exchange. On the one hand, they affix the chain of equivalents to lived experience and daily life. On the other, they detach and shatter it. In the 'micro', conflicts between these elements and the chains of equivalence are continually arising. Yet the 'macro', the pressure of the market and exchange, is forever limiting these conflicts and restoring order. At certain periods, people have looked to these moments to transform existence ...

Lefebvre often writes of 'moments'. 'What is Possible', the final chapter of the first volume of the *Critique*, written in 1945, contains this:

> Mystics and metaphysicians used to acknowledge that everything in life revolved around exceptional moments. In their view, life found expression and was concentrated in them. These moments were festivals: festivals of the mind or the heart, public or intimate festivals. In order to attack and mortally wound mysticism, it was necessary to show that festivals had lost their meaning, the power they had in the days when all their magnificence came from life, and when life drew its magnificence from festivals.

And in the opening chapter of *The Production of Space* he identifies another kind of *moment*:

> The fact is that around 1910 a certain space was shattered. It was the space of common sense, of knowledge (*savoir*), of social practice, of political power, a space thitherto enshrined in everyday discourse, just as in abstract thought, as the environment of and channel for communications; the space, too, of classical perspective and geometry, developed from the Renaissance onwards on the basis of the Greek tradition (Euclid, logic) and bodied forth in Western art and philosophy, as in the form of the city and the town ... Euclidean and

perspectivist space have disappeared as systems of reference, along with other former 'commonplaces' such as the town, history, paternity, the tonal system in music, traditional morality, and so forth. This was truly a crucial moment.

This paragraph had already appeared in 1990, quoted in David Harvey's *The Condition of Postmodernity*, also published by Blackwell, and Harvey quoted it again in his afterword for Blackwell's edition of *The Production of Space*. Harvey's interest in the passage arises, I assume, from its identification of the beginning of a period that ended with the 'profound shift in the "structure of feeling"' that signalled the onset of postmodernity in the early 1970s, with the break-up of the Bretton-Woods fixed-exchange-rate system and the subsequent slide to neoliberalism. In the autumn of 2008, it began to seem possible that this period might be giving way to another.

If such moments of historical transition, however questionable their identification, open possibilities for creativity, for those moments to which, in Lefebvre's words, people have looked to transform existence (1910 was, among other things, the year in which Apollinaire invented the art of going for a walk), it seems strange that Surrealist and Situationist techniques—*flânerie*, the *dérive* and psychogeography—should have become the subject of so much attention, even if they were not quite 'revived', in London during the 1990s. At the time, I suggested that their purpose had been overlooked: psychogeography and the *dérive* were conceived, in a more politically ambitious period, as preliminaries to the production of new, revolutionary spaces; in the 1990s they seemed more likely to be preliminary to the production of literature and other works, and to gentrification, the discovery of previously overlooked value in dilapidated spaces and neighbourhoods.

In an essay on 'contemporary London Gothic', Roger Luckhurst has suggested that the Gothic genre that he and others identified as characteristic of London in the 1990s was a response to 'that curious mix of tyranny and farce that constitutes London governance', particularly the dominance of the City of London, with its medieval peculiarities and its untiring pursuit of an ever more unequal, damaged world. Among the writers Luckhurst identified with the contemporary London Gothic, several have invoked the techniques of Situationist urbanism, as if the power of the financial sector is such that subjective re-imagination offered the only possibility for change that had become unattainable in other ways.

In 2008, cycling along Harrow Road, I did not encounter any explosion of the 'intense forces of "atmosphere"' that are undoubtedly concealed there; but unexpected memories of earlier discoveries, at a time when it seemed possible that a dysfunctional economic orthodoxy was finally collapsing, suggested that such experiences still have some value.

Reading

Apollinaire, Guillaume, *The Heresiarch & Co.*, trans. Rèmy Inglis Hall (Boston: Exact Change, 1991).

Aragon, Louis, *Paris Peasant*, trans. Simon Watson Taylor (Boston: Exact Change, 1994).

Benjamin, Walter, 'Surrealism: The Last Snapshot of the European Intelligentsia', in *One-Way Street and Other Writings*, trans. Edmund Jephcott and Kingsley Shorter (London: New Left Books, 1979): 225–39.

Freud, Sigmund, 'On Beginning the Treatment (Further Recommendations on the Technique of Psycho-Analysis I)', in *The Standard Edition of the Complete Psychological Works*, Vol. 12 (London: Vintage, 2001): 123–44.

Greater London Industrial Archaeology Society Newsletter, February 2007 (http://www.glias.org.uk/news/228news.html)

Harvey, David, *The Condition of Postmodernity: An Enquiry into the Origins of Cultural Change* (Oxford, Cambridge, MA: Blackwell, 1990).

Hauser, Kitty, *Bloody Old Britain: O. G. S. Crawford and the Archaeology of Modern Life* (London: Granta, 2008).

Jones, Edward and Christopher Woodward, *Guide to the Architecture of London* (London: Weidenfeld & Nicolson, 2000).

Keiller, Patrick, *Robinson in Space, and a Conversation with Patrick Wright* (London: Reaktion, 1999).

Lefebvre, Henri, *The Production of Space*, trans. Donald Nicholson-Smith (Oxford: Blackwell, 1991).

Lefebvre, Henri, *Critique of Everyday Life, Volume 1*, trans. John Moore (London: Verso, 1991).

Lefebvre, Henri, *Critique of Everyday Life, Volume 3: From Modernity to Modernism (Towards a Metaphilosophy of Daily Life)*, trans. Gregory Elliott (London: Verso, 2008).

Luckhurst, Roger, 'The Contemporary London Gothic and the Limits of the "Spectral Turn"', *Textual Practice* 16 (2002): 527–46.

O'Brien, Flann, *The Third Policeman* (London: Picador, 1974).

Phillips, Christopher (ed.), *Photography in the Modern Era: European Documents and Critical Writings 1913–1940* (New York: Metropolitan Museum of Art/Aperture, 1989).

Poe, Edgar Allan, 'The Fall of the House of Usher', in *Selected Writings of Edgar Allan Poe*, ed. David Galloway (Harmondsworth: Penguin, 1967): 138–57.

Rifkin, Adrian, 'Benjamin's Paris, Freud's Rome: Whose London?', *Art History* 22 (1999): 619–32.

Sinclair, Iain, *London Orbital* (London: Penguin, 2003).

Sterne, Laurence, *The Life and Opinions of Tristram Shandy, Gentleman*, ed. Melvyn New (Harmondsworth: Penguin, 2003).

Vaneigem, Raoul, 'Self-realisation, Communication and Participation', in *Leaving the Twentieth Century: The Incomplete Work of the Situationist International*, trans. and ed. Christopher Gray (London: Free Fall Publications, 1974): 131–51.

Vaneigem, Raoul, *The Revolution of Everyday Life*, revised edition, trans. Donald Nicholson-Smith (London: Rebel Press/Left Bank Books, 1994).

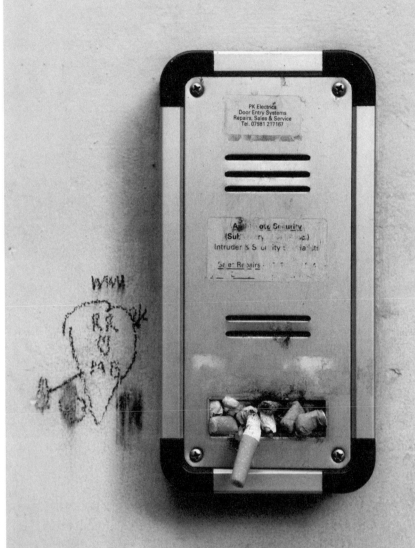

Inhabiting

Geoff Dyer

For many years I lived in various flats either on or just off Brixton Water Lane in south London. So I was always walking, cycling or taking a bus down Effra Road. How many times did I walk down Effra Road? How many hours did I spend walking down Effra Road? If I was going to Brixton Rec to play squash, or to Franco's for a pizza or a cappuccino (this was before I acquired the refinement of taste in cappuccino that, in the years since then, has invariably been a source of torment and frustration rather than enhanced satisfaction) or to the aptly named Effra to meet friends for drinks, or just to take the tube to some other part of London, I always had to trudge or cycle down Effra Road. Wherever I was going the journey began and ended on Effra Road. One of the reasons I moved away from Brixton was because I could not face trudging, cycling or taking the bus down Effra Road again. Effra Road was so deeply lodged in my muscle memory that I could have made my way home blind or after some kind of seizure or stroke had completely wiped out part of my brain. Assuming I was able to walk I could have made my way down Effra Road when I was no longer capable of going anywhere—or doing anything—else.

The route never varied but, in small and large ways, the experience changed over time. In the mid-'80s, when a lot of my friends lived in the area, the fact that I was always bumping into someone I knew as we made our respective ways up and down Effra Road added to the cosy sense that this was exactly where I most wanted to be in the world. Over time, the road itself changed also. The disused Cool Tan factory was co-opted for various alternative ventures: pre-rave-type parties; a sensory-deprivation flotation tank. My friend Heather Ackroyd grew the first of her grass sculptures there in the 1980s. Then it became the European Business Centre or something like that. Then branches of Halfords and Currys opened (very handy for the one time I needed to buy a fridge). What struck me about this was how completely each new development obliterated the previous one. At first you would notice that the Cool Tan plant had been knocked down, that something was being built in its stead. But once that new thing was completed it was as though the previous thing had never been there. It was the opposite of the model of the unconscious offered by Freud: a version of Rome in which all successive stages of construction are preserved simultaneously. I struggle to remember the Cool Tan factory. To all intents and purposes Currys and Halfords have been there forever, even if they are no longer there. I don't know. I haven't been to check, haven't walked down Effra Road for ages (thank god) and hope I never have to do so again.

I say Effra Road but it could be any road. We are always taking the same routes through cities. The tube or metro forces us to do this, and so—less claustrophobically—do buses. Even on a bike, when we can take any route, we allow ourselves to get funneled along familiar paths, preferring the often slightly longer but nicer cycle lanes because they are ostensibly safer, even though they can actually be more dangerous because one is in a state of less than heightened alert. As pedestrians, too, we not only stick to the same routes, but prefer to cling to the same side of the road (north side of Effra Road going into Brixton, south side coming home, in the same direction as the traffic). This tendency to the habitual expresses in linear terms the way that, in a vast city like London, we avail ourselves of only a fraction of the numerous other opportunities—all those concerts, films and lectures listed in *Time Out*, a magazine which I stopped buying years ago—and alternative routes open to us. As the routes prescribed by habit grow more and more familiar so we become increasingly oblivious to them. Alex, the protagonist of Alan Hollinghurst's *The Spell* (1998), lives in Hammersmith, but he speaks for all of us when his immediate environment gets reduced to 'a block or two worn half-invisible by use'.

We tend always to approach a given place from the same direction, via the same route. I am always surprised how thoroughly disorienting it is if I arrange to meet someone at a café I know well but, for whatever reason—an earlier appointment somewhere else—end up approaching it from an unusual direction. It's completely bewildering, as if the place we are supposed to be meeting at has disappeared. What's happened to it? Where did it go? Psychologically, the location of a place is not fixed. It is determined not by *where* it is but how we get to it.

Even though I was unhappy and lonely for much of my time there, I always think of the period when I lived on rue Boulle in the eleventh *arrondissement* of Paris as an idyllic phase of my life. Partly this was because I liked the *quartier* so much, partly it was because I was able to leave and approach my apartment in such a multiplicity of ways. Depending on where in the city I was going I could use one of three Metro stops served by three different lines. I could get buses at the Bastille. If I was walking somewhere I could set off in all sorts of directions. Now, obviously, your home is always the hub from which you branch out; but when I lived off or on Brixton Water Lane, 90 per cent of the time I would be heading east, into Brixton, along the Effra Road. Whereas when I lived on rue Boulle, my routes were divided equally between the ten options that were available. All points of the compass were equally alluring. There was always some reason to go in a new direction. Having said that, being a creature of habit, I did tend to go to the same place every morning for my coffee and croissant—a café on rue de la Roquette—and I always took the same route there, just as I always took the same route to the same café—the Croissant D'Or—when I lived on Esplanade in New Orleans, or as I did when I trudged down Effra Road for a cappuccino in Franco's (or Franca Manca as it has now become). I am like Michael Hofmann in his poem 'Guanajuato Two Times':

I could keep returning to the same few places
till I turned blue, till I turned into
José José
on the sleeve of his new record album
'What is love?'

I like to go back to the same few places all the time—then, as soon as I
break free of the prison of routine, I am left wondering why I kept
going to a place I had stopped enjoying years earlier. For many years,
whenever I had errands to run or meetings to attend in Soho, I would
have a cappuccino at the Cappuccetto. Then, for reasons I can no
longer remember, I started going to Patisserie Valerie's a hundred
yards down the road, on Old Compton Street, and wondered why I'd
wasted so many years in the Cappuccetto which, by comparison, was
a dismal and unatmospheric place. I kept going to Patisserie Valerie's
for years after it had stopped being any good, for years after it had
become a source of constant and terrible disappointment, for years
after the nice Spanish waitress, Maria (who worked there for years,
who always flirted a bit with my friend Chris and me) had left, so
that instead of this nice, unchanging waitress–customer relationship
we were faced with such a rapid turnover of staff as to suggest
that Valerie's might not be an entirely happy ship. The pastries got
bigger and bigger, I no longer liked the coffee, and the staff, though
rapidly changing, seemed always to be drawn from the same ex-
Soviet republic where the idea of service or charm was anathema. On
the larger stage, meanwhile, Valerie's began opening new branches
across London, thereby undermining the idea that you were at a
unique quasi-bohemian hang-out and creating the feeling that you
were part of a mini empire, a Starbucks in the process of formation.
But I kept going anyway, even though I ranted on to anyone who
would listen about how terrible the service, coffees and pastries had
become.

Nietzsche loved what he called 'brief habits', but he so hated 'enduring habits' that he was grateful even to the bouts of sickness or
misfortune that caused him to break free of the chains of enduring
habit (though most intolerable of all, he went on, would be 'a life

entirely devoid of habits, a life that would demand perpetual improvisation. That would be my exile and my Siberia.'). Unlike Nietzsche
I succumb all too easily to enduring habits. Programmed by habit, I
kept going to Patisserie Valerie's until I met the woman who became
my wife. She persuaded me to meet her in the Monmouth Street
Coffee Shop or, later, at Fernandez and Wells on Beak Street, one of
the new wave of antipodean cafés that is revolutionizing the coffee
scene in Soho. Once I had taken my custom to Fernandez and Wells
or to Flat White (on Berwick Street) I never thought of Patisserie
Valerie's again except with regret for all the years I had loyally
wasted there. I would like to claim I am now in a state of bliss, but the
truth is that the pastries at Fernandez and Wells and Flat White could
be a lot better, are actually a bit on the dismal side.

Which brings me to the thing I really want to talk about: namely
the donuts of New York.

In September 2004 I rented a studio apartment on 37th Street,
between Park and Lex, in Manhattan. It was a very busy period for
me; all sorts of things had to be sorted out with some urgency, but
although there were other, ostensibly more serious things to sort out,
nothing was more urgent than the need to find a local café I could go
to every day for my elevenses.

Given that so many conditions had to be met this was easier said
than done. First, the coffee had to be exactly as I liked it, although I
would have been hard pressed to define exactly how this was. Second,
the pastry had to be exactly as I liked it. By pastry I mean a croissant
or donut—I don't like those American staples, muffins or bagels.
Third, I would never drink my coffee out of a paper cup; the coffee
had to be served in a proper china cup. This is not as easy as you
might think. There are plenty of places in Manhattan where, although
the coffee is good, it is only served in a paper or Styrofoam cup.
Fourth, when I said 'cup' I meant cup (i.e. a cup not a mug). And,
fifth, it had to be the right size cup. This question of size is not simply
a matter of size; I have never ever had a nice cappuccino in a place
where they serve them in those jumbo-size cups; all you get is a great
bucket of foam.

In the excited hope that it might be possible to fulfil these conditions I began to explore the neighbourhood, which turned out to be far more promising than I'd initially thought, especially if you walked east a couple of blocks to Third Avenue. I went into a place called Delectica on the corner of Third and 38th. It looked like the kind of place where people had a quick lunch or picked up a coffee on the way to work—but they did at least have proper cups. It wasn't atmospheric but I saw that as well as proper cups they had a wide selection of pastries. I ordered a cappuccino and it was OK—a bit too frothy but it came in a cup the right size. I also ordered a croissant. It wasn't up to much, but great croissants are increasingly hard to find anywhere in the world, even in France. I went back to Delectica the following day and ordered another cappuccino and a donut. The donut I ordered that day was a ring donut and it was an amazing donut. It had a slight glaze of icing—but not too much—and this icing wasn't too sweet. And the texture ... What can I say about the texture except what I said to myself on that fateful morning: 'Wow-ee,' I said, 'this is really something, this is a *major donut experience* I'm having here.' The donut experience was perfectly complemented by the cappuccino experience, which had been quite nice the day before but which today was right on the money. It wasn't a coffee with a scum of foam floating on the top; no, the foam was *integrated* with the coffee. Foam and coffee were one. It had been made by a different person and she had made it perfectly. I had not made any specific requests, but this waitress, quite by chance, had made my cappuccino exactly as I liked it, and had in the process made something much more than that—namely my day. And not just *that* day because from then on, if I was in the queue and the other waitress offered to serve me, I would say I was still making up my mind—even though I had exactly the same thing every day—and wait until the waitress who made my cappuccino exactly as I liked it was free.

And so my life fell into the unvarying routine I crave and need. I would wake up, have my muesli at home, work for a bit and then go to Delectica for my elevenses. I said 'unvarying' but gradually, as my eagerness to go to Delectica increased, I found it impossible to concentrate on my work because all I could think about was my donut and coffee, and so I started having my elevenses earlier and earlier until I ended up skipping breakfast and having my elevenses at nine. At the latest. I went to bed at night looking forward to my nineses and then, as soon as I woke up, I stumbled out of bed, dressed and went to Delectica before I was even properly awake. I got dressed in a hurry, I hurried down there, and then although I loved them and should have savoured them, I started gobbling my donut and drinking my coffee in a hurry, gobbling and slurping them down in such a frenzy that I barely tasted a thing. Before I knew it the high point of my day was over with. It was only 8:45 and there was nothing to look forward to. I also found it increasingly difficult to keep my rapture to myself. One morning, as I gobbled my donut and slurped my coffee, thinking to myself, 'What a fantastic donut, what an amazing coffee', I realized that I had not just thought this but was actually saying aloud, 'What a fantastic donut!', 'What a totally fantastic experience!', and that this was attracting the attention of the other customers, one of whom turned to me and said,

'You like the donuts, huh?'

'And the coffee!' I said. 'The donut would be nothing without the coffee—and vice-versa.'

'Where you from?' he said.

'England.'

'Don't they have donuts like that in England?'

'Not like this they don't', I said. 'I've spent twenty years searching for just such a donut. Now that I've found it I can go to my grave a happy man. I've achieved everything I wanted from life.'

'Well, enjoy,' he said, as though I had been making a joke.

'Sure will,' I said and resumed my chewing.

Time passed. I was only subletting this apartment for six weeks. I arranged to sublet another place, for another six weeks, in the heart of the East Village, on 9th Street between First and A. As the time for moving grew close I realized that I had actually come to love my apartment and my neighbourhood and that I was blissfully happy there. No sooner had I realized this than I realized I was in count-down mode, that I only had five mornings left to take my coffee and donut in Delectica. Then I had just four, then three ... It wasn't just the thought of leaving that was terrible; it was the knowledge that as soon as I moved into my new place I'd have to start over again. Eventually I had no more days left. I moved in to my new place and once again began rolling the stone up the steep hill of consumer choice. The problem here was almost the opposite of the one I'd faced on 37th Street—there were too many cafés. I hardly knew where to start, so I sought guidance from my friend Jaime who lived a couple of blocks away and who explained that the donuts I loved at Delectica came from a place called the Donut Plant and that the aptly named Donut Plant distributed their donuts to quite a few places, one of which was on the corner of Third and A, opposite Two Boots, the Cajun pizza place that I had been completely obsessed by and utterly dependent on when I lived in New York in the late 1980s. They did have the donuts at this place on the corner of Third and A but the coffee came in a mug and wasn't so nice. It was too frothy and rather bland. After a while I discovered that I could get Donut Plant donuts even closer to home, on my street, on the corner of Ninth and A, but the coffee there was really not up to much so I preferred to go down to Third and A. Well, it was OK and I trudged down there every day, but with nothing like the spring in my step that had characterized my trips to Delectica. In every other respect this was a perfect neighbourhood: it was full of cool people, there were tons of cheap places to eat, and the St Marks bookstore was only a five-minute walk away ... Yes, it was a great neighbourhood; but in my cups I often fell to thinking about Delectica, and although I never walked up there just for coffee, if I had any excuse to go up that way, however flimsy, I would stop off at Delectica. Delectica had been my base, it was the point from which my sense of familiar and localized happiness had spread. It was the epicentre of my well-being—what Marx, in a non-pastry-related context, termed the heart of a heartless world.

I've always been dependent on places like this wherever I've lived. In New Orleans it was the Croissant D'Or, in Rome it was the bar San Calisto in Trastevere, in Brixton it was Franco's. Even if I am only in a place for a short while I quickly build up a routine: I want not just to visit a city but to *inhabit* it as rapidly as possible. A few years ago I was in Turin for a conference. I was only there three days but, in a classic instance of the Nietzschean 'brief habit', I came to love having my coffee and cornetto in the café across the road from my hotel. (Turin, of course, is where Nietzsche suffered his final breakdown—a desperately successful attempt to break free of the habit of sanity?) If I were in Turin tomorrow I would return to that same café immediately and it would be a completely satisfactory experience, but when you've had an ongoing relationship with a place, when you've built your life around it as I had built mine around Delectica, there is no going back. Sometimes this is literally the case: places close or change hands, the disused Cool Tan factory where Heather grew her grass sculptures turns into a branch of Halfords; the lease runs out or the management changes or a new chef comes along and where previously you found delight now there only lurks the grim spectre of the kind of disappointment that haunted my last years at Patisserie Valerie's when I kept going back there even though I knew, in my heart, that it was time to move on. But even if nothing changes, even if the place and the food and the staff remain unchanged, there is still no going back, even though, of course, one does exactly that: one goes back. When we went to New Orleans for a wedding earlier this year, I took my wife to see my old apartment on Esplanade (I could not find it exactly, was not sure that the building that seemed in roughly the location was actually my building or was a new building that had been built on the same site) and then we took exactly the walk that I used to take to the Croissant D'Or. It was still there and we ordered cappuccinos and croissants, and the croissant, while just about tolerable, was nowhere near as good as I remembered, and the coffee was pretty terrible (too milky and the foam was all bubbly and, although it seemed OK at first, by the halfway stage I decided it was totally revolting). That was nothing, though, compared to the disappointment of my return to Delectica about a year and a half after first discovering it.

I was staying at a hotel on 48th Street and Seventh Avenue, but such is my compulsion to repeat experiences that I trudged across town and went to Delectica. It took about 40 minutes to get there. They still had the donuts but I recognized none of the staff. I ordered a cappuccino. When it was prepared I looked in horror: it was like a

Knickerbocker Glory or something with foam piled high like cream in a tall glass.

'What on *earth* is that?' I demanded.

'A cappuccino,' she said proudly

'Well that's where you're wrong,' I said. 'It's not a cappuccino. It's an abominaccino! If you knew how much this place meant to me...'

I couldn't go on. I felt so angry and so sorry for myself that I stormed out of the door and into the street, where I began asking people, randomly, if they knew any cafés where they stocked Donut Plant donuts, getting myself into more and more of a frenzy as I did so. Obviously most people had not heard of Donut Plant donuts and the few who had heard of them did not know of a café that stocked them, but eventually someone said that they thought Orin's Daily Roast stocked Donut Plant donuts and that there was branch of Orin's in Grand Central station. And so, like a commuter hurrying for a train, I made my way to Grand Central station. Finding Grand Central station was easy enough but finding Orin's Daily Roast within the vast station complex was extremely difficult. Eventually I found it, saw a line of people queuing up, saw that although it was essentially just a stall they did indeed stock Donut Plant donuts, but that only one vanilla donut remained. I joined the queue. If anyone had taken the last donut I would have pleaded with them and argued my case—'If you knew what I have been through this morning...' If after pleading with them to take something else, they had refused, I would have snatched the donut from their hand and started chewing on it frantically, but no one wanted this last donut and so I ordered it together with a cappuccino, and although I had to drink my cappuccino out of a paper cup, standing, like a commuter who has missed the train he had been hurrying for, I was grateful, in the circumstances, to have got a coffee and a donut at all.

Thereafter, whenever I was in New York, I checked online at the Donut Plant website to find a Donut Plant outlet close to wherever I was staying. When I was staying at the Maritime in Chelsea for a week the best bet seemed to be Joe's Art of Coffee on Waverly Place. A 15-minute walk, often in terrible weather, but it was well worth it. The coffee was amazing, and they had the donuts, though it was often touch-and-go whether they had *enough* donuts. On two occasions there was only one donut left and, as had happened at Orin's Daily Roast, I found myself in a state of great tension, waiting to see if someone would take the last donut, girding my loins to say, 'Excuse me sir/madam, but I wonder if there is anything else that takes your fancy because, frankly, I *must* have that donut.' It never came to that; miraculously, there was always at least one donut left for me, and the combination of donut and excellent coffee was bliss, even better, in a way, than Delectica, because unlike Delectica this was a cool and atmospheric place in a fun neighbourhood. I went there so often in the course of my week-long stay that I took out a loyalty card and, on my last morning, my loyalty was rewarded with a free coffee: a perfect example of Nietzsche's ideal of the brief habit.

My last trip to New York was nothing like as happy. I was staying at a hotel on 55th Street and Broadway, very near the N and R subway lines, so I took the train down to Joe's Art of Coffee on 13th Street near Union Square. They had Donut Plant donuts alright but not the ones I like, only the more exotic flavours, and so, thinking quickly—I had a hectic schedule, was pressed for time, should not really have been schlepping down all this way just for a coffee and a donut—I decided to walk back to the Waverly Place branch. I got there and it was the same story, except it was even worse than the same story because in addition to not having the donuts I wanted the coffee was too milky and the donut I opted for—coconut glaze, filled with coconut cream—was actually a bit horrible, and as I sat there chewing I found it hard to fathom what could lead anyone to abandon the basic donut, the default donut from which all others are derived, in favour of the more elaborate versions which may appeal to some tastes. To be honest, I made my way to the subway with my tail between my legs, wishing, at some level, that I was not forced to live this way, was not compelled to seek out things I have decided I like in the face of terrible odds. Sitting on the subway car as it clanged and hurtled back to midtown I reflected on the way that wherever we live we are always compelled to repeat the same thing over and over, that at some level, perhaps every level, all we ever do is trudge up and down Effra Road, and that whatever we are talking about, whether it is something pleasurable (like finding the supreme donut) or something onerous (like taking the subway or tube), when we talk about life we might just as well talk about trudging up and down Effra Road, irrespective of where we are in the world.

The story could have ended there—I intended to end it there—on a note of glum resignation, but to present a truly global picture of how things stand, mention must be made of a recent trip to Tokyo. It seems to me that we are always trying to re-create our particular ideal of a city in whichever actual city we happen to find ourselves. Before going to Tokyo I remembered reading, on the Donut Plant website, that they had opened a branch in Tokyo, not a concession in the sense of a place where Donut Plant donuts cooked in New York were available for purchase in Tokyo but an actual donut-producing Donut Plant. As in New York these donuts were available at a number of locations throughout the sprawling megalopolis that is Tokyo. We were staying at the Peninsula in Marunouchi and by studying the Donut Plant website carefully we saw that the nearest location was a branch of Dean & DeLuca, a mere 15 minutes' walk away. There were other reasons for going to Japan, of course. There were ancient temples and carp ponds, there were geishas and cherry blossom, there were incredible feats of retail architecture and there was the sci-fi neon of Shinjuku, but at the back of my mind, in contrast to the untranslatable otherness of Japan, was the familiar prospect of Donut Plant donuts which, far from being reminders of home, were, for most of the year—the part of the year spent in London—site-specific New York treats, edible emblems of everything that New York was and London was not. So that what I was looking for was not *London*-in-Tokyo but *New York*-in-Tokyo. Ryszard Kapuściński claimed that whereas in the past an encounter with 'the Other' meant an encounter between a European (white) and an easterner (non-white), increasingly there would be contacts between these Others and *other* Others (Indians and South Americans, say, or Chinese and Africans). That, it seemed to me, was what we had here. The donut as Other (i.e. not England) being consumed in Dean & DeLuca (the quintessential upmarket New York deli) in a part of Tokyo (the quintessential urban Other) that looked incredibly like downtown Chicago. I am not quite sure what I mean by this, am worried slightly that I am using 'Other' in the sense of 'Same', but it doesn't matter because we went kind of insane in Tokyo. Because it was not New York (home of the donut), because it was a kind of double treat (a place where one did not expect to find donuts *where donuts were miraculously available*), my wife and I ordered two donuts each and two coffees each, each and every day. We would sit there with vanilla icing stuck to our faces and noses, smiling and chewing. In a sense this was everything that was bad about the homogenizing effect of globalization, an upmarket equivalent of finding a McDonald's in every city on earth, or a branch of Patisserie Valerie's in every area of London, but the thing is, the point I want to emphasize, is that I love donuts and I wouldn't mind if there were a Donut Plant outlet on every city block in London—the world would be a better place.

We arrived at Dean & DeLuca at ten on the dot every day. One day it wasn't open, would not be open until eleven, because, we discovered, this was a Japanese national holiday. We stood outside. There was nowhere to sit but there was a keen wind which made standing even more irksome. There was nothing to do but wait. We were in a pedestrian version of the London double-bind whereby if we walked back to the hotel—and we had already begun to find this walk onerous; in less than five days Naka Dori had taken on some of the qualities of Effra Road, stroll had turned to trudge—we would have had to set out again the moment we got back there. So we had pure dead time to kill. We were in this strange, strangely familiar city, and we stood there as time congealed around us on the nearly deserted, litterless street. We stood and waited and it was like being one of the undead, because whatever we thought of doing, there was nothing to do, and so we just stood there in the keen wind, wishing time would pass, wanting one thing and one thing only: for time to pass, to get out of the wind and into Dean & DeLuca so that we could order our donuts and coffees and sit down, eating and drinking them in this distant part of the world that, at this moment, at the moment which was not yet at hand but which was drawing closer at an agonizingly slow pace, contained everything that we wanted from a city, namely *donuts*. Eventually, Dean & DeLuca opened, we scoffed our donuts and swilled our coffees and then, when we had finished scoffing and swilling, walked back to the hotel, noticing, as we had failed to on the way down (I was blind to everything except the prospect of donuts) the Japanese flag—the red circle on a field of white—flying from many buildings. It seemed that although there were many nice flags in the world none was nicer than the Japanese flag, even though when I was growing up, reading about Japanese atrocities in the Pacific War, it had seemed a symbol of pure evil. It did not seem like that at all now; now it became a symbol of the healing potential of the donut, of a world community of donut lovers living in peace and harmony, bound together by the vision and ambition of a Czech immigrant who went to New York, opened his Donut Plant and then forged a donut empire, extending from New York to Tokyo, but regrettably bypassing London, where we still have to make do with croissants that are like stale buns, so that at times the whole of the London seems like nothing so much as an interminable extension of Effra Road.

Reading

Hofmann, Michael, *Corona, Corona* (London: Faber & Faber, 1993).

Hollinghurst, Alan, *The Spell* (London: Chatto & Windus, 1998).

Kapuściński, Ryszard, *The Other*, trans. Antonia Lloyd-Jones (London and New York: Verso, 2008).

Nietzsche, Friedrich, *The Gay Science: With a Prelude in Rhymes and an Appendix of Songs*, trans. Walter Kaufmann (New York: Vintage, 1974).

Lodging

Michael Newton

For seven years, I lodged in an attic room in a four-storey house on the edge of Hampstead Heath. On the lowest two floors the landlady lived with her son, two Persian Blue cats, a chocolate Labrador and a fish-tank. Besides myself, there were four other lodgers on the upper floors, dispersed in various cycles of despair. Recumbent in some purgatorial place devoted to lassitude lived the other long-term lodger, the only woman I've ever met for whom the term 'spinster' seemed inescapable. For seven years, her evening meal did not once vary, a nutritionist's nightmare of spaghetti hoops, a pot of raspberry yoghurt and a chocolate biscuit. The other residents were more fleeting: foreign students, the arty down on their luck, and the terminally single.

Lodging in Hampstead brought its confusions, its disadvantages, and some very few benefits. The confusion arose every time someone asked me where I lived. 'Hampstead' implied trust funds and settled opulence, presenting an image of my prospects that everything else about me belied. So after each fresh introduction I would be forced to explain away the locale, by laying out the terms in which I lived: one low-ceilinged room (romantically pictured by my landlady as a *chambre de bonne*) lit by a large window directly over the bed and a small opaque skylight in the north-eastern corner; a shared kitchen; a table in the hallway for dining; a pay-phone; and a shared bathroom with Victorian plumbing overlooking a plenitude of garden and a glimpse of Parliament Hill. No, I am not rich, I would inform them. I am a lodger.

The disadvantages grew obvious in time. My amorous life stalled, unable to evade the constriction of the room; I succumbed to the ambiguity of the lodger's status. Within a few days of leaving the building, I had a girlfriend again. Icy as Anchorage in the winter, sticky as Tangiers in the summer, the room itself prompted only thoughts of escape. Standing up, the ceiling was never higher than two feet above my head. Lodging smeared the prospect of comfy domesticity, and after a couple of years I became rabidly social in part at least in order to escape from those four walls.

There were, however, two benefits. The first was the Heath itself. It invaded my room that first summer there, with improbable insects that had drifted in from the grasses gathering around the electric light. The window over my bed allowed me to fall asleep while gazing up at the stars, and I would sit up on its ledge and peer out over the rooftops to the trees beyond. The house was located somewhere between the homes of two renowned Hampstead lodgers—John Keats and George Orwell. Both men had also belonged to the area on sufferance.

The other benefit derived from the sheer misery of lodging. Recently returned from America, newly single, post post-graduate, post-young, my life was unutterably boring. I would work all day in the British Library, or in my room, and then face a television-less evening of more of the same. In order to escape the dulling consequences of my living arrangements, I headed for the cinema. A walk across the Heath brought me to the Everyman, in the days when it still showed a rolling repertoire. I developed the habit of dropping off there, after a day researching or writing, and catching a movie or two. Soon I was there daily, turning an ordinary interest in films into a passion for the cinema. It is for this reason perhaps that I connect the movies with lodging, one circumstantially involved with the other.

However, it also became apparent that the link was more than circumstantial. Many of the directors whose work stirred me most had themselves been intrigued by the circumstances of the lodger. Alfred Hitchcock, Michael Powell and Roman Polanski had all explored the ambiguous place in which I found myself. Although their image of the lodger exerted an uncanny force that nothing in my own experience could lay claim to, their grasping of the contingent oddity of the lodger's situation nonetheless resonated with my own condition. There was, it appeared, something baffling about lodging, something that both required explanation and defeated it.

Yet the imagined lodger of their films—that reticent, creepy solitary—was a surprisingly recent invention. It was just before the First World War that this new urban character sprang into being. The terms of the innovation were first set out in Marie Belloc Lowndes's novel, *The Lodger* (1913), which unfolds in a shabby house on the Marylebone Road in London. During a series of murders committed by the mysterious Avenger, a middle-aged couple, the Buntings, take in a Mr Sleuth as a lodger. Entranced by her well-spoken tenant, Mrs Bunting slowly realizes that he is the killer; but rather than turn him in she decides to protect her paying guest.

The juxtaposition of rich and poor common to all urban settings found its confused microcosm in such relationships. Both Robert and Ellen Bunting have worked as domestic servants, living in with their aristocratic masters in 'pretty country houses'. In seeking a lodger, they are both hoping to save themselves from debt and also to reproduce in their own home the 'happy' and 'secure' social relations that had defined their lives as servants. Lodging is, after all, a domestic relationship, though one that bears the traces of master and servant. Mr Sleuth, the lodger, fits this pattern perfectly; he is without doubt a gentleman, his eccentricities the marks of his superior station. It is soon just like old times, with Mrs Bunting serving the gentleman upstairs, though the roles are now blurred: after all, she is not just 'doing' for Mr Sleuth, she is also his landlady and the owner of the rooms that he rents.

The story blends complicity with curiosity, the criminal with the lodger. Like many crime fictions, Lowndes's novel exploits our fascination with crime, and reproaches us for it. Murder brings its frisson of illicit pleasure, and Mr Bunting proves addicted to its gruesome retelling. Co-opted by the newspapers' purveying of ghastly secrets, the city voyeur turns their gaze outwards to the strangers who pass them on the street, revealed now as potential victims or killers. The paper brings news of the outside world into the home, where domesticated reading lingers comfortably over horror elsewhere. It is Mrs Bunting's fate to discover that the strangeness may reside at home, both in the figure of her lodger, and in her own willing entanglement with his fate.

Mr Sleuth is 'queer'; Lowndes worries at this word, reiterating it as a mantra intended not to define the man's strangeness, but to gesture towards it. Lodging itself is eccentric; only someone queer would choose not to live with friends or relations. The solitude that lodging implies proves a questionable property. Yet Mrs Bunting similarly becomes 'queer'; through her reprehensible passion of concern she catches the lodger's contagious strangeness.

When Mrs Bunting visits the Black Museum, the collection of criminal artefacts held at Scotland Yard, the guardian of those grim relics expresses the thought that evil resides in material things. This notion informs most of the films and literary works under discussion here. It is there in the Buntings' grotty furniture. The squalid corporeality of the house, the materiality of the corpse, load the book with a sickening weight. Mrs Bunting prides herself on being 'nice', refraining from using words such as 'stomach'. On being exposed to the odours produced by Mr Sleuth's 'experiments', she feels herself 'to be all smell'. Her fastidious disgust implies fascination, one that ties in with her longing to discover more about Mr Sleuth and his crimes. Mr Sleuth lives in Mrs Bunting's imaginings as much as in her rooms. When a lodger enters, part of the house is alienated from its owner; it becomes a mysterious privacy. For Lowndes's heroine, the lodger's locked chiffonier embodies this process. This article of furniture contains a secret, one whose origins are not domestic, but come from the streets.

Action is largely confined to the house itself. Claustrophobia is the essence of such narratives; they hardly stray outside at all. Roman Polanski's film, *Repulsion* (1965), for instance, similarly surrenders to this agoraphobic intensity. Here, a woman is locked into domestic space, an interior that harasses her and from which she cannot and will not escape. This confinement is the clue to the development of Lowndes's archetypal story in the cinema. With its entanglement of strangers in temporary intimacy, the auditorium mirrors the murky exchanges on the screen.

Lowndes staked a new territory, laying claim to the sinister face of a city relationship that had previously passed for normal. The mode that Lowndes discovered and that Hitchcock and others would emulate was a form of metropolitan Gothic, a gloomily fantastic fairy-tale re-imagining of a perennial city type. The lodger's situation that suddenly came to seem so perversely unusual was in fact an enduring and entirely familiar social establishment. Rather than sinister, lodgers had once seemed comic, like Charles Dickens's Newman Noggs, an element in the cluttered ludicrousness of domestic life. The image of home was anyway more makeshift then, the family not separated off by a rigid demarcation, but a porous structure. Up to the mid-nineteenth century, living arrangements were more fluid, and tenanted houses might mix together members of heterogeneous social classes. The lodger was just one wild card among many.

Given this accustomed piebald cosiness, why should the lodger have suddenly appeared so unaccountable? What made the figure's long-standing ambiguity all at once seem so sinister? The term 'lodger' itself was anyway an ambiguous one; in 1885, for instance, while tidying up inconsistencies in the franchise, the government struggled to define this slippery character. The distinction then was between householders and lodgers, the permanent and the temporary, lodgers being defined by their transience.

While hard to pin down, lodgers remained a social fact. Lodging, sharing houses, was a matter of convenience; but it was also a triumph of human optimism. Sharing a space depended upon the optimism and the equanimity necessary for city life as such: it was remarkable that through a combination of indifference and amiability a close bond to others, unconnected by relationships of kith or kin, should nonetheless flourish. The solitude often imagined, at least since the social analysis of Wilhelm Heinrich Riehl (1823–97), as the essence of city experience here attains its equivocal limit; it remains a solitude, but finds itself contingently linked to others' lives.

Yet towards the end of the nineteenth century, a note of disapproval enters into discussions of the lodger. Social commentators and legislators worry about the phenomenon of the 'boarding-house young man'; leader writers declare that lodging is altogether too transient; married couples are encouraged to achieve domestic independence, and the ultimate goal became a distinct and discrete oasis of familial bliss. Privacy settles down as the aim of life. Lodgers start to seem weirdly temporary, their identities resistant to definition, their desires anomalous. It was this new worry that was to find its earliest artistic expression in Lowndes's seedy novel.

While the theme was played out in works by Alexander Mackendrick and Joe Orton, and played out for real in 10 Rillington Place and 25 Noel Road, it was in the work of a handful of directors—Alfred Hitchcock, Michael Powell, Roman Polanski and Nicolas Roeg—that the dark lodger would find its best expression. These artists acquired and absorbed the lodger's story, exploiting its peculiar energies. Some of the most vivid urban films express a startling lack of interest in the landscape of the city. Instead their attention is directed indoors; the house as microcosm of the city experience determines their scope. These films argue that, in the city, to share rooms is to share more than a space; it is to fall together into narratives of merging and murder. Landlord and lodger, or fellow tenants, dwell in a guilty connection that erodes their separate selves; they stand opposed and yet melded together, either side poised to expunge the other. These stories of complicity adhere to a particular urban moment, stretching from the 1910s to the 1970s. There are Parisian and New York versions, but the majority belong to London: to *The Lodger* (1927) and *The Ladykillers* (1955); to Rillington Place, where Reginald Christie strangled his victims, and Powis Square. The key instances of the archetype—among them, *Peeping Tom* (1960), *The Servant* (1963), *Performance* (1970), *Brimstone and Treacle* (1976)—do not so much constitute a metropolitan genre, as possess a space that has been possessed before. Tracing the progress of these tales, from their earliest example to their demise, maps a shift in our understanding of this improvised domesticity. The focus moves from Dickensian whimsy into Dickensian darkness, and then, via Lowndes, to guilty connivance, through psychological fusing, to the end of the lodger's anxious evanescence back where it had started, in a bright metropolitan acceptance; from *The Lodger* through *Performance* to *Coupling* (2000–4).

The fictions of Hitchcock, Polanski, Powell and Roeg offer a dark space of lodging narrative between two comic realms. Their works interpret the tenant's situation differently. While the defining experience of the city is being surrounded by too many strangers, the home offers a refuge of familiarity. Yet the lodger, the sub-tenant, the randomly found flatmate, they bring the stranger into the home. The lodger is the outsider who is invited in, but remains an alien. The lodger theme fuses strangeness and familiarity. The outsider rapidly becomes one of an imagined family: in Dennis Potter's *Brimstone and Treacle*, Martin promptly calls Mrs Bates 'mumsy'; in Barbet Schroeder's *Single White Female*, Ellen soon annexes Allie as her twin sister. Yet the lodger pays money to live with us; his or her presence depends on a financial transaction. The landlord/lodger relationship complicates the position of the host: the lodger is a stranger invited over the threshold, and yet is no guest. The money that changes hands places both parties in an equivocal position. The host provides a service for the tenant, and yet that rendered service is a function of his higher status as proprietor. Owning property should endow the landlord with authority, but instead he is under obligation, compelled by economic necessity to take in a stranger.

It is hardly accidental that murder should form the focus of the city's Gothic lodging stories, with violence being merely the necessary consequence of merging. In these stories, murder is both a constituent of the cosiness and its breach. Everything depends on the horror. Murder raises the stakes of the relationship, its erasure a neat figure for the urban fear that the city itself will erode our identity.

If Lowndes had discovered the dark potentialities of the lodger for prose fiction, it was Hitchcock who moulded the image for cinema. In his film adaptation of *The Lodger*, Hitchcock shifts the focus to romance; Daisy, the landlady's daughter, finds herself caught in a triangular love story between the effete gentleman lodger and her brutish policeman boyfriend. The casting of Ivor Novello as the lodger fixes sex appeal onto the role. (The film opened on Valentine's Day 1927.) In keeping with this, the murders are no longer prompted by insane revulsion at sin, but are fetishistic: it is not drunkenness that condemns the Avenger's victims, but their blonde hair. In this vein,

Hitchcock's *The Lodger* brings into play the thrill of glimpsing nude women in the compromised privacy of their rooms. Yet the truly eroticized figure is Novello himself; the film contentedly gazes at his vulnerable beauty, his whitened tragic mask of a face, with its lipstick and eye shadow. Novello's good looks make him cinematically sympathetic; even Hitchcock seems to have appreciated his effeminacy.

The lodger's lustful propensities were proverbial, the source of innumerable dirty jokes and comic songs, a lingering element of that early nineteenth-century coherence. Hitchcock's film plays with this urban legend, notably in the anxiety that Daisy's boyfriend and father feel about their gentleman tenant. The landlord considers the lodger a 'stranger' and therefore no fit person to be giving his daughter presents. In due course, the posh lodger (his sister was killed by the Avenger after a debutantes' ball) marries the landlord's daughter.

Though doubled with the Avenger and accused of his crimes, Hitchcock's lodger is not a killer, but a righter of wrongs. With Novello in the role, there was no chance that the lodger would turn out to be the murderer. In Hitchcock's film, as eventually happens in Lowndes's novel, the attention shifts from killer to victim. It's the customary Hitchcockian theme: the innocent man accused of murders he has not committed. Yet there are indications that Hitchcock clung to Lowndes's more subversive account: in talking about the movie, Hitchcock consistently described Ivor Novello's character as Jack the Ripper. And though the film apparently plays safe, there is plenty of evidence that the killer finds his counterparts elsewhere. Newspapers, neon signs and radio disseminate news of the Avenger's murders around the city, the information circulating for hungry audiences. The public's desire for vicarious mayhem merges with various moments where Londoners imitate the killer. The Avenger's tastes are shared too: Joe, the bumptious policeman, declares ghoulishly that he too is keen on 'golden hair'.

When Hitchcock left Britain for America, he took his concern with the lodging theme with him: in particular, *Shadow of a Doubt* (1943) may be seen as re-moulding *The Lodger* in an American context. Although often falsely described as Hitchcock's first film set in America (it follows the remarriage comedy, *Mr and Mrs Smith*

[1941] and the wartime thriller, *Saboteur* [1942]), this film nonetheless exploited its American setting with a new subtlety and force. Above all, with Joseph Cotten, Hitchcock could finally do what he had failed to do with *The Lodger*: the leading man, the temporary lodger, would be both an attractive figure and a killer.

The film depicts the relationship between Uncle Charlie (Joseph Cotten) and young Charlie (Teresa Wright), his small-town niece. After many years apart, Uncle Charlie unexpectedly comes to stay at his sister's family home. Although the niece dotes on the uncle, she slowly realizes that Uncle Charlie is a serial killer, the so-called Merry Widow Murderer, on the run from the police. Rather than break her mother's heart by exposing her brother's crimes, young Charlie colludes with her uncle in the hope that he will simply leave the family alone. However, Uncle Charlie understands that he must kill his niece in order to destroy the last evidence of his guilt; while attempting to do so, she instead causes his death, as he falls from a moving train.

If, to European observers, the central fact of American life once seemed the dispersal of the family, the habit of uprooting, then *Shadow of a Doubt* exemplifies that arbitrary pulling apart. The midwestern Oakleys scatter eastwards and westwards, breaking apart and coming together as their trajectories permit. The Santa Rosa home looks permanent enough, but mother still yearns nostalgically for that lost childhood home, which is as distant now as the previous century. As first imagined by scriptwriter Thornton Wilder, the modernity of the film's opening scenes set in a New Jersey landscape of vacant lots and rooming houses contrasts with the *Our Town* world of west-coast Santa Rosa, the latter place an 'Anywhere, USA' as quintessentially ubiquitous as Frank Capra's Bedford Falls. Uncle Charlie's coming to Santa Rosa transposes an urban arrangement to a small town milieu. He reproduces the uncanny aspects of the rooming-house in his sister's family home. So it is that the uncle occupies young Charlie's room; she, a typical girl; her room, a typical girl's room. Though more of a house-guest than a lodger, Uncle Charlie's history is certainly that of a rooming-house young man, his addresses impermanent, his movements across the States vague and undetermined. His sister, young Charlie's mother, owns her house, whereas her brother is a chronic renter. Moreover, Uncle Charlie seduces widows, his chosen role that of assuming a dead man's place; he is a natural stand-in.

Santa Rosa strikes us as guileless, the 'kind of home where you didn't lock the doors'. However, the town is no bastion of innocence, but a modern locale, open to the influences of the big city through the jukebox, the dive bar, the radio and the cinema. It was the *New Yorker* writer Sally Benson who added the modernity that was central to Hitchcock's vision of Santa Rosa, supplying the glow of neon that Thornton Wilder's draft of the script had excluded.

After the dark introduction of Uncle Charlie in New Jersey urban sprawl, the early scenes of small-town life are played as comedy; it is the uncle's presence that draws the inconsequential humour towards the urban Gothic. Central to that turn is the sense that the two name-sakes mirror each other. The number two haunts the picture, and the two Charlies are somehow doubles, even though they in no way resemble each other, their duality a shared fantasy, a family legend. The two share a name, and feel themselves to be 'twins', psychically connected. They take over each other's gestures, and share a certain knowledge. She knows that evil, or at the least the capacity for vio-lence, exists in her too; she becomes complicit with her uncle's crimes, protecting him, shielding her mother from knowledge, a young girl who knows too much.

In the opening minutes of the film, young Charlie's reclining languor coincidentally echoes Uncle Charlie's recumbent pose, as he lies in bed in his lodgings, the two disclosing each other's physical grace. For one, a concerned landlady looms over; for the other, an inquisitive father. Their kinship hinges on an incestuous sexual attraction between uncle and niece; Uncle Charlie is, after all, one of two older men who pursue the young girl (the other is the policeman hero). Goodness in the shape of the policeman, young Charlie's *beau*, is a rather uninspiring prospect (the result, Hitchcock declared to François Truffaut, of being unable to attract a strong enough actor for such a minor role). Joseph Cotten's insinuating charm is, aestheti-cally speaking, a far more captivating prospect. Yet this appeal has its paradoxes. According to Hitchcock, it is young Charlie's attentiveness to her uncle that unmasks his guilt; because she loves him, she watches him closely, and so detects his evil.

Young Charlie may resemble her uncle in his murderousness too. She loves her uncle, and destroys him. After all, in the end her stated wish is to kill him, and kill him is what she does, bundling him out of the door of the speeding train, as each struggles with the other. Gordon MacDonnell's original treatment for the story had Uncle Charlie's death as more obviously an accident, the cliff under his feet giving way while he attempts to murder his niece. In the film itself things would be more active. As Teresa Wright, the actress who played young Charlie has reported, people have often said to her, 'That was quite a shove you gave him.'

While *Shadow of a Doubt* began with comedy and merged into Gothic, Michael Powell's *Peeping Tom* (1959) employed an even blacker tone, between farce and tragedy. It depicts Mark Lewis (Carl Böhm), a cameraman and serial killer, who is composing a 'documentary' of fear in which he films his victims at the moment of their murder. Mark may identify himself with either his father, the house's previous owner, and his bleak childhood self, or with his lodger, Helen Stephens (Anna Massey), and the innocent child in him. In one sense, it is Mark's childlikeness that offers the best chance for his redemption. Mark and Helen's potential collaboration on a children's book proffers a guarantee of continued naivety. Yet at the same time Mark's refusal of maturity remains an index of his potential for evil, the sign of his damage. Mark reveals his resistance to adulthood in his refusal of ownership. While we see Helen's twenty-first birthday party and her symbolic present of the keys to the house, Mark wants nothing to do with keys. He shuns the independence they represent, and persists in assuming the status of tenant, not landlord. He acts, as Helen tells him, like a guilty lodger. Yet Mark's murders are themselves acts of ownership. He grasps his victims' souls with the picture of their fear, that image itself becoming an act of merging. Their fear repeats his own; in killing them, he makes them a version of himself. In this way, all his murders resemble acts of suicide, as the film speeds towards his self-immolation.

It was during the 1960s that filmmakers worried over the lodger's fate. All Roman Polanski's 'apartment' films merge performance with the tenant's experience. They tell us that the foolish and tragic characters are themselves performers. In particular, *Rosemary's Baby* (1968) investigates the directorial relationship, the intertwining of actor and director. The appearance of the director, or of the directorial relationship, within the film itself seems a consistent element in the lodging sub-genre. Hitchcock's screen appearances are legendary, while in *Peeping Tom*, in home movies, Michael Powell spookily plays Mark Lewis's cruel scientist father, while his own son, Columba Powell, takes the part of the child, Mark. In *Shadow of a Doubt*, Hitchcock had given Uncle Charlie aspects of his own history, with the two sharing the effects of the same childhood bicycle accident. In the case of *Rosemary's Baby*, both Roman Polanski and John Cassavetes, who played Rosemary's husband Guy, are actor-directors; head-witch Roman Castevet shares Polanski's name, though this name 'Roman' is an alias employed by Steven Mercato; Mia Farrow's father was the film director, John Farrow. Complexities ramify and identities amalgamate, as Castevet echoes Cassavetes, and Rosemary's abbreviated name, Ro, stands in for Roman too. Rosemary mistakes the girl in the laundry room for the actress who actually plays her, Victoria Vetri (though she appears in the credits under her Playboy bunny pseudonym, Angela Dorian). Tony Curtis, Mia Farrow's pal, speaks, uncredited, on the phone to Rosemary, as Baumgarten, the actor put out of work by her husband, Guy. The Pope appears as a show-business figure too; Adrian Mercato's Satanic religion masquerades as the work of a 'theatrical producer'.

In those apartment films of Polanski's, the tenant performs—and it is this embracing of performance that underlies his or her merging. This version of the lodger's experience receives its fullest expression in Nic Roeg and Donald Cammell's film, *Performance* (1970). This too is a movie about acting, though one with only one professional actor in a leading role, James Fox. The film's other male lead, Mick Jagger, both plays himself and impersonates Rolling Stones bandmates Brian Jones and Keith Richards; it is the lack of clear distinction between these personalities that gives the role its composite force. *Performance*'s cast of amateurs and players manifests the arbitrariness of performance; anyone can be called upon to enact their identity to others. Here performance is both enactment and possession, and the film itself the stand-in for a magical act.

The film portrays the relationship between two characters: the gangland enforcer, Chas (James Fox), and the reclusive ex-rock star, Turner (Mick Jagger). After murdering another gangland villain and old friend, Joey Maddocks (Anthony Valentine), Chas goes on the run from his furious gangster bosses. He overhears that Turner will sublet a black musician's basement room at 81 Powis Square. (Turner is therefore first known to us, not as a reclusive former rock star, but as a 'landlord'.) Chas takes refuge in Turner's Notting Hill house, mixing it up with the middle-class dandy rock star and his continental pair of girlfriends. Hostile at first to his new tenant, Turner becomes increasingly fascinated by him, Chas embodying the demon that he has lost. Scenes happen in half-light, or behind gauze, like a breathed-on looking-glass, a heavy scented atmosphere of Aubrey Beardsley and the Arabian Nights. In the era of R. D. Laing and Kingsley Hall, the film celebrates madness as the only performance that matters: Chas 'goes down' into madness, a process that incorporates his merger with Turner. The gangsters pursue business mergers. Although pop music is a business too, Turner seeks a radically deeper integration. Though class and identities formed on local city loyalties remain present in the film, Cammell and Roeg unravel the concept of a stable self through the presentation of a deeply unstable film.

Like *Vertigo* (1958), *Performance* splits in half, doubling itself; its second section echoes dialogue and images of the first (for instance, the scene of Maddocks being murdered while cowering under the sheet connects to the threesome's lyrical moment of love-making, light filtered through the covers). During the whipping of Chas, a moment that repeats his earlier S&M sex scene with the young woman, Joey Maddocks is clear that, despite the visual echo, boundaries must still exist: 'I'm not him', he asserts. For all the desire to keep personalities distinct, the film's energies depend upon the identification of things, the involvement of one world in another world.

These psychological games express urban class loyalties. When Chas crosses the river, heading from south London to Notting Hill, he passes the bisecting line of the film. Marked in the *A to Z* as 'not continuous', Powis Square, Notting Hill was the perfect locale for the merging to take place, as the first black area in London, and a home for slumming hippies eager for working-class authenticity. Chas brings the authenticity with him. Notting Hill had also been the centre of the slum landlord Peter Rachman's realm (his first significant property acquisition had been in nearby Powis Terrace), and as such was infamous for an institutionalized violence between landlord and tenant. Pherber (Anita Pallenberg) will herself try to set up an 'extortionate' arrangement with Chas as sub-tenant. Meanwhile Turner is no owner, merely standing higher than Chas in the hierarchy of impermanence.

Our few glimpses of the streets of Notting Hill show a red-haired hippy girl taking out milk and bread, young blacks, white working-class middle-aged men, an old lady, and cigarette-smoking hipsters. Chas's negotiations to get into Turner's house are spied on by a black girl staring at him, at the camera, from behind a landing window, and then a white child and mother looking down from an upstairs window across the way. Though the film is soon to retreat into the fastness of the house's interior, it lingers for a moment, placing the district, giving us the urban context in which the collapse will happen. Even after the deal that will see Chas established as sub-tenant has been arranged, the film glances outside, catching again images of passers-by, a multi-ethnic London out of which emerges, with her mother, the young working-class girl who acts as cleaner in the house.

The film flirts with cross-cultural connections, hooking Chelsea up with Bethnal Green, Romantic England with fabled Persia, the gangster with the rock star. Its 'Dialogue Consultant and Technical Advisor', David Litvinoff, was the patron saint of such couplings, simultaneously *au fait* with the Kray Twins, dodgy West End gambling clubs, and the Anglo-American jet set. *Performance* plays out London's class tensions through the mixing or merging of classes. It reverses and repeats a previous James Fox film of house-sharing and merging, Joseph Losey's *The Servant* (1963), with upper-class Fox this time taking the role of the working-class interloper. Jagger's casting was equally evocative. Rock music had come to seem one route by which a working-class lad might ascend into the elite. The new aristocracy of fame welcomed equally photographers, writers, artists, movie stars, rock musicians and criminals. In their different ways, all were dangerously edgy embodiments of social fluidity; cool sustained their difference from the masses, though the mass-taint was itself an element in the attraction.

Here mergers happen on the level of urban style, stealing a look from one another. Characters play with mirrors, adoring themselves narcissistically, dressing up as each other, appropriating others, abandoning themselves; it's a childlike cavort with dissolution. Cropped hair, dyed hair, long hair, wigs—a medley of modes determine the surface of the person; a velvet jacket makes a rock star; below the surface there's only a hole, merely leading inwards and outwards to more images still.

At the time, the Stones were moving towards symbolic violence, the aggression of 'Jumping Jack Flash' or 'Midnight Rambler' an unmistakable come-on for the passive audience. Shades of Altamont were closing around the growing boys. The film cannot justify the idea that Chas personifies violence itself; he just seems a cocky chancer. His disintegration therefore lacks any real force; as the film proceeds, there is drift rather than dynamism, instead of menace, bathos. When Chas murders Turner, it should mark the end of the merger, a vicious way out of the collapsing of identities. In fact, as it plays, the violence permits the final absorption of one self into the other, for as 'Chas' is driven away, he turns to look back at Powis Square with Turner's face.

Performance had attempted to take lodger Gothic to its ultimate verge. However, it was Polanski who had the last word on the subject. If *The Tenant* (1976) plays differently than the London or New York versions of the tale, that may be because the French version of 'le locataire' manifests so different a tradition. The '*locataire*' as such requires no social explanation; in Parisian terms to be a tenant is a natural fate. However, suspicions about the nature of the tenant remain, enforced by the peculiar French collision of privacy and proximity. The Parisian apartment house is a miniature police state, one where individual freedoms clash with the petty rules of communal living.

Both Polanski's *Repulsion* and *The Tenant* present a central character alienated from the city they live in and undergoing psychological disintegration in the apartments they inhabit. Like Catherine Deneuve's character, Carole, in *Repulsion*, Trelkovsky in *The Tenant* (played by Polanski himself) is a foreigner; like Hitchcock in America, he's a tenant in France too, a Polish immigrant, who, despite being a French citizen, fails to convince anyone that he is sufficiently French. In 1988, Polanski spoke of the hostility he has felt in Paris; in *The Tenant*, based on a novel by Roland Topor, this hostility finds its expression in the intimate war waged within an apartment block. The neighbours keep each other awake, and spy on each other, caught between closeness and alienation. Trelkovsky cannot comprehend the previous tenant Simone Choule's suicide; yet it is precisely this inexplicable deed that he will also end up attempting. Here another aspect of the tenant's predicament emerges: their relation to those who once resided in their rooms. The fact of the previous tenant signals the current tenant's impermanence, though in

Polanski's film that temporary belonging becomes an inescapable loop, as his arrival on the scene replays at the film's end. He will always be replacing the previous tenant, and that previous tenant will always be a version of himself. He merges with her, caught up in her suicidal desires. For Trelkovsky, to metamorphose into Simone Choule means living in her room, adopting her habits (drinking chocolate and smoking Marlboro) and trying on her clothes. To become her is to perform her personality traits, the self a matter of location and a composite of urban styles.

More recently, the conceit of the lodger as uncanny double has faded, and this particular social microcosm has largely returned to the happy incongruities of comedy. Dennis Potter's play for television, *Brimstone and Treacle* (1976) was the last great British expression of this metropolitan legend. Manhattan would prove the myth's nemesis. In *Single White Female* (1992), the image has become a marketable quality. Allie Jones's (Bridget Fonda) job involves advertising herself; her self that desirable commodity—the New York woman. Watching her brisk transformation, her lascivious client even fears that he 'won't be able to afford [her] any more'. Her new roommate Hedy Carlson, otherwise known as Ellen (Jennifer Jason Leigh), absorbs Allie by adopting her 'style', her 'personality', all those aspects of herself that Allie has herself constructed (for Allie was once a small-town girl). It is precisely the extrinsic, artificial nature of these things that renders them susceptible to theft. Allie's self was ersatz anyway, a beautiful apparition for a glamorous city. With this Hollywood apartment horror film, the makeshift shoddiness of London was replaced by a New York sheen. Crucially, the economic basis of the relationship was over: Allie requires a roommate for emotional reasons, someone to be there for her now that she has left her boyfriend.

Thereafter such stories ended. There was the swansong of Danny Boyle's *Shallow Grave* (1994), but, rather than adding to the fable, that film explained why it was over. Just as the myth of merging had formed from the conditions of city life, so the story was put to rest when social life changed. The new cultural model was group living, the old-fashioned enforced intimacy and ambiguous privacy of the lodger and subtenant replaced by the collection of 'friends'. In this late instance, it was greed that would render the flat-sharing relationship Gothic and undo the improvised intimacy; the stylishness of youth barely concealing its sneaky rapacity.

And there the cycle came to a stop. Like the living arrangements themselves, it was not meant to last for ever; like cinema, it plays out over and over again. In the new century, lodging looked as though it belonged to a past, its intensities as outmoded as *Rising Damp*. For me, the experience of lodging has taken on the nostalgic appeal of an 'episode'. By the time I left that room by the Heath, the early twenty-first-century property boom had begun to swing into life. Already lodgers looked all too anomalous in Hampstead, where houses might fetch unheard-of sums—a million pounds, it was rumoured, for 'our' house. The itinerant lodger who had temporarily belonged to those high streets, to that history, would soon find himself priced out of the city. The scaffolding went up; the builders moved in; the shambolic and tatty were banished. The Atkinson Grimshaw twilights of the Heath remained, but there was nothing uncanny about the bubble of prosperity that was coming.

Reading

Cronin, Paul (ed.), *Roman Polanski: Interviews* (Jackson, MS: University Press of Mississippi, 2005).

Kennedy, Ludovic, *10 Rillington Place* (London: Victor Gollancz, 1961).

Lowndes, Marie Belloc, *The Lodger* (Oxford: Oxford University Press, 1996).

Marks, Leo, *Peeping Tom* (London: Faber & Faber, 1998).

Spoto, Donald, *The Dark Side of Genius: The Life of Alfred Hitchcock* (London: Collins, 1983).

Phoning

David Trotter

Anyone old enough to have made use of public phone-booths on a regular basis will know that they were more often than not damp, cold, filthy and foul-smelling, and while amply supplied with the phone numbers of prostitutes, practically impossible to make any sort of call from. So folk memory insists, at any rate. So literature insists. A quick online search or waft through the bulkier paperbacks at the airport bookstall will confirm that urban phone-booths in particular have become indelibly associated in the literary imagination with urine. What invariably greets the protagonists of genre fiction as they open the door of a booth to make some life-or-death call is the stickiness left behind by a previous user. Expecting to speak and to listen, they instead inhale the anonymous yet fiercely intimate odour of population itself. They have seen and smelt, and may still touch or even taste, the fact of the crowd, the fact of the city.

The protagonist of Howard R. Simpson's Vietnam spy-novel *Someone Else's War* (2003) has information to gather. He makes a call. 'The phone booth smelled of urine; someone had spat generously on the floor and a loud argument in Cantonese was going on at the stamp counter.' Booths should keep sound both out and in. They should be secretive. But Simpson, like many other novelists, has felt it necessary to compound secrets with secretions; not just urine, but phlegm, too, for good measure. A spilt body has preceded and prefigured espionage's spilling of minds. Simpson wants us to understand that all the spilling in spying is a dirty business. The implication he draws on, the implication of the folk memory endlessly recycled in genre fiction, is that we don't fully recognize a phone-booth as a phone-booth until we've felt just a little bit sick at the sight and smell of it. The disgust *is* the recognition. But what exactly has it recognized?

Of course, better things do happen to patrons of public telephone systems, at least in fiction. Clark Kent and Dr Who regularly disappear into booths maintained to high standards of hygiene in order to pick up where they left off as extra-terrestrials. The time-travelling booth which launched *Bill and Ted's Excellent Adventure* (1989), and as a result Keanu Reeves's even more excellent career, had a curious retractable tripod fizzing with static on top, but no sign of insanitary behaviour below. Phone-booths have continued to provide Reeves with lift-off, most notably in *The Matrix* (1999), where he plays Thomas Anderson, a.k.a. Neo, a company man turned hacker turned messiah. At the film's conclusion, Neo phones in a final proclamation of defiance from a booth on a busy street in the virtual world into which the bulk of the human species has been absorbed, before stepping outside, donning dark glasses, and ascending into heaven, while Rage Against the Machine break out their heavy-metal anthem 'Wake Up'. But it isn't all CGI, yet, at reality's interface with illusion. Harry Potter, for example, nips into a sanctuary of rather more traditional design to place a call to the Ministry of Magic. J. K. Rowling has enough respect for folk memory to register his surprise that the phone actually works.

A lot depends on genre. Don't go there, would be sound advice to characters in most kinds of Hollywood movie. They invariably do. Why, when Hitchcock's homicidal birds swoop down in earnest on the main drag in Bodega Bay, does Melanie Daniels (Tippi Hedren) rush out of the diner from which she's witnessed the onset of the attack and headlong into what is about to become the most famous phone-booth in the history of cinema? If she had wanted to make a call, there's a perfectly good phone inside, which she's just used to tell her father about an earlier attack on the local school, and then to summon her boyfriend and the police. Hitchcock, of course, knows why. What he gets from Melanie's mistake is an image of isolation and exposure, as she twists and turns in torment in her transparent cubicle, and the glass shatters. Generations of commentary have led one to suppose that the danger stems from inside rather than outside the psyche.

The Bodega Bay cubicle was the first to serve as a lightning-conductor for the unconscious. After that, it was only a matter of time before someone made *Phone Booth* (2002), in which a sniper armed with a high velocity rifle traps publicist Stu Shepard (Colin Farrell) behind glass on a street in New York, forbidding him to put the receiver down until he has agreed to confess his sins (that is, his desire); or *Run Lola Run* (1998), in which Man communicates despair and self-hatred from the Berlin equivalent, while Woman does something about it, in postmodern fashion, three times over.

As these examples demonstrate, phone-boxes have led an exciting imaginary life, and not always in big cities. A good deal of folklore attaches to the booth which once stood on the Aiken Mine Road in the Mojave Desert, in California, about 15 miles from the nearest highway. It even earned a cameo in an *X-Files* episode. Technology's far-flung outposts in the wilderness have fulfilled a variety of tasks, up to and including the reconfiguration of traditional communities by international capital. In Bill Forsyth's comic-utopian *Local Hero* (1983), the young executive sent to Scotland to buy a fishing village on behalf of Knox Oil and Gas has no other means of communication with his boss in Houston, Texas, than a public phone-box on the quayside across the road from the hotel. The locals have a whip-round to supply him with 10p coins, and thereafter attend assiduously on each visit to the box, wiping the receiver for him (folk memory dies hard), or supplying a glass of whisky. On one occasion, the outside of the cubicle is repainted while he frets inside; on another, a previous user, who has fallen asleep *in situ*, bolt upright, emerges to relay an important message. The phone-box is the point at which traditional community forms and re-forms in mildly carnivalesque fashion around the connection to modernity, a connection which once made will never be un-made. At the end of the film, as the executive gazes out at Houston from the penthouse apartment to which he has reluctantly returned, Forsyth cuts to a long shot of the quayside portal, in which the phone rings.

In cities, by contrast, we enter phone-boxes off the street in order to be private in public. That is, we once did, before we all had mobiles. Nowadays you don't go somewhere special to phone in unless your mobile's broken, or out of juice, or you've left it at home. The new urban spectacle consists of people apparently in earnest conversation with themselves, whom we might once have crossed the road to avoid, or broadcasting the gory details of a personal fiasco to a railway carriage full of strangers. It is in fact the prospect of the phone-box's imminent supersession by the mobile which has most effectively laid bare its original purpose. For each of these mobile-users is engaged, as we once were when we stepped into a phone-box, in constructing privacy in public. The difference is that they rely upon an understanding of the distance between themselves and the next person whose expression is social and cultural, rather than physical. That understanding has not yet quite become a consensus. But it is already powerful enough to have altered urban experience. The history of the urban phone-box, which is also the history of the city since electrification, is the history of the construction of privacy in public by physical as well as social and cultural means.

The history is a complicated one, and its complication reveals that public privacy—call it living in a city—is always under construction. In a phone-box, we are impersonally personal, in that we communicate with someone we know well or at least can identify, but not in person; and personally impersonal, in that previous users, whom we do not know and cannot identify, have indeed been there in person, have left us themselves to touch, taste, smell, while those yet to come gaze at us from outside. Where, exactly, is the intimacy in all this, the being private in private? And where is that consensual acknowledgement of common purpose, that being public in public, forever built into the city's other communicative and regulatory systems, into postbox, bus stop and road sign, into traffic lights and speed and security cameras, into all those items of street furniture which, unlike the phone-box, we have agreed not to vandalize? For vandalism there has always been, where phone-boxes are concerned. Many have left their mark on one who would not look twice at a No Entry sign. It's hard, for example, to see Martin Amis's prose style (never mind his more pathologically inclined protagonists) passing up on an opportunity for booth-rage. In *Money* (1984), John Self duly lets rip. 'I had been wanting to smash a telephone for a long time. The bakelite split obligingly, then retaliated with an electric shock. I got to my feet and left the hot receiver dangling from its mauled base.' In Britain, there is a further complication to this long history, in the fact that ownership of the booths in which we once learnt to be personally impersonal and impersonally personal has passed during the last hundred years from private into public hands and back again.

My aim here is to examine the uses made in literature and film of the feelings aroused by the (once) commonplace phone-box, -booth, or -kiosk. These include rage, and terror, of course. But descriptions of privacy constructed in public are often at their most subtle, inventive and compelling when in a minor key. The two feelings I shall have most to say about here are disgust and tenderness. The Romantic view, formulated by Blake, Wordsworth, Baudelaire and others, and still amply evident in urban theory from Benjamin and Simmel to Michel de Certeau, is that urban experience is defined by bewilderment, shock and resistance to shock. They were wrong. Urban experience has always included practical affect. For Benjamin, the telephone was a shock, because it rang peremptorily and without warning in the depths of the bourgeois home. Booth life, which thrives on practical affect, does not seem to have interested him. We need to ask, instead, what disgust and tenderness might know about living in a city that could not otherwise be known. The examples I have chosen from literature and film concern London, for the most part, but not only London.

Bacteriological Boxes

The telephone was invented in March 1876, by Alexander Graham Bell. Queen Victoria witnessed a demonstration of the new device on 14 January 1878. On 7 April 1882, the *Aberdeen Weekly Journal* reported that the establishment of a rudimentary telephone system in London had 'justified the most sanguine expectations of its proprietors'. The commercial development of such systems encountered a variety of obstacles, but by the turn of the century the telephone had nonetheless become a necessary basis for the proper organization of middle-class social, economic and cultural life in major cities around the world. Using the device was one way to be modern, in public and in private.

'In Berlin, Zurich and Hamburg, telephonic kiosks have been established, so that anyone walking along and desirous of sending a communication by telephone, or asking a question, or giving an order, or making a correction overlooked in recent conversation, may do so, and the charge is twopence halfpenny.' The directors of the London Telephone Company were hoping to make a similar provision. The term 'kiosk' drew at once on a faint association with the Turkish pavilion or summerhouse, and on a rather more palpable one with the familiar outdoor stands offering newspapers, or tea and buns.

'Today', trumpeted the *Daily News* on 1 April 1891, 'the new Telephone line between London and Paris is open to the public.' A person with eight shillings to spare could gossip with anyone in Paris she or he could find to gossip with for a period of three minutes. What most preoccupied the *News*, however, was not the science behind this latest technological triumph, but the material construction of the 'chamber' in which calls were to be made. The marvel lay as much in the raising of a social and cultural barrier between one person and another in London as in the lowering of the physical barrier between one person in London and another in Paris. For the person in London wishing to call Paris 'steps into a little sort of padded sentry-box, the door of which is edged with india-rubber.'

> When this closes upon him he is hermetically sealed, and might rave himself hoarse without conveying the faintest sound to anyone outside. There is a pane of glass in the door, so that the officer in charge could see the inmate of the box, though unable to hear him. On stepping in, the interior of the little cupboard is in darkness, but the telephoner by sitting down on the seat establishes connection, and an arc light instantly blazes out until he again rises, when it goes out till the next comer takes his seat. The telephone box is a wonderfully

compact and all but perfect little institution, the only drawback being that it is entirely unventilated, and the person sitting in it is literally hermetically sealed up.

As the repetition of the phrase 'hermetically sealed' makes clear, the emphasis in this early assessment of this new method of telecommunication was on enclosure. The guarantees offered concerning privacy had literally to be iron-clad. From the outset, there was a certain excess in the construction of privacy in public by physical as well as social and cultural means. The box had to be sealed, yes. But *hermetically* sealed, so that one could scarcely breathe inside it?

On 1 January 1912, the General Post Office, a government department, became to all intents and purposes the monopoly supplier of telephone services in the United Kingdom, and was to remain so until the creation of British Telecom in 1981. In 1912, phone-boxes entered public service. They had thereafter to be ubiquitous, and uniform in design. The first kiosk satisfactorily to combine form and function, the K2, built out of cast iron to a neoclassical design by Sir Giles Gilbert Scott and painted a glossy Post Office red all over, came into service in 1927. It was as much emblem as shelter: ventilation came from holes pierced through the top fascia in the shape of a crown. The smaller and more durable K6, also designed by Scott, and set up in villages across Britain to celebrate George V's Jubilee in 1935, acquired the status of an institution. In August 1986, a K2 kiosk in London Zoo's Parrot House became the first phone-box ever to receive listed building status. By that time, British Telecom had become British Telecom PLC, flagship of the Thatcher government's ambitious privatization programme. In 1987, BT's phone-box monopoly was broken up. So began the conversion, memorably described by Patrick Wright, of the only remaining 'public' element of a now otherwise privately owned service into a (privately owned) heritage industry. Boxes now came in different shapes and sizes. Respectable neighbourhoods could hope for a bit of roof, and two or three walls. 'The new and growing underclass, meanwhile, would have to settle for a sawn-off metal stump with an armoured cardphone bolted onto it.' Scott's totemic cubicles disappeared from the streets. Many of them have since found their way to the United States, where they do duty as interior or exterior decoration. One now resides in a room at Twitter HQ in San Francisco, its sole contents a plastic chair.

The K6 was supposed to be an amenity as well as an emblem and shelter. According to the *Post Office Electrical Engineers' Journal*, a 'modernistic touch' had been supplied by the 'horizontal glazing scheme', which 'furnishes a remarkably free view from the inside of the kiosk'. The interior surfaces were of bakelite-faced plywood, and the stainless steel fittings included a pipe- or cigarette-rack and a hook for umbrellas. By converting the original hermetically sealed sentry-boxes into a middle-class room with a view, the Post Office designers had built a supplementary layer of social and cultural distance into the physical construction of privacy in public. It was a futile gesture (albeit one that today's mobile-users have unknowingly taken to heart). What people wanted in a phone-box was a box, even if they didn't always much like some of the consequences.

However lavishly furnished, the phone-booth was at once an enclosure and a facility accessible to all and sundry; that is, a health hazard. In August 1906, a 'call office attendant' wrote to the *Lancet* to complain about 'the growing danger arising from the use of the common mouthpiece by promiscuous callers at public telephones'. Cleaning up after a caller with a particularly violent cough, the hapless attendant had found the instrument still damp with 'congealed breath'. A year later, the journal returned to the theme, remarking that the telephone call station should rather be described as 'a bacteriological box in which pathogenic and other organisms are carefully nourished'. In March 1908, a correspondent reported on a wide variety of London booths in which 'the condition of the apparatus was unsatisfactory, the vulcanite mouthpieces frequently containing debris with a more or less bad odour'. In June, Dr Frances J. Allan, Medical Officer of Health of the City of Westminster, reported the results of tests done on swabs taken from the mouthpieces of transmitters in public call boxes. One had attached to it a 'mass of whitish-grey viscid substance'. The viscid substance was injected into two guinea-pigs. One died after 23 days, the other after

27. Nor did the transfer into public ownership altogether solve the problem. In February 1924, the *Lancet* reported on a series of further tests carried out in February 1912 by the aptly named Dr H. R. D. Spitta at St George's Hospital in London, which had shown that the transmission of tuberculosis by means of the telephone mouthpiece was 'practically impossible'.

The phone-box is the place where one kind of communication—one way to be in contact—intersects another. Tuberculosis may no longer have been a worry. But the disgust provoked by the debris, odour and viscid substance previous users had promiscuously left in and around the mouthpiece did not diminish. Indeed, it strengthened. It took shape as a common perception of the phone-box as phobic object or site. Few things give greater pause for thought to the amnesiac ex-commando in John Lodwick's *Peal of Ordnance* (1947), who has been laying explosive charges on monuments across central London, than the state of the box from which he rings the BBC to tell them there's a bomb in one of their studios.

> The booth smelt of urine and spittle gouts. He opened the directory; obsolete, tatty and well thumbed ... signatures into the bargain (Jack H. Rossbach; U.S.N. Yonkers, N.Y.), and here and there addresses underlined with words of advice: 'Call her up any time. She'll be there.'

The nausea anchors and provides some kind of justification for a free-floating anxiety which also includes sex and foreigners. Phone-boxes have always been 'obscene'. One of the accusations levelled against Leopold Bloom in the Nighttown episode of James Joyce's *Ulysses* (1922) is that 'Unspeakable messages he telephoned mentally to Miss Dunn at an address in d'Olier Street while he presented himself indecently to the instrument in the callbox.' In so far as he 'presented himself' to the instrument, rather than to the more or less oblivious Miss Dunn, Bloom, too, might be thought to have left a viscid substance behind him. In Christopher Isherwood's *Mr Norris Changes Trains* (1935), the homosexual Baron Kuno von Pregnitz, pursued by the police on charges of political corruption, locks himself in panic into a cubicle in a public lavatory. Next day, the newspapers uniformly report him as having finally been run to ground in a telephone-box. By the end of the 1990s, it was costing Westminster City Council's Street Enforcement Department around £250,000 a month to remove prostitutes' cards from booths in central London. On 1 September 2001, Sections 46 and 47 of the Criminal Justice and Police Act came into force, making it an offence to place such advertisements in, or in the immediate vicinity of, a phone-booth. According to Jonathan Glancey, what's wrong with the new deregulated London is too much instant availability. 'Unprotected sex with eastern Europeans on the make for a few quid just a piss-streaked telephone-kiosk's call away.' It certainly doesn't help that the sex on offer is from some of those east Europeans who have been invading England imaginarily ever since Count Dracula first landed his coffins at Whitby. Like Howard Simpson, and many others, Glancey feels the need to be absolutely precise about the location and extent of the traces of piss (at least the punters in his part of London aim high).

It is possible, however, for disgust to express a sense, if not of community, then of a construction of privacy in public which includes rather than excludes the acknowledgement of strangers. Tony Harrison's 'Changing at York' takes place in a phone-booth in York railway station, where he has gone to inform his son that his train has been delayed. The booth is replete with phobic objects and sensations: a vandalized directory, the smell of alcohol and dossers' pee, and (a touch the *Lancet* would have appreciated) 'saliva in the mouthpiece'. Harrison thinks himself away from phobia into a sorrowing account of the deceptions interactivity at a distance has enabled him to inflict on those he loves. He concludes the poem by returning to the son he now has to call, and remembering him

> in this same kiosk with the stale, sour breath
> of queuing callers, drunk, cajoling, lying,
> consoling his grampa for his granny's death,
> how I heard him, for the first time ever, crying.

To bring the material remnant back in is to think with phobia, rather than away from it. Phobia replaces Harrison in the company of strangers. For the chronicle of the activities undertaken by previous callers—cajoling, lying—carries straight over the line-break into the son's tearful consolation, which has been bound further into them by rhyme (crying/lying) and half-rhyme (cajoling/consoling). The consolation the poem itself finds could be said to lie in phobia's bitter-sweet acknowledgement of our intimacy with people unknown to us who do as we do.

The key to these experiences was inadvertency. You went into a booth in search of one kind of privacy in public and ended up with another; and the experience made you think. For smell, touch and taste were not the only kinds of inadvertency you might find yourself shut in with. During the public payphone's *belle époque* you would after all have been as likely to witness somebody else using one as to use one yourself. Closing the door in order to speak and listen, these people were also there to be seen, if you wished to see them. A view of a person in a phone-booth works wonders, in literature and film; and because sight, unlike taste, touch and smell, has distance built into it, the sensations provoked are often gentler. The experience has to do with stimulation by fellow-feeling rather than with stimulation by threat.

Aquarium

George Harvey Bone, the protagonist of Patrick Hamilton's *Hang-over Square* (1941), suffers from psychotic episodes, begun and concluded with a curious click, which separate him off from ordinary existence, and eventually induce him to murder Netta, the woman of his obsessions. The closest he gets to understanding the nature and scope of these episodes is when he calls Netta from a public payphone in Earl's Court station.

> In the line of telephone booths there were a few other people locked and lit up in glass, like waxed fruit, or Crown jewels, or footballers in a slot machine on a pier, and he went in and became like them—a

different sort of person in a different sort of world—a muffled, urgent, anxious, private, ghostly world, composed not of human beings but of voices, disembodied communications—a world not unlike, so far as he could remember, the one he entered when he had one of his 'dead' moods.

The 'ghostly world' Bone inspects, of people 'locked and lit up in glass', is like his dead moods in its separation off from ordinary existence, but unlike them in that its inhabitants enter it and leave it at will. What he in fact sees, perhaps, is an alternative version of those moods, in which his own anxiety, though scarcely diminished, at least resembles everyone else's. Entry into the booth is the only occasion in his adult life on which he can be said to have *become like* a 'few other people'. The likeness is too fleeting to mature into liking. But Bone's awareness of a shared experience of spectatorship—he could be a tourist in the Tower of London, or a slot-machine addict—has drawn him momentarily out of obsession. He has been touched into that awareness by the pathos of strangers.

Buchi Emecheta's *Second-Class Citizen* (1974) is a novel about the early phases of London's gradual, uneven and incomplete post-war transition to a multi-ethnic metropolis. Adah joins her husband Francis in London, where he has taken and continues to take interminable accountancy exams, from Lagos. She works as librarian, gives birth, is beaten up and humiliated, but keeps going. The crucial narrative development concerns her exchange of the status and function of second-class citizen as a wife under Ibo patriarchy for the status and function of second-class citizen as an immigrant under institutionalized racism. Emecheta manages this development indirectly, by telling the story of Adah's friend Janet, a white girl married to another Nigerian student, Babalola. Babalola had first met Janet while standing outside a phone-booth waiting for her to finish a call. 'It started to drizzle and he was getting soaked to the skin, so he banged on the kiosk door, and shook his fist at the girl to frighten her. Then he looked closer, and saw that the girl was not phoning anybody, she was asleep, standing up.' Janet had at that time been 16, and pregnant. Babalola had taken her home, lent her to his friends, then fallen in love with her, and married her. Janet does not in fact feature extensively in Adah's story; she is there primarily as an image of a person in a phone-box. Her introduction into it opens the story out: to new dangers, but also to the potential for change, in Adah herself and in others.

Such images seem in an obvious sense cinematic, and there are indeed phone-booth virtuosos among directors: Hitchcock, undoubtedly, and Margarethe von Trotta, who learnt much from him. Von Trotta's controversial films about the politics of the person offer an incisive and deeply felt analysis of the gendering of public and private spheres in post-war middle-class German society. The uncompromising activism of her intellect requires that middle-class women not only cross over from a private sphere understood as feminine into a public sphere understood as masculine, but feminize the latter in the process. They must *speak out*, as women, on the hustings, and in the law court, the lecture theatre and the television studio. But crossing over also involves the occupation of civic as well as political and cultural space. The domestic interiors which immobilize the more anxious among her protagonists have often been described as labyrinthine. Recessive might be a better term: frame within frame within frame, a vista narrowed down at its far end to a boxy cell or incubator of depression. In these films, enforced privacy kills (or provokes to murder) by absorption into an unfathomable interior depth or black hole. A phone-booth is, of course, a recess of a kind. But it is a recess projected into the world, a recess with an apprehensible outside to it—a place you go in order to be private *in public*.

Von Trotta dramatizes inadvertency. Her protagonists are at their wits' end when they seek refuge in the booth. They lift the receiver and dial. The person they wish to communicate with cannot be reached. There is no one, friend or functionary, to speak out *to*. In the meantime, like it or not, they see and are seen. They find themselves, in more than one sense, in public. And finding themselves in public, flee—if they get the chance. In *Sheer Madness* (1982), Ruth (Angela Winkler), an artist smothered by a protective, bullying husband, finally overcomes her fear of other people to the extent of leaving the house on her own to call her closest friend from a public payphone in a post office. The payphones nestle in spacious booths transparent from three sides. Ruth lifts the receiver. She stops listening, and looks: down the row of occupied booths to her left, then across at the bank of postboxes on the wall opposite, then down the row of booths to her right. In the booth next to hers, a face looms grotesquely. This is her George Harvey Bone moment. Bone had become like these strangers locked and lit up in glass. Ruth, knowing that she will never become like them, flees, as Christa (Tina Engel) had, in *The Second Awakening of Christa Klages* (1979), when spotted by someone she knows. Carla (Carla Aldrovandi), trailed by a mafia assassin in *The Long Silence* (1993), does not even get the chance to flee. For von Trotta, the phone-booth *is* the public sphere in its civic dimension: a dangerous place for women who have been taught to invest all they have in staying private.

Phone-booths encourage us to think about one city in relation to another, one film in relation to another. André Bazin once chose a scene in William Wyler's *The Best Years of Our Lives* (1946) to exemplify the long-take deep-focus style he regarded as a 'liberal and democratic' alternative to the standard manipulation of point of view through rapid-fire editing. The scene, set in a bar in Boone City, involves three variously damaged ex-servicemen who have become friends on the flight home. Homer (Harold Russell) plays piano in the near foreground, while Al (Fredric March) looks on, and Fred (Dana Andrews) makes a call he would rather not make from a booth in the distant background. Wyler filmed the scene in long shot, with both planes of action in sharp focus. Homer's playing (he has hooks for hands) absorbs our interest and admiration, and Al's. But the 'true drama', Bazin suggests, may be that which is taking place in the 'little aquarium' at the far end of the room, where Fred renounces his love for Al's daughter, who has offered him a way out of a miserable marriage. Wyler cut in two close-ups of Al looking over towards the booth. The final look Al gives Fred, as he stands rigid in the booth after putting the phone down, could easily be construed as tenderness. It is indeed a look *given*.

One person who may have noticed it was a young Japanese director, Akira Kurosawa. Kurosawa's tenth film as director, *Stray Dog*

(1949), is a Simenon-like thriller about a young detective, Murukami (Toshiro Mifune), whose gun goes missing. With some help from the older and wiser Sato (Takashi Shimura), Murukami eventually tracks the culprit down in Tokyo's seamy criminal underworld. Towards the end of the film, Sato, arriving at the hotel where the culprit has holed up, calls Murukami from a booth in the lobby. There is confusion and delay at the other end. Kurosawa almost literally suspends Sato in the booth, in a long shot held for 25 seconds, while the hotel manager flirts clumsily with the receptionist in the foreground. The thief escapes. As Sato leaves the booth in pursuit, the receiver dangles. He is shot down outside. Kurosawa, unlike Wyler, does not provide an intermediary gaze. But we don't need help to feel for the haunted Sato. We know that the balance of power and responsibility between veteran and novice, such an important theme in Kurosawa, has just tilted towards the novice, as the veteran's vulnerability is laid bare.

Such is the hauntedness of telephone-booths that they can distract attention from foreground drama even when empty. Towards the end of Carol Reed's *The Third Man* (1949), Anna (Alida Valli) and Holly Martins (Joseph Cotten) wait for Harry Lime (Orson Welles) in the Café Marc Aurel. An empty booth glows faintly behind Anna, in the depth of the shot, as she paces restlessly up and down. In Martin Scorsese's *The King of Comedy* (1982), fantasist Rupert Pupkin (Robert De Niro), on a first date with barmaid Rita (Diahnne Abbott), hopes to impress her by leafing through his autograph album. It's not long before our attention has been drawn away from his dismal performance to the area of the restaurant behind him, where two illuminated booths stand empty. This is not someone we want to feel sorry for. Another patron, who has witnessed the performance at close range, withdraws into the nearest booth, apparently to report on it in amazement. A waiter enters the booth behind him. Pupkin has been out-magnetized by less than zero. Scorsese has said that his aim was to make *The King of Comedy* in '1903 style', without close-ups and virtuoso camera movements. Here, the phone-booths, a featureless feature in the depth of the shot, enabled him to isolate his anti-hero without moving his camera an inch. Usually, though, in cinema, it's people we know who make the calls, and in so doing appear to us in a different light.

In a scene in Pedro Almodóvar's *Women on the Verge of a Nervous Breakdown* (1988), Pepa (Carmen Maura), who spends most of the film trying to get in touch with her faithless lover Iván (Ricardo Gullón), and realizes in the process that she can perfectly well do without him, has established herself across the road from the building in which Iván's ex-wife Lucía (Julieta Serrano) lives. In homage to *Rear Window*, the camera passes from one illuminated window to another, revealing as it does Madrid's answer to Miss Torso, and Lucía's son Carlos (Antonio Banderas) packing his suitcase for departure, to her considerable distress. Pepa crosses the road to the phone-booth in front of the building. A poster on which a grinning young girl holds a grinning young boy upside down by the ankles partly screens her from us. This is a harmless enough aquarium, as aquariums go. Pepa rings home. The only message on the machine is from her hapless friend Candela (María Barranco), who's got mixed up with terrorists. There's a violent thud, and the booth begins to shake. Like Melanie in *The Birds*, Pepa is under attack. Almodóvar shoots her from above as she twists and turns, as Hitchcock had shot Melanie; and then at knee level, as the receiver she has dropped dangles, while Candela intones 'Pepa, I'm in big trouble.' But this is a film which diminishes trouble rather than aggravating it. The thud was Carlos's suitcase bouncing off the roof. Its contents spill out. Pepa, stepping out of the booth, picks up a framed photograph and inspects it. The photograph, of Iván and Carlos, carries the inscription 'From your dad, who doesn't deserve you.' Carlos and his girlfriend Marisa (Rossy de Palma) argue obliviously across Pepa (even Miss Torso is somehow his fault), while she gazes intently at him. Marisa bundles her back into the booth ('Weren't you making a call?'). Accident, and a little by-the-book urban discourtesy, have broken into her obsession with the truly undeserving Iván. In a later scene, Pepa marches resolutely back towards the building she lives in, having dumped Iván's belongings in a skip across the street. She occupies the foreground, in sharp focus; while Iván, a blur in the phone-booth in the middle distance, smooth-talks her answering

machine. As she enters the building, Almodóvar pulls focus to capture Iván, still in the booth, still burbling, but also, in the far distance, Lucía on the warpath.

In all the examples I have considered so far, the phone-box is a matter of geographical rather than historical interest. That this cannot long remain the case is amply demonstrated by the first series of the cult TV drama *The Wire* (2002), in which a public payphone on the end wall of one of the low-rises in and around which the bulk of the drug-dealing is done features prominently. The dealers re-supply by means of a system involving pagers and public payphones which one of the detectives refers to as a 'throwback'. *The Wire* is insistently elegiac. It dreams of 'back in the day': the day of trade unions and investigative reporting, of policing before arrest statistics ('I love this job'), of gangsters who obey a code. No wonder it sometimes resembles a Western. And no wonder there's a phone-booth in there somewhere, in the first series. A middle-management gangster uses it to alert his boss to the whereabouts of a rival scheduled for kidnap, torture and elimination. The camera aligns one 'throwback' with another, conscience-stricken thug with public payphone: the booth glows coolly in the night, a blue-green aquarium against the warm red brick behind it.

So what is to be done with phone-boxes? Or, increasingly, without them? Some will no doubt enjoy an afterlife as tourist attraction, temporary internet office, or excuse for performance art. The rest will vanish. But the question these cubicles have posed for more than a century is as pertinent today as it ever was. How are we to go on being private in public? The lesson to be learnt from the history of the phone-box is that the construction of privacy in public by physical rather than social and cultural means always tends to excess. The physical structure (box, booth or kiosk) brought about experiences which, although they did not concern telecommunication, became indelibly associated with it. The lesson to be learnt from the representation of the phone-box in folk memory, and in literature and film, is that we remember the piss and the phlegm, and the hauntedness. There is knowledge in that remembering, knowledge we wouldn't otherwise have, of what ordinary co-existence in dense populations might actually amount to. In short, we'll miss out on a lot of inadvertency, both good and bad, if we give up constructing privacy in public by physical means. We may find ourselves in a world in which the boundary between public and private is either non-existent or policed by surveillance and legal constraint. That doesn't sound to me like much of an improvement on those anxious, savoury minutes spent locked and lit up in the toxic aquarium.

Reading

Benjamin, Walter, 'A Berlin Chronicle', in *Selected Writings 1927–30*, Vol. 2, trans. Rodney Livingstone et al., ed. Michael W. Jennings, Howard Eiland and Gary Smith (Cambridge, MA: Harvard University Press, 2005): 595–637.

Collins, Alan, *Cities of Pleasure: Sex and the Urban Social Landscape* (London: Routledge, 2005).

Emecheta, Buchi, *Second-Class Citizen* (London: Allison and Busby, 1974).

Glancey, Jonathan, *London: Bread and Circuses* (London: Verso, 2001).

Hamilton, Patrick, *Hangover Square* (Harmondsworth: Penguin, 2001).

Harrison, Tony, *Selected Poems*, 2nd edition (Harmondsworth: Penguin, 1987).

Lodwick, John, *Peal of Ordnance* (London: Methuen, 1947).

Rodaway, Paul, *Sensuous Geographies: Body, Sense and Place* (London: Routledge, 1994).

Scorsese, Martin, *Scorsese on Scorsese*, ed. Ian Christie and David Thompson (London: Faber & Faber, 2003).

Urry, John, 'City Life and the Senses', in Gary Bridge and Sophie Watson (eds), *A Companion to the City* (Oxford: Blackwell, 2000): 388–97.

Potting

Kasia Boddy

Sitting demurely on windowsills, filled with flora of all kinds, pot plants don't attract much attention from the type of observer for whom the whole point of city life is to get out of the house and into the pulsating streets as fast as possible. But for most of us, there can be no absolute separation between public and private space, only permeability. As we go out and come back in, we cross or pass through a variety of thresholds—doorsteps, stoops, hallways, vestibules, courtyards—each of which triggers a complicated sense of transition from one social role or persona to another. We don't usually climb through the window, but windowsills, on both sides of the glass, provide another important dividing-line between public and private space.

When houses were places where people worked as well as lived, these flat surfaces often functioned as boundaries across which goods and money were exchanged. During the nineteenth century, after industrialization definitively separated work and home, and as buildings became ever taller, windowsills acquired new uses: keeping milk or food cold, airing shoes and drying washing, as temptation to burglary or to suicide. Windowsills also reinvented themselves as sites of symbolic interaction between home and the city. Looked at from inside, these ledges seem to be bits of private space exposed to the public; from the street, however, they appear as public space appropriated for private use. Who, then, is the plant in the window for: the person inside looking out, or the person outside looking in?

In order to answer this question, we need to consider shifting attitudes to urban life during the modern period, in particular the way in which, in Britain at least, the city and the home came to be seen, despite their continuing mutual reinforcement, not simply as distinct but as fundamentally incompatible. The city was public, impersonal and evocative of transitoriness; home (ideally) private, personal and evocative of permanence. The city inflicted injury that the home healed. This view solidified through the nineteenth century as population increased exponentially. That the newly cramped urban-dwellers were, for the most part, the displaced rural poor meant that the modern dichotomy between street and home became even more closely associated with a more traditional one: that between country and city. The exemplary city homes of the Victorian imagination—the worker's cottage and the suburban villa—were anti-urban in spirit, not only in their domesticity, but in their studied emulation of rural existence. One of the ways in which that emulation was undertaken was through gardening.

Pots plants, once happy merely to brighten the place up, were drawn into the debate. As participants in countrified domesticity, the plant's job was to screen out the city, to stand in the frontline of 'defence' (as Elizabeth Gaskell put it) against its very existence. As participants in urban life, however, they continued to address the street, distinguishing a house or flat from its identical neighbours, or, like a freshly scrubbed doorstep, providing a means to keep up with them. In discussions about the function and future of the city—conducted by novelists, doctors, urban planners and priests—pot plants became valuable symbolic currency.

The Scarlet Geranium

While many plants—ivy, nasturtiums, chrysanthemums, mignonette, ferns, the aspidistra—proved popular for pot culture, the archetypal Victorian flower pot contained a scarlet geranium. Mostly native to southern Africa, geraniums (still the common name for plants of the genus pelargonium) were introduced into Europe in the seventeenth century. For more than a hundred years, they remained the glasshouse exotica of wealthy collectors, and when they appeared in poems, it was usually to represent sex or, in various versions of the 'language of flowers', folly. This was largely by virtue of what Cowper in 'The Task' (1785) calls the 'crimson honours' of particular varieties and perhaps the way in which their petals overlap. Sexy women, said Robert Rabelais (pseud.) in 1814, have 'pouting and geranium'd lips'. 'The Geranium' (1795), by Thomas Erskine, was unusual in thinking about the form of the whole plant rather than simply its petals, and thus in figuring the plant as male. If you find it drooping in the shade, Erskine says, give it a little sunshine (perhaps from the eyes of 'sweet Sue') and 'it shall rise':

> 'Oh, me!' cried Susan, 'When is this?
> What strange tumultuous throbs of bliss!
> Sure, never mortal till this hour
> Felt such emotion at a flower!'

Erskine here seems to be thinking of an ancestor of the zonal or 'scarlet geranium', an upright plant with lobed palmate leaves and dense balls of flat, opaque, overlapping petals at the end of each short stem. While the trailing ivy-leafed geranium was adopted in many European countries to curtain the façades of buildings, the erect zonal became, and remains, more popular in Britain.

By the 1830s developments in glasshouse technology began to provide the urban middle classes with conservatories and greenhouses to fill, and geranium hybrids in a range of forms, colour and scent became fashionable choices. For the 'smallest' houses, J. C. Loudon's *The Suburban Gardner* (1838) proposed adding a two-foot bay to an ordinary window to create an aquarium-like 'plant cabinet' as 'an allusion to the green-house of the villa, or the conservatory of the mansion'. The next step down in aspirational miniaturization was the window box or flower pot. Rather than 'choice' hybrids, however, these pots tended, from the 1840s on, to contain cheap commercially produced scarlet geraniums.

Like aspidistras, zonal geraniums were considered ideal urban plants because they thrive in confined spaces and can survive considerable neglect without dying. Nevertheless, deprived of proper care, the plants do tend to look 'sickly', as Victorian commentators often pointed out. This is largely because the plant holds on to, rather than drops, its dead flowers and leaves. If it is to produce further flowers, these need to be removed. Unlike aspidistras, geraniums need several hours of sun every day, their soft young stems naturally bending towards the sun. In insufficient light, they can become lank and untidy. In Browning's 'Pippa Passes' (1841) Ottima asks her lover to open the window where 'tall/Naked geraniums straggle'. They can survive a certain amount of drought but if over-watered are prone to fungal infections. They are not frost-hardy. And yet, and yet … as *Amateur Gardening* magazine noted in 1935, no other plant provides a 'braver show', flowering an eye-catching scarlet from May to November. The OED gives examples of 'geranium-coloured' from the 1830s and 'geranium' as itself the name of a colour from the 1840s. What the noun identified was a shade of red with a flat, solid concentration not often found in nature, and, as Ruskin noted in his *Lectures on Art* in 1870, of a 'beauty' difficult to reproduce in paint. 'The brightness of the hue dazzled the eye', he writes. A similar hue was adopted by British pillar boxes (in the 1870s) and phone-boxes (in the 1920s). Today we describe these as 'pillar-box red', but perhaps they too were intended to emulate 'geranium'.

For Octavia Hill, one of many nineteenth-century social reformers who read Ruskin and championed the home against the city, a distinctive characteristic of urban housing was its 'miserable monotony'. 'All bright colour exhilarates and gives a sense of gladness', Hill told the Kyrle Society in 1884. 'Till you stay a little in the colourless, forlorn desolation of the houses in the worst courts, till you have lived among the monotonous, dirty tints of the poor districts of London, you little know what the colours of your curtains, carpets, and wall-papers are to you.' It is not only because these items are bright and cheerful, however, that the poor might be expected to find 'exhilaration' in placing a geranium in the window, or in fixing a 'coloured print' to the wall or throwing a 'gay quilt' on the bed. For Hill and Ruskin, decoration expresses the individualism that the monotonous city was determined to stamp out.

Too many geraniums, however, could make one 'disagreeably conspicuous'. That at least is the premise behind M. E. Braddon's description, at the opening of her 1867 sensation novel, *Birds of Prey*, of 14 Fitzgeorge Street. The 'unsullied brightness' of the house does not convey gladness but rather acts as a 'standing reproach' to its neighbours.

> It was as bright, and pleasant, and rural of aspect as any house within earshot of the roar and rattle of Holborn can be. There were flowers in the windows; gaudy scarlet geraniums, which seemed to enjoy an immunity from all the ills to which geraniums are subject, so impossible was it to discover a faded leaf amongst their greenness, or the presence of blight amidst their wealth of blossom ... The freshly-varnished street-door bore a brass-plate, on which to look was to be dazzled; and the effect produced by this combination of white doorstep, scarlet geranium, green blind, and brass-plate was obtrusively brilliant.

But all is not what it seems in Fitzgeorge Street. That obtrusive brilliance can be worse than miserable monotony is confirmed when we learn that the house's new tenant, Philip Sheldon, is a dentist, specializing in false teeth. Not content to advertise with a brass-plate, he attaches to his house a 'neat little glass-case, on the level of the eye of the passing pedestrian', containing, in a grotesque echo of the white door-step and scarlet geraniums, 'glistening white teeth and impossibly red gums'. The house, despite itself, succeeds in expressing its tenant's (murderous) personality.

Different kinds of urban-dweller needed different kinds of protection against the city, as Elizabeth Gaskell acknowledged in *Mary Barton*, her 1848 'tale of Manchester Life'. The Barton home is warm, cosy and 'almost crammed with furniture (sure sign of good times among the mills)'. Mrs Barton displays her abundance—furniture, food and a cupboard kept open to display various 'nondescript articles, for which one would have fancied their possessors could find no use—such as triangular pieces of glass to save carving knives and forks from dirtying table-cloths'. These comforts—examples of

what Richard Hoggart was to dub 'the working-class baroque'—
exist for family and friends, and not for envious eyes. Mrs Barton
draws her blue-and-white check curtains, 'to shut in the friends met
to enjoy themselves. Two geraniums, unpruned and leafy, which
stood on the sill, formed a further defence from outdoor pryers.'
While Philip Sheldon's unblemished geraniums indicate suspicious
behind-the-scenes engineering, Mrs Barton's baroque suggests care
and attention. Both novels, however, present their luscious plants
as rather anomalous. Braddon states directly (and rather takes for
granted) that Sheldon's house of rural aspect exists, incongruously,
amid the 'roar and rattle' of Holborn. For Gaskell, the shift from
country to city life deserves more deliberate consideration. *Mary
Barton*, therefore, opens in the last-gasp rural setting of Green Heys
Fields. Only two miles from Manchester, Green Heys, with its rose-
covered farmhouse set in a garden of 'scrambling and wild luxuriance', speaks of 'other times and other occupations', an idyll against
which ensuing events will be measured. Mrs Barton's 'unpruned and
leafy' geraniums, splendid though they are, are a poor imitation of
that garden's luxuriance, and the defence they offer proves insufficient to protect the Barton family from scandal or destitution. The
lovingly described furniture is sold off, and the novel's action moves
further and further from Green Heys into the depths of the city. *Mary
Barton* could be understood as a story of the Fall; in the bourgeois
Bloomsbury of Braddon's novel, innocence is from the outset a
distant memory.

The Philanthropic Geranium

But not everyone was so pessimistic about the absolute nature of the
division between city and country, between smokestacks and geraniums (as the 1917 San Diego mayoral election styled it). A great deal of
the impetus behind nineteenth-century philanthropy was stimulated
by a desire for reconciliation. Among the many problems of urban
poverty, two were most often singled out for discussion—up-rooting
and over-crowding. What better metaphor for both than the country-
grown plant in its city-ledge pot?

While some schemes existed to provide *more* space for city-dwellers, most of the emphasis was on giving them a different, better *kind* of space. Large or small didn't matter, a continuum between garden cities, parks, communal gardens, backyards and window boxes was assumed. But while there was some similarity between these attempts to 'restore the people to the land' (in Ebenezer Howard's phrase), there were also some differences. Once more it seemed to come down to a question of perspective. Was the window box a private or a public space? Given that the potted geranium could not return to its country-cottage origins, what were its dreams? Did it, in other words, hope to become a city park or a suburban garden?

Arturo Soria y Mata believed that the geranium and its cultivator were committed to metropolitan life. In *The Linear City* (1892), he invents a scenario in which 'the worker's wife' makes a 'simple' but 'very eloquent' gesture of revolt against poor urban planning:

> She will place a flower pot with some bright geraniums on her attic window ledge. This flower pot is a living and perennial protest from nature against the arts forgotten by men … From there we find the impulse that engenders the public gardens in plazas, boulevards. With time, these flowers will kindle the hope for a true urban life and the desire to harmonize the sweetness of country life with the undeniable advantages of the city.

Most of the great city park designers of the nineteenth century, however, conceived their project less in terms of achieving harmony with the city and more as providing 'the greatest possible contrast'. The aim of New York's Central Park, said its architect, Frederick Law Olmstead, was to 'completely shut the city out'. Olmstead had firm ideas about the way that parks should be used, as ruralized retreats but also as civilizing influences. The reality did not always match the intention, however, with parks often providing a hospitable environment for the very activities they were meant to counteract: 'loitering', 'loafing', drinking, drug-taking, sex, crime and political protest all flourished within their gates.

A different kind of urban *cordon sanitaire*—associated with a different kind of leisure—was offered by the private garden, even in its miniaturized window-box form. In the park, pruning, planting and mowing are jobs for municipal employees; everyone else can be 'idle'. In the garden, allotment or at the windowsill, there is always work to be done. Gardeners, it was asserted, cannot help but feel responsible for their *own* little plots of soil; this feeling would lead inexorably towards industry of a vigorous but encouragingly pre-industrial hue. For middle-class Victorians, gardening's unique blend of aspirational self-help and rural connectedness made it the ideal recreation for the urban poor. Slum investigators such as Margaret Harkness, in *Toilers in London* (1889), found it 'wonderful to witness the love which the poorest and lowest people in London have for flowers'.

> They watch over their sickly geraniums and blighted dwarf rose-trees with more devotion than a gardener bestows on hot-house plants … This love of flowers is one of the most hopeful symptoms in the condition of the *very poor* in London.

If men were imagined receiving their moral education in a garden or an allotment—'gardening filled up the hours' and became 'a habit far more gratifying than seeking gratification in dogs or beer' (as *Gardener's Chronicle* pointed out in 1875)—the windowsill was more often seen as the woman's domain. No one could claim that a pot or two would occupy the gardener—thus keeping her away from the bottle—for great lengths of time. Its effect, rather, was homeopathic. In learning how to dead-head their geraniums—in acquiring pride in their public personae—women would gradually acquire a 'taste' for, and be 'brought over' to, 'cleanliness, regularity, order, and self-respect' in their most private lives. 'I must keep everything extra clean,' says the eponymous heroine of *Dot's Scarlet Geranium* (1890) by the Christian children's author Harriet Boultwood, 'or the geranium will make the room look dirty—the flower is so bright.' Tending one's geranium was a bit like tending one's conscience. It encouraged what many called 'love of the home' but also the godliness that was next to cleanliness. Once more the metaphor, and the ambition, proved flexible.

For most commentators, looking after a pot plant had less in common with washing the floor than with caring for a baby. 'Plants are just like children', declared the bossy Mrs C. W. Earle in *Pot-Pourri from a Surrey Garden* (1897); 'it is a keen, watchful, ever-attentive, thoughtful eye they require'. Victorian fiction consistently associates good—that is, maternally inclined—women with the pot-plant nurture that turned a house, a lodging-house room or, in the case of the prisoner's wife in *The Pickwick Papers* (1836), a debtors' prison, into a home. Aware that the scene was already a bit of a cliché, Dickens presents 'a lean haggard woman ... who was watering, with great solicitude, the wretched stump of a dried-up, withered plant, which, it was plain to see, could never send forth a green leaf again;— too true an emblem, perhaps, of the office she had come there to discharge'. The solitary, perhaps childless, woman (the sempstress, governess, invalid, or the lonely teenager—such as the eponymous Dot or Amy in *Little Woman*, 1868) was also often depicted with a 'pet geranium'. The motherless 14-year-old heroine of *Jenny and her Geranium* (1841), exiled from her country home, treats her plant as 'a cherished companion, to whom she confided her thoughts and feel-ings, and who responded to them in an eloquent language all its own', while in his Bloomsbury parish, the Revd. Parkes recorded the grati-tude of a widow to whom he had given a pot: 'I did not believe before that I should care for anything again in this world like I have cared for that geranium. Indeed, sir, I've almost got to love it as if it could speak.'

But the intended benefits were not only personal and moral. In *Jenny and her Geranium*, after the girl's plant is restored and her father reformed—to the extent of buying new furniture so that the gera-nium has 'decent company to look at'—the neighbours begin to take notice. 'Stirred by some dim remembrance of better things', they too resort to geraniums and are thus, in turn, 'reclaimed from drunk-enness'. The seed of house-pride, or rather pot-plant-pride, has blossomed into neighbourhood-pride. In 'a world of general disorder', concludes the anonymous author, introducing another metaphor, 'good example is catching'.

Philanthropists described themselves as merely encouraging a tendency 'latent' in the poor. But, as with today's TV equivalents of the Victorian middle-class makeover, no one really believed that self-help was a reward in itself, and so 'incitements' and 'encouragement', that is cash prizes, were offered. Competitive flower-shows—run by enthusiasts such as the Stoke Newington Chrysanthemum Society (founded in 1846) and Tower Hamlets Floricultural Society (founded in 1859)—provided a model for window-box evangelicals. In 1860 the Revd. Parkes, of St George's in Bloomsbury, launched a campaign which he later described in *Window Gardens for the People, and Clean and Tidy Rooms, Being an Experiment to Improve the Homes of the London Poor*. In addition to awarding prizes for well-kept rooms, he supplied his parishioners with plants to grow for competition. Regular inspections were conducted to ensure that no-one cheated and tried to pass off as their own specimens from Covent Garden flower market. Parkes organized window-gardening shows throughout the 1860s and '70s. One was held in Russell Square; the first time, he noted, that any of the large, private London squares had been 'thrown open for the recreation of the masses'. In 1863 the Earl of

Shaftesbury handed out the prizes, praising Parkes as 'just as much a benefactor as the man who invented the steam engine'. Many similar schemes followed and the idea was later taken up by the transatlantic Settlement Movement. In 1867, one successful show took place in the grounds of London's Middlesex Hospital. Plants 'grown in the rooms or on the window-sills of very poor persons living near the hospital' competed against pots cultivated by patients on its wards. 'The flowers were quite remarkable for beauty when the circumstances under which they were cultivated are considered', reported the *Lancet*. The against-all-odds quality of the window display only increased its moral worth.

But the *Lancet* also had medical matters in mind, and was pleased to note that 'many a good hint about air, water, warmth and ventilation, of no slight service to delicate human plants, is conveyed to the poor flower-growers by the kind ladies who superintend these competitions'. The comparison of human and flowering plants here is mildly humorous. Other more melodramatic sources anthropomorphized the plants completely and imagined them sharing a 'torpid life' with their owners in the 'musty courts and alleys' of the pathological city. The pot geranium featured as the floral equivalent of a canary sent down the mine to see if there was any clear air or sunlight. Sometimes its troubles were correlated with a specific problem, such as the presence of a gas factory: 'No improvement can ever reach that infected neighbourhood,' reported the *Illustrated News* in 1864, 'no new streets, no improved dwellings, not even a garden is possible within a circle of at least quarter of a mile in diameter, and not so much as a geranium can flourish in a window-sill.' More often, however, the problem, for people, as for their plant representatives, was simply the over-crowded, soot-filled city itself. In 1855, the gardening journalist Shirley Hibberd observed that 'thousands of beautiful plants are every spring and summer brought from the nurseries around London, and sold in the city to undergo the slow death of suffocation—dying literally from asphyxia, from the absorption of soot in the place of air'.

Talk of the diagnostic, and curative, value of plants was the legacy of the miasmic theory of disease, popular since the medieval plagues, which proposed a close connection between disease and 'bad air'. Even as germ theory took hold in the 1850s and '60s, many continued to emphasize the medical consequences—the 'pestilential miasma'—of enclosed space.

Those geraniums that did survive asphyxiation, said the Christian Socialist Charles Kingsley, were able to diagnose a wide variety of diseases:

> The sickly geranium which spreads its blanched leaves against the cellar panes, and peers up, as if imploringly, to the narrow slip of sunlight at the top of the narrow alley, had it a voice, could tell more truly than ever a doctor in the town, why little Bessy sickened of the scarlatina, and little Johnny of the whooping-cough, till the toddling wee things who used to pet and water it were carried off each and all of them one by one to the churchyard sleep.

And the geranium could also attempt a cure. In an 1869 lecture, entitled 'The Two Breaths', Kingsley elaborated on the 'mutual dependence and mutual helpfulness' that existed between people and plants:

> The delicate surface of the green leaves absorbs the carbonic acid, and parts it into its elements, retaining the carbon to make woody fibre, and courteously returning you the oxygen to mingle with the fresh air, and be inhaled by your lungs once more. Thus do you feed the plants; just as the plants feed you; while the great life-giving sun feeds both; and the geranium standing in the sick child's window does not merely rejoice his eye and mind by its beauty and freshness, but repays honestly the trouble spent on it; absorbing the breath which the child needs not, and giving to him the breath which he needs.

The geranium provided, in miniature, the exchange of good air for bad that many reformers, even as they abandoned miasmic theory, continued to believe was necessary for city living. But even where parks were concerned, the 'lungs of the city' argument didn't make much sense. 'It takes about three acres of woods to absorb as much carbon dioxide as four people exude in breathing, cooking, and heating', Jane Jacobs has observed: 'the oceans of air circulating about us, not parks, keep cities from suffocating'.

The medical argument for plants easily slipped back into the moral. Geraniums could only do their detoxifying bit if, in turn, a window-gardener took 'trouble'. In Kingsley's *Glaucus* (1855), Little Bessy tries to fight off her scarlatina, and Little Johnny his whooping-cough, by tending their geranium, but the plucky trio cannot overcome the pernicious influence of their father and mother, who tried 'to supply by gin that very vital energy which fresh air and pure water, and the balmy breath of woods and heaths, were made by God to give':

> the little geranium did its best, like a heaven-sent angel, to right the wrong which man's ignorance had begotten, and drank in, day by day, the poisoned atmosphere, and formed it into fair green leaves, and breathed into the children's faces from every pore, whenever they bent over it, the life-giving oxygen for which their dulled blood and festered lungs were craving in vain.

The Red Light

It wasn't all oxygen-transfusions and self-help. If, by the 1850s, most geraniums had become angels in the house, some retained a little eighteenth-century sex appeal, even if this was only invoked in order to be cast aside. When the narrator of Robert Browning's 'Evelyn Hope' (1855) expresses grief at the death of a 16-year-old who had 'scarcely heard his name', he also confesses to being 'thrice as old' as the girl with lips of 'geranium's red'. Folly, here, had been averted, but it wasn't always so easy to avoid geranium'd temptation.

The scarlet geranium was Dickens's favourite flower. He liked to wear a sprig in his coat buttonhole and, his daughter recalled, they made 'a blaze of colour in the front garden'. So far, so respectable. In *David Copperfield* (1849–50), however, the homely and erotic associations of the plant prove confusing. At the beginning of the novel, Clara Copperfield, David's mother, is a widow. We can tell that she is a 'childlike' (i.e. bad) mother because she cares more about looking good than looking after her son. When her servant Clara Peggotty suggests this, she retorts,

> Would you wish me to shave my head and black my face, or disfigure myself with a burn, or a scald, or something of that sort? ... on his account only last quarter I wouldn't buy myself a new parasol, though that old green one is frayed the whole way up, and the fringe is perfectly mangy.

Maybe so, but where Clara does manage to put on a good show is in the Blunderstone 'parlour-window' where a 'famous geranium' is displayed. Dickens does not say whether Clara Copperfield herself gives the plant maternal attention or whether this task too is delegated to the good mother, Clara Peggotty, a woman who likes to 'clean everything over and over again'. It is Mrs Copperfield, however, who takes advantage of the geranium's showy blossoms. One Sunday, she invites Mr Murdstone, the mysterious gentleman who has been pursuing her, to look at the plant.

> It did not appear to me that he took much notice of it, but before he went he asked my mother to give him a bit of the blossom. She begged him to choose it for himself, but he refused to do that—I could not understand why—so she plucked it for him, and gave it into his hand.

David Copperfield was Freud's favourite novel and reading this scene one can understand why. If young Davy fails consciously to 'understand' what it is going on and to recognize his feelings for his mother, his unconscious has lodged a direct association between geraniums and desire. David next encounters the plant at the height of his infatuation with the 'enchanting' Dora Spenlow. A 'lackadaisical young spooney', he visits her in suburban Norwood, where she takes him through the 'beautifully kept' (by someone else) garden to see the greenhouse geraniums.

We loitered along in front of them, and Dora often stopped to admire this one or that one, and I stopped to admire the same one, and Dora laughing, held the dog up childishly, to smell the flowers; and if we were not all three in Fairyland, certainly *I* was. The scent of a geranium leaf, at this day, strikes me with a half comical, half serious wonder as to what change has come over me in a moment; and then I see a straw hat and blue ribbons, and a quantity of curls, and a little black dog being held up, in two slender arms, against a bank of blossoms and bright leaves.

'I Fall Into Captivity' is the chapter's title, but it is a fall that might have been predicted. Dora among the geraniums—a combination of 'girlish' 'curls' and 'blossoms', a childlike woman who poses among the plants but does not tend them—repeats Clara Copperfield precisely.

Perhaps we shouldn't blame the young spooney, for how was he to disentangle the signals for sex from those for good-housekeeping. It was all too easy to misread a geranium. On setting up Waverly House, one of Manhattan's first detention houses for prostitutes, Maude Miner decided to 'post no sign which would distinguish this from other red brick dwellings on the street'. She 'had not realized that it was marked until one of the girls returning to visit us said, "I knew where to find it all right. I just looked for the red geraniums."' Miner, born in 1880, was a probation officer, determined to save women from the 'slavery of prostitution', and determined to convert the red geranium from sex to respectability. Her near-contemporary, T. S. Eliot, born in 1888, had fewer hopes for women. Eliot's 'sunless dry geraniums', both brazenly red and satisfyingly 'withered', advertise nothing more uplifting than 'female smells in shuttered rooms'.

Modern Nature and Artifice

By the end of the nineteenth century, the geranium had undergone the latest in its rapid evolutions as a social and cultural emblem. In 1820, it had been a hothouse exotic; in 1850, a humble resident of garret windows. By 1880, it bore the stamp of mass-production. No longer a spot of colour breaking up urban monotony, the plant was now thought to contribute to the 'darkness of ugliness that has covered all modern life'. At least that was William Morris's view. His 1879 lecture on 'Making the Best of It' attacked the 'over-artificiality' of various commercial hybrids, 'inventions of men' rather than nature, but with particular venom reserved for the 'scarlet geranium', whose 'bad' colour demonstrated that 'even flowers can be thoroughly ugly'. In the Edwardian 'golden age' of garden writing, the championing of species over cultivars, of pastels over primary colours, of plants that sway in the breeze rather than stand upright, became commonplace, and to a considerable extent those tastes endure today. 'My eye has had too much tender tutoring', wrote Gertrude Jekyll, a disciple of Ruskin and Morris, 'to endure the popular "Henry Jacoby" [*pelargonium*]—a colour that, for all its violence, has a harsh dullness that I find displeasing.'

A few geraniums lingered on in their traditional roles. In the 'modern story' of D. W. Griffith's epic film *Intolerance* (1916), the Dear One (Mae Marsh) takes comfort in the city from her 'Hopeful Geranium', while Flannery O'Connor's first published short story, 'The Geranium' (1946) made similarly conventional points about urban uprooting and containment. But others began to recast geraniums as emblems of petit-bourgeois conventionality and 'stiffness'. An extreme example of this is Richard Riching's short story, 'The House of Blood', published in the modernist little magazine *Coterie*. Garfield Lovell's disgust with family tradition and 'bloodless' propriety finds its focus in the blood-red geraniums that have 'always flowered' in the window-boxes of the family home. 'How infuriatingly trim and stiff it all is,' he muttered, 'and how unnatural. Oh, you geraniums, why can't you nod in the breeze—or do something.' Nodding in the breeze won't cut it for Garfield. When he finally does something, it's to brandish a revolver at his aunt, and then shoot himself instead.

During its final evolution, the geranium could be redeemed in one of two ways, as the antidote to, or perfection of, artificiality. D. H. Lawrence filled his writings with appreciations of the 'redness of the red geranium', which for him could never be 'anything but a sensual experience'. For Lawrence, the sun-loving flower was not an industrial product but an expression of sexual nature at its most undiluted, forceful and, as his contemporary Amy Lowell concurred, 'raw'. For those who, by contrast, held modern life to be an inevitably artful performance, the appeal of the red geranium lay rather in its almost-artificiality. So Laforgue, in 'Pierrots', describes a clown's mouth as 'comme un singulier géranium', while Proust—a rather different disciple of Ruskin than Octavia Hill—isolates the effect of sunlight on a red carpet as 'une carnation' (or 'flesh-glow') of 'géranium'. In Nella Larsen's novel *Passing* (1929), Irene knows that her friend Clare is a fake, because her lips, 'painted a brilliant geranium-red', show up 'the ivory of her skin'. (Variations on 'geranium' have remained popular in the naming of lipsticks since the 1920s.) Detailing the Berlin apartment building of his turn-of-the-century childhood, Walter Benjamin recalled the defamiliarizing effect of seeing its courtyard from a train. From this point of view, 'the red geraniums that were peeping from their boxes accorded less well with the summer than the red feather mattresses that were hung over the windowsills each morning to air'. Who needs nature when lipstick or a feather mattress will do the job?

Window Gardens for the People

Flowers today are not the moral agents they once were. Varieties of pelargonium such as 'Lipstick', 'Cover Girl' and 'Ginger Rogers' have been created with the sole intention of smearing some red or shocking pink across the cityscape, while, as Salman Rushdie proposes in *The Satanic Verses* (1988), generations of immigrants have tried to 'tropicalize' the metropolis by introducing 'outrageously-coloured' flowers in shades of 'magenta, vermillion, neon-green'. But if blossoms are now mere agents of brightening up the place, the window-box remains an important site in the ongoing debate about city and country life, and about the symbolic interaction between home and street, interior and exterior. What Jane Jacobs calls the 'magical fetish' of good air for bad still attracts believers, witnessed in the success of books such as *How to Grow Fresh Air* (1997). However, much of the impulse behind today's window-box philanthropy centres around 'bad food'. Once again, all sorts of medical and social ills are diagnosed in terms of what we ingest, and once again, the suggested cure—that we cultivate our gardens—divides the respectable from the unrespectable poor by virtue of their potting up. As politicians fall over their spades in an effort to turn their conspicuous lawns into conspicuous vegetable gardens, the rest of the population is reminded that no space is 'too small' to do its bit in tackling obesity and climate change. In 2009, the National Trust (founded by Octavia Hill in 1895) launched a campaign to encourage 'people living in the UK's five million flats' to take advantage of the '600 acres of growing space' available on their windowsills. 'Amidst high food prices and concern about sustainable food, it's the perfect time to grow your own delicious, cheap and local "window food". Even with just two window boxes you can grow your own meal.'

Don't have 'just two' window boxes? Well, make do with milk bottles and baked bean cans instead. 'Inspiration' on a 'low budget' was the theme of 'Edible Spaces with Capital Growth', unveiled at the 2009 Hampton Court Flower Show. The display featured three small gardens and six balconies. 'Gardens in cities don't have to be big', announced Rosie Boycott, Chair of the London Food Board. 'It is amazing how much you can grow in a converted builder's bag, a recycled polystyrene box, an old market tray, even in disposable coffee cups, plastic food containers and old wellingtons. You just need imagination and the will to grow.' London Food, the National Trust and all the other organizations devoted to grow-your-own presumably do not believe that the harvest of a window box or two will provide many meals. As was the case with the Victorian geranium, homeopathic vanity seems to be the drive. The pride instilled by growing, and displaying, two carrots or four radishes will magically redirect window-gardeners, whatever their income, from the takeaway towards the organic farmers' market and the peasant recipes of their rural ancestors. The window ledge's public show will sow the seeds for private goods and will also instil civic pride of a reassuringly small-scale rural kind. Boycott, who owns a 'London home' near Portobello Road and, until recently, a farm in Somerset, recently wrote of her visit to the '30 small, neat growing spaces' granted to Tower Hamlets Women's Environmental Network:

> All was neat, tidy and, above all, loved. The community, which once sat indoors in frightened isolation, now had a focal point around which to gather and, like us on apple day in Somerset, a good excuse for parties when the vegetables were flourishing and ready for cropping.

If only it could always be apple day in Somerset. The Victorian philanthropist's dream of a green-fingered urban feudalism—in which the poor are 'like us', but on a miniature scale—persists into the twenty-first century.

Reading

Boycott, Rosie, 'Reconnecting our Food, Culture and Community', *The Garden* (January 2009): 54–5.

Gaskell, S. Martin, 'Gardens for the Working Class: Victorian Practical Pleasures', *Victorian Studies*, 23 (Summer 1980): 479–501.

Hill, Octavia, 'Colour, Space and Music for the People', *The Nineteenth Century* (May 1884): 741–52.

Horwood, Catherine, *Potted History: The Story of Plants in the Home* (London: Frances Lincoln, 2007).

Malchow, H. L., 'Public Gardens and Social Action in Late Victorian London', *Victorian Studies*, 29 (Autumn 1985): 97–124.

Matheson, Julia, '"A New Gleam of Social Sunshine": Window Garden Flower Shows for the Working Classes 1860–1875', *The London Gardener*, 9 (2003–4): 60–70.

Wilkinson, Anne, *The Passion for Pelargoniums* (Stroud: Sutton Publishing, 2007).

'Our Garden City', *Evening Standard* (2 July 2009): 27.

The Victorian Gardener (Stroud: Sutton Publishing, 2006).

Recycling

Esther Leslie

Wastelands

The city is an immense machine for creating waste. The city's inhabitants ingest, eject, digest, disgorge, discard, acquire, stockpile. The city is full of rubbish. The city gets older. Oldness lingers. As the cities age, their rubbish grows old with it. New types of waste come into being too. Today our homes and offices are cluttered with intangible waste, clogging, recalcitrant all the same. It is the digital stuff, spam, old files, viruses, interferences, unbidden photos of babies or sunsets, unmanaged blogs and websites, and spreading 'link rot'. Toshers, mud-larks, dustmen, pure-finders, sewer-hunters, bone-grubbers, ragpickers and gatherers, zabbaleen, Link Sleuths and checkers, 404 widgets, Wayback Machines are the figures called up to deal with the dead and the dangling, the stuff that has slipped out of use.

The city's ability to generate but not deal with its accumulating waste was recognized in earnest in the nineteenth century. The Ashes-and Dustmen could cope no longer. The dust piled up and up, such that many battled miserably with it their life long until they finally returned to it. And Dickens's 'golden dustman', in *Our Mutual Friend* (1865), made his fortune from the very excess of it, capitalized and multifarious in form:

he grew rich as a Dust Contractor, and lived in a hollow in a hilly country entirely composed of Dust. On his own small estate the growling old vagabond threw up his own mountain range, like an old volcano, and its geological formation was Dust. Coal-dust, vegetable-dust, bone-dust, crockery dust, rough dust and sifted dust,—all manner of Dust.

But dust was just a part of it. The cities, with their concentrations of populations, concentrated vast amounts of organic waste, not least the tons of excrement of the urban masses that needed management. In 1842 Edwin Chadwick's 'Report on the Sanitary Condition of the Labouring Population of Great Britain' inaugurated the 'sanitary movement' in Britain. It concentrated on the waste produced by households—ashes from the fires, food wastes and excrement. Chadwick identified a problem of filth, but he also suggested the productive transformation of that filth into something useful, even marketable. He imagined pipes bringing drained water from the countryside and taking away, on its return journey, wastes from the town to be used as manure. In this way, as he wrote in a letter to Lord Francis Egerton, 'we complete the circle, and realize the Egyptian type of eternity by bringing as it were the serpent's tail into the serpent's mouth'. Such a perfect cycle, from waste to utility, also appeared in Henry Mayhew's description of dustmen, nightmen, sweeps and scavengers in the second volume of *London Labour and the London Poor* (1861). He recycles a study of his own, from two years earlier, in which he describes nature's circularity, where exchange of chemicals and minerals sustains life in different parts of nature's body. He describes how plants are both scavengers and purifiers. Plants live off our excreted gases and '*remove the filth from the earth, as well as disinfect the atmosphere, and fit it to be breathed by a higher order of beings*'. It is this cycling that pushes Mayhew to propose that human waste be utilized, an act as natural as breathing, even if Mayhew's characterization of it uses a more historically bound metaphor: 'what appeared worse than worthless to us was Nature's capital, *wealth set aside for future production*'.

Justus von Liebig then contributed to these debates on waste, coining the phrase *Stoffwechsel*, exchange of stuffs. This is, he observes, the state of affairs that rules in the natural world—for example, in the body or in the relationship between plants and carbon, animals and oxygen. But it is not the state of affairs that ruled in British farming, where Liebig observed a 'robbery system', an undermining of soil's fertility through overuse, consumption without replacement. Marx was struck by Liebig's observation of how the failure to recycle waste would exhaust resources. Like Engels, whose diagnosis of the condition of the working classes had extended Chadwick's analysis of urban filth to include industrial pollution, the blackening smoke, the contaminated waters, by-products of factory production, rather than just the ordure of the poor, Marx was especially interested in the waste of industry, and, like Liebig, in the waste of waste. He saw how capitalist industry recycled 'the excretions of production and consumption' only when it seemed directly profitable to so do. He noted the waste of human bodily excretions from four-and-a-half million Londoners pumped into the Thames at heavy expense.

The poor, for their part, were well practised at some sort of recycling and making value out of the abject. A contribution to the weekly magazine *Household Words*, in July 1850 (which may have been Dickens's inspiration for his Dust story), 'Dust; or Ugliness Redeemed' by R. H. Horne, tabulates the ways in which an unsightly pile of dusty remains is picked over by various agencies, the searchers and sorters, squeezing value out of the discarded. Various interests were sought in the heap. Some scrabbled for the bits of coal that had found their way into the ashes mistakenly. Others went for the cinders, selling the largest bits to braziers and the breeze to brickmakers. Some sifted through what was known as 'soft-ware'—vegetable and animal matter, sold on as manure, or dead cats for fur trims. Others gathered 'hard-ware', fragments of crockery, old pans and oyster-shells, sold to make new roads. Bones went to the soap-boiler, who extracted and sold the fat and marrow and crushed the remains for manure. Woollen rags fed the hops and white linen rags made paper. Metals and glass went to dealers. Even so, Horne's heap grew so large that not all could be sifted and reutilized. Eventually it was bundled up and sold as materials for bricks in order to rebuild Moscow after the fire of 1812 that accompanied Napoleon's invasion.

There were also, noted Marx ironically, more intangible transformations of waste into commodity. The rubbish of the city transmuted in form with the arrival of mass means of ideological influencing. Marx's riposte to the Swiss spy *Herr Vogt* (1860) makes an analogy between the effluvium of the cities and ideological drivel—'social filth'—outlining another way in which money can be made from muckraking:

By means of an artificial system of hidden piping all the lavatories of London empty their physical filth into the Thames. In the same way the world capital daily spews all its social filth through a system of goose-quills into one big central paper sewer—the 'Daily Telegraph'. Liebig correctly criticizes the senseless waste that robs the waters of the Thames of their purity and the soil of Britain of its manure. But Levy, the proprietor of the central paper sewer, is an expert not only at chemistry but also at alchemy. After transforming all the social filth of London into newspaper articles, he transforms the newspaper articles into copper and finally the copper into gold. On the gate that leads to the central paper sewer are inscribed di colore oscuro the words 'Hic ...

quisquam faxit oletum!' Or, as Byron has already beautifully translated it in verse: 'Stop, traveller, and—piss!'

Art as Rubbish

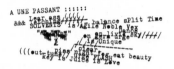

The city's filth found new uses, not least of which was its figurative transformation into tawdry prose. In this same moment, as Marx identifies boulevard journalism's muckraking over city lives, artists find themselves degraded. They are bereft of old modes of support, such as church and noble patronage. These have been swept away in the processes of industrialization and rationalization. Remaindered and unsupported, thrown up against each other and onto the market, artists stand exposed and without means.

Cities have long inspired—or better expired—their own aesthetic, which might be characterized as a poetry of the streets. A key figure in this history is Charles Baudelaire, who depicts and mocks the position of the poet who struggles and fails to transcend the conditions of city life, but forges thereby new lyric articulations. Baudelaire was for Walter Benjamin a commentator on a commodity-producing society, in which the new was shown to be a return of the ever-same, the mass a seductive veil for the lonely *flâneur*, who pounds the streets, not as an idle dandy, but as a labourer seeking booty to write about, material for hack work to sell wherever he can. Baudelaire is the poet who thematically and formally tracks capitalism's moves, from the perspective of someone who, as poet, intellectual, bohemian and seller of his albeit mental labour power, is fully exposed, because he exists at a time when artists have been compelled to scurry to the margins, representing no one clearly, and certainly not officialdom or a heroic ascendant class. In this context, Benjamin describes how the city, with all its refuse and rags, detritus and ephemera, becomes a resource for writing for those who have little else and are condemned to scrabble their lyric together in a hard new environment. Benjamin quotes Baudelaire's own description of the ragpicker, before stating that it amounted to a self-characterization:

> 'Here we have a man whose job it is to gather the day's refuse in the capital. Everything that the big city has thrown away, everything it has lost, everything it has scorned, everything it has crushed underfoot he catalogues and collects. He collates the annals of intemperance, the capharnaum of waste. He sorts things out and selects judiciously: he collects like a miser guarding a treasure, refuse which will assume the shape of useful or gratifying objects between the jaws of the goddess of Industry.' This description is one extended metaphor for the poetic method, as Baudelaire practised it. Ragpicker and poet: both are concerned with refuse, and both go about their solitary business while other citizens are sleeping; they even move in the same way. Nadar speaks of Baudelaire's 'pas saccadé'. This is the gait of the poet who roams the city in search of rhyme-booty; it is also the gait of the ragpicker, who is obliged to come to a halt every few moments to gather up the refuse he encounters.

Waste as poetic booty. The jerky step of someone on the lookout for something to transform into lyric and not just for the love of it but to sell it. Degraded experience elevated into art, then sullied once more, if the poet is lucky, for commerce. And this, in turn, published as a small entry, perhaps, buried in a newspaper or magazine, and destined itself to become tomorrow's rejectamenta, or maybe recycled as wrapping paper.

James Joyce's Leopold Bloom, sauntering into the Dublin cityscape a few years after Baudelaire had been trashed by Paris, similarly treats the streets as the scene of imaginative forgeries, a place of recycling banal experience into 'copy'. Significant experience occurs amidst urban detritus. Towards the close of the book Bloom is at rest, having travelled, his mythic journey completed. In bed, the remains of the day, the fragments of the workaday, batter between conscious and unconscious mind. His last waking thoughts before falling into dreamsleep are word and image coagulates designed to trip up a modern man, especially one who works in the world of advertising. In the chapter 'Ithaca' the following is noted:

> What were habitually his final meditations?
> Of some one sole unique advertisement to cause passers to stop in wonder, a poster novelty, with all extraneous accretions excluded, reduced to its simplest and most efficient terms not exceeding the span of casual vision and congruous with the velocity of modern life.

At the gateway to Bloom's unconscious is the advertisement. This is no surprise. Soon after, the Surrealists also discover the proximity of advertisement and unconscious. Bloom imagines a poster that would grab the attention, a piece of street debris so meaningful and absolute it arrests the pedestrian, if only for a moment.

An erratic step, a stopping and starting, forever delaying. This going forward is interrupted, in order to allow the attractions of the street to trip up passers-by, to hold them still, to process and re-process the multiple stimuli. Such delaying is the core around which Surrealism collects. Delay is there in the love of dreams, a reprocessing of the day in the night and then, subsequently, another mining of those night contents the following day. Delay is the retrospective surfacing of previously unseen contents or significance into the present: as in the surreal gesture of recycling or rescuing the lost as found, the affection for the flea market item or the deployment of the ready-made or the embrace of discarded technologies or fashions. Surrealism was an art of delayed reception. It rediscovered in the solid, substantial Victoriana of days gone the uncanny, the flimsy, the layered and absurd. This was Surrealism's reception of the immediate past—an aftertime in which they went hunting for ghosts. But there was also different accord of culture and time proposed. Delay is not the reception of the past that is outmoded or distant enough for its defamiliarizations to speak. Delay is not just a lapse of time but also describes the rhythm of art *vis-à-vis* life. The avant-garde is meant to come before—it precedes. In relation to it life is delayed—normal vision catches up with artistic insight. But from the start it was also the other way round. Art is delayed, limps behind the new visions forged in the crinkles of everyday life, manifest in new technologies, jostling for attention in print culture, coined in the mangle of polyglot languages in growing urban centres. Benjamin described it as the discovery of the extraordinary in the everyday.

According to Benjamin, it was Mallarmé who predicted the future of art, for he was one of the first to recognize the graphic nature of script, incorporating in his 1897 poem 'Un coup de dés' all of 'the graphic tensions of the advertisement'. Surrealism extended this. Likewise, even Dada's name may have been purloined from something visible in the Zurich urbanscape: Dada was the name of a hair lotion that was advertised in Swiss newspapers before the First World War. Its poster featured a strange little girl, like John Tenniel's Alice, with hair so thick it seemed unnatural and absurd. The poster proclaimed the wonders of Dada hair-and-scalp-strengthening headwater, which promised to improve on nature's efforts. Did it in turn take its name from the Yoruba word 'dada', meaning a girl with curly hair, intimating the commodity's acknowledgement in itself of what might be viewed as its 'pre-civilizational' other? In any case, Dada, the art movement, brought chips of actuality into the image world. It concentrated on rubbish, the scraps and worthless bits, that which had been thrown away, left to decay or fade. As such it was a form of recycling—to take just one example—like Duchamp's use of the Sapolin enamel ready-made altered to namecheck his friend Apollinaire.

It is not just delay that motivates a surreal sensibility—decay too plays a crucial and connected part in this. For example, inspired by surreal procedures, Benjamin uncovers things, impulses, matter and objects that have decayed. In his first forays in 1927 into the arcades, Benjamin follows the Surrealist procedure to the letter, montaging a pile-up of disparate industrially produced fragments, trash and parodies of natural form to be found inside the junk shops of the arcades. Benjamin lists the umbrellas and canes, with ocarinas for handles, the orthopaedic belts and bandages wound round the bellies of naked mannequins, frog-green and coral-red combs swimming 'as in an aquarium',

RECYCLING

balls of string and silk tangled up with stamps, trumpets like conches, birdseed lying in the fixative pans from a photographer's darkroom, the odalisque waiting by the inkwell. All this detritus waits for a new owner, new uses or is simply dust-gathering trash on display. The 'rags, the refuse', notes Benjamin, in a comment on his own methodology, is what is deployed. Waste comes into its own, here for philosophy and art. It comes to voice in an act of recycling and it tells histories of exhausted desires and the relentless march of consumption under the rule of capital. In his 1935 Exposé of his *Arcades Project* Benjamin writes that it was Balzac who first spoke of the ruins of the bourgeoisie, but it was Surrealism that first allowed its gaze to wander uninhibitedly across the field of rubble that the capitalist development of the productive forces had left in its wake. Balzac could see the ruination contained in that order—immanent to it—but it takes time and a liberated consciousness (or rather the awakened consciousness, which remembers the dream) to cash this out fully. In Benjamin's moment of writing, the 1930s, the ruins of past promises were visible, and even more devastation was to come. Delay commutes into decay and both make the flow of experience and the pile-up of objects accessible to social knowledge—a knowledge that the one thing most delayed is revolution in all states of affairs.

Marginal figures, outsider poets: they recycle detritus as lyric and it in turn becomes a critical commentary on what is valued and unvalued socially and economically. If recycling is a matter of sending things round again, of making a circuit of production–consumption–production, then those artists who imagined ways in which this could be accomplished outside established capitalist circuits perhaps provide an emblem of this in the wheel. The first found-object sculpture is commonly seen as Marcel Duchamp's 'Bicycle Wheel' from 1913. The found object, the ready-made, recycles the banal as art or as anti-art. In either case, a transformation is at work. And, as a possibly unintended by-product, monetary value is eventually squeezed from this re-spun object. Kurt Schwitters made the boldest attempts to recycle rubbish as art. In the fracturing into shards of scraps, such as wrappers, cogs, tickets, textured surfaces, and objects, such as feathers or netting or buttons, new meanings are won of mass-reproduced and found materials, including meanings that are purely aesthetic, to do with composition and rhythm, surface and line.

Schwitters knew of scraps, in many senses. Two of his extraordinary homes, or *Merzbauten*, were scrapped by circumstance, or at least 'unfinished out of principle', making them ultimately failed or incomplete works. Arguably, though, these were works, like Benjamin's methodologically scrappy *Arcades Project* perhaps, that were made never to be finished, that were rather reasons for living. Scraps were also the matter of Schwitters's collages and montages, and these were captured and re-directed in order to expand and extend the vocabularies of art. In 'The Aim of My Merz Art', written in 1938, in a period when the vocabularies of art were being decidedly truncated in his homeland, in the Degenerate Art touring exhibition, he stated that 'there does not appear to be a rule which prescribes that one can only make artworks from specific materials'. So rubbish from waste bins presented itself a fine enough material for the task of composition. Schwitters also treated his own work as scraps, as remouldable, as odds and ends. He recycled postcard versions of his own works, such as the more conventional *Still Life with Challice* or *The Pleasure Gallows* or *Revolving*. He turned them into collages for friends, obliterated partially by purloined bucolic scenes or other scraps. He scrapped his own image in promotional postcards too, merging himself Merzstyle with his creation Anna Blume, or with women's ready-to-wear clothing, or a wheel.

Schwitters used wheels in his work repeatedly. There is the 'Picture with the Turning Wheel' from 1920. The version of 'Arbeiterbild' (1919), printed in the June 1927 edition of the journal *Transition*, shows a wheel (which fell off or got recycled in another work). And in his English translation of his poem about Anna Blume 'Anna Blume has wheels'. The wheel turns. The wheel revolves. The wheel, in its act of revolution, might be a symbol of one. But revolutions are meant to change everything. Revolutions that fail—like the German one of 1919, which maybe finds its way in some form into 'Arbeiterbild', with its red worker word, its reference to strikes, its smashed up machine-like form—revolutions that fail, revolutions that fail to turn things over, simply spin on the spot, grinding things down, crushing, flattening out. Just such a 'revolution', which even called itself one, but was really, in all truthfulness, a mode of salvaging all that already existed in terms of the distribution of money and power, was made by the Nazis, and it led to the expulsion of Schwitters from Germany. As it called itself a revolution it had to filch some of the trappings of the revolution whose activists and achievements it sought to obliterate. To this end it borrowed too— in gruesomely parodic form—some of the tactics of the avant-garde that was its nemesis. This recycling was grim. Re-circulations: modernity's proposal for communal living and creativity returns cynically as *Gleichschaltung*, a suffocatingly mass society. Modern promises of technological liberation turn into techno-enslavement in the camps. And the realms of art and politics collapse in the worst ways: aestheticized politics of charismatic dictatorship and the politicized aesthetics of propaganda art.

Rubbish Theory Now

The city as a rubbish tip of ephemera, degradation and the thrown-away, in which artist-ragpickers might profitably rummage, endures—even if, as Ivan Chtcheglov put it in his *Formulary for a New Urbanism* of 1953, 'the poetry of the billboards lasted twenty years', and even, or especially, once waste and rubbish loom as ethico-political issues drummed into the consciousness of Mr and Mrs Everyman. Iain Sinclair, sometime haunter of Dalston's Waste Market, has navigated this trash heap for aesthetic and political purposes; alert, for example, in *London Orbital* (2002), to the corruption and scandal at London Waste Ltd in Edmonton, with its toxic ash used for road construction and breezeblocks for homes on new satellite estates. Over this book towers that waste-heap recycled as pleasure ground, the anti-Romantic Alp at Beckton. The film of the book, made with Chris Petit, repeated the strategy of thrusting rubbish, the discarded, the wasted, under the noses of its audience. This time, though, brought back to light is found film, including surveillance camera footage that was only made to be seen in the case of the exceptional, the accident. This is pure contingency. *London Orbital*, the film, rescues rubbish, forwarding it as the prime hunting ground of cultural significance, while simultaneously condemning it as perceptual landfill.

Certainly ours is an age of returns, a making do with ever more enervated replications. We move amongst the dead presented as the best there was and is. Che Guevara's stylized image, derived from Alberto Korda's photograph of 1960, re-returns as an icon of rebellion in the service of revolution and commercialism alike. But an image not so dissimilar, a black and white stylization of a photograph of the model Twiggy from 1967, appears on a recyclable tote bag issued by the global chain store Marks & Spencer in 2009. Past beauty is recycled as the desideratum of contemporary cool. We should make do with past splinters of beauty, because we are not worthy of new ones. Left to us is the task of making new beauty out of the old. Nicolas Bourriaud articulates the watchword of the age when he insists that the question posed by modernists—'what can we make that is new?'—needs to be replaced by the question 'how can we make do with what we have?'

Walter Benjamin some 70 years ago wrote of Charles Baudelaire as 'the lyric poet of high capitalism': his poetry sampled capitalist alienation and reification in the city, even as it battled to express these new experiences in older lyric forms. Baudelaire's various translations into English, or as Benjamin noted, German, have not always been able to account for that original context, composed as they have been in more complacent times, or under different aesthetic imperatives. But recently a respinning of Baudelaire seems to have scraped him up off the mean streets of Paris. His spleen is being vented once more on the hard pavements of a post-global ugly megalopolis such as London.

Sean Bonney found some Baudelaire poems—because these are also a part of the more or less tangible junk under which we buckle. He rendered a brace of them into vicious verse. His versions are compressed, the translation not faithful in any strict linguistic sense. They tear at language, at the French they mockingly translate and at the English into which they are conveyed. English is the global language and here it splurts out in new, urgent and socially communicative rhythms, a world away from the lyrical subjectivism of Baudelaire.

This is language damaged, language as damage, language as register of damage. Compare Edna St. Vincent Millay's and Bonney's versions of 'Reve parisien':

Hers:

> I woke; my mind was bright with flame;
> I saw the cheap and sordid hole
> I live in, and my cares all came
> Burrowing back into my soul.
> Brutally the twelve strokes of noon
> Against my naked ear were hurled;
> And a gray sky was drizzling down
> Upon this sad, lethargic world.

His:

> I live in shit
> MY needle life a
> bruteist clock—
> its always mid-day///
> the sky is rolling shadows
> all over the choking earth—

The sentiment is degraded, from 'cheap and sordid hole' to 'I live in shit'. 'MY needle life': drugs enter these homes as shitholes, drug dens, and this then diverts the metaphor into that of the drugs wearing off and the cares returning to the soul, or rather the body. The motifs that are embedded in Baudelaire in chains of words are placed directly—so the distancing reference to time the chiming clock with its funereal accents becomes simply a clock. The cluttered and languid language of Baudelaire—deployed then as revolt against speed-up, register of emergent temporalities—reduces to shock, the spluttered, paratactic mutterings of someone stranded after the new era, and hyped up on anger's energy. The experience is extended—it is always midday—not a singular poetic glimpse, but a universal, and so more horrible, more trapped. And the earth is no longer this passive thing, this melancholic object of contemplation, a poetic object; rather it is choking. The earth, which is our body, chokes for us and with us. It is another version of the old pathetic fallacy, but it is one that figures in a contemporary imagination of ecological crisis, as greenhouse gases choke it and us and the boulevard gives way to escalators and shopping malls.

The visual format of Bonney's Baudelaire poems is a part of its meaning. The lines trample over each other. They skew and clash on the page. Unpronounceable characters—brackets and commas, asterisks and carets—force their way in and some words are erased by typings over. The whole looks like a toppling pile of words, which cannot be easily read. This is a crucial part of an anti-writing, which

means a denial of poetry's complacency, just as Baudelaire in his day stretched lyric form to incorporate new contents and in so doing ruined, in a sense, poetry, in order to make it anew.

Bonney's poems realize Mallarmé's dreams for the future: graphic articulations, as nightmares, as excess signification in the landscape, the aural and oral pollution of official, political and commercial languages against which the fragments of underdog speech struggle to be heard. In life, Bonney declares poems through a megaphone at anti-war rallies. He chalks them on the ground. He performs them like someone spitting. One of Bonney's poems from 2003 is an assault on language and its capacity to lie. Bonney took a speech by Tony Blair delivered in Glasgow on 15 February 2003, just as the second Gulf War began, and shredded it literally, tearing and slashing the newspaper in which it was printed. The resulting poem defamiliarized language, exposing its politeness as vicious political violence. The words are mangled such that they can only be spat or shot out on the edge of comprehensibility, but traces of their ideological force, countered in an almost homeopathic act of debarbing, are still audible, if only because of the predictability of political rhetoric. The graphic nature of the poems impedes their easy reading, their untrammelled communicative ability, because their so obvious truths find it hard to make a passage into the world. Their visual and graphic form suggests something splattered on the pavement, words that rose up in advertising and avant-garde poetry smashed back down to the ground.

The charge inherent in found materials, re-contextualized ready-mades, is that they dislodge things from a context once made for them into a space of free play, of unbounded significance, connotation and, thus, re-personalization. Radical subjectivity is found in the abandoned because its abandonment means no one else has a stake in it. There is much junk still to hunt and gather, and not least the recalcitrant at the heart of the digital. As Sinclair's archaeologies of London and elsewhere indicate, junk engulfs us. Where it was once the tangible junk of flea markets that attracted the Surrealists, our age groans under digital junk. An abundant form of this is spam—email inboxes clog daily with offers of sex aids or loans. This unceasing data-waste, like the outmoded trash that attracted the Surrealists, becomes at least potentially interesting because it has a history, because it changes, and so tracks something other than its own useless (non)appeal: it is evidence of technological shift, of commercial adaptation, of social realities, and it proposes, quite unknown to itself, an aesthetic, a shock of montaged words, obscenity, coincidence, intimate appeal. There was a period—around 2004/5—when it came to us as if from people bearing the most extraordinary names: Unreservedly P. Niggardliness; Groundhog R. Cytology; Ellipse B. Queers; Doggiest J. Freethinker; Hydraulicking A. Sleazes, Chrysler Q. Dalmatian, and so on. All those randomly generated names proposed an imaginary population who were sending in the same period emails of randomly generated verbiage or cut-ups stolen from zombie computer hard drives or online texts. These linguistic concoctions, known as 'hash busters', were an effort to evade the anti-spam filters that incorporate Bayesian analysis techniques, which calculate the probability of an email being spam based on the message's contents—the more words that are not Viagra or loan the better. Is there a new beauty of words, now a silicon and electrical product belonging equally to everyone, to millions at a time? Is there a possible beauty in the 'infinite continuum of spewage', a phrase extracted from the commented code of an anti-spam filtering programme and cited in Finn Brunton's PhD, 'Spam in Action: Social Technology and Unintended Consequences'?

'Humans make history, but not under conditions of their own

choosing', observed Marx. It is a statement of making do in order to make anew. We make the new from what we have—that is simultaneously the revolutionary break and the revolutionary tradition. Take Joachim Schmid's photographs collected from the streets of Europe and Brazil for the past 25 years. They are recycled: Schmid's watchword is: 'No new photographs until the old ones have been used up.' These failures of representation are redoubled failures, for they often come with traces of decay: misprintings, footprints, tears. Schmid's conservation preserves damage and loss, finding beauty in both. The stories behind their distress will probably not be known, nor will the histories of those represented. More certain is the origin of Schmid's spliced faces—half-boy/half-girl, half-adult/half-child—made from a commercial photographer's abandoned archive —the negatives had been cut in two to prevent their re-use. The hybrids might well bear names like those made up by the junk mail spammers of 2005, Seaweed T. Mercurochrome, Immortalize R. Hypermarket or Ingratitude Q. Dustiness. These recyclings are not just signs that circulate and re-circulate, but self-transforming, consumable things that alter themselves and us in their re-settings. These failures of representation offer themselves for re-subjectification. Both Schmid and Bonney re-circulate the found, turning the errors and horrors to productive and re-subjectivized use. (Making do or reusing is not necessarily a vehicle for postmodern cynicism and data disorientation, as Bourriaud has claimed in his hymn to semionauts, voyagers in the realm of signs, all recombining, re-spinning, re-articulating, reshuffling in an aesthetics of re-programming, in the absence of the need for anything new. The point being that only the already valued—art—is re-spun.) In any case Schmid finds in the found a possibility of cathexis and presents it to us as such. Art encourages looking, and with that, the anticipation of finding. Like the collector in Benjamin's typology, an object, especially one that arrives unbidden, provides a site for a social dreaming that is, actually, historical archaeology. Art is the frame of an experience that is everywhere and in flow. Strategies might yet be developed to exploit the dispersed surrealism of everyday industrialized life.

Streets as Touchstone Still

Ben Wilson paints little acrylic paintings on discarded chewing gum that has been stamped into the pavement. His pictures are emblems of contemporary social life—some are declarations of love, some commemorate the absent or dead, some celebrate a gang or the bonds of friendship, others record memories or tokens of identity. Over a number of days or weeks, passers-by, from alcoholics to housewives to community police officers, are held up for a while, in order to involve

themselves in discussions and affective relations with the artist, who appears as a mad drunk, prostrate on the ground for hours on end, painting his miniatures, as city life rumbles around him. Passers-by propose their own images, or have their images' contours drawn out of them through long processes of conversation and enquiry. They contribute sketches, suggest colours, tussle with the artist over what could and should appear. They give their consent to be photographed, which produces, alongside the colourful micro-paintings, an archive of the London public in the first years of the twenty-first century.

Through this activity, which he has pursued for over five years, nearly every day, along the roads from Barnet to Central London, Wilson has challenged the seemingly exclusive rights of the commercial image-scape to decorate our environment. The images and their commissioning generate in micro-form a redistribution of the ability to participate in the system of patronage. Wilson has also contributed to a mapping of urban relations as they exist on the ground, has brought people and their affections to expression. And he has stepped over lines of property and perceived property. He has been assaulted once by young men, arrested twice, and beaten seriously by City of London police as they forcibly extracted DNA from him—though in painting a discarded item raised a few millimetres from the ground he had not committed the crime of which he was accused: criminal damage.

His is a politics probed by an art practice that tests its own possibility of being in the most exposed way. Wilson was involved in a court case brought by the Crown Prosecution Service. He was charged with obstruction in 2008, for he dallied in handing over his camera

when asked to do so by a policeman. His argument was that he had not completed and documented his commission and would be breaking the terms of the relationship with his patron. This little incident is part of a shift of power relations on London streets. It is significant that it happened in the City of London, where paranoia about terrorism is rife. But it is also a reflection of an attitude, reinforced by the police, that unlicensed—or unprofitable—activities in socially shared space are illegitimate or 'mad'. Only the waste remains for 'us'. Discarded waste recycled as intimate expression, as spot of delight. Nose to the ground. Nose to the grindstone. An image to recycle for 'our' urbanized futures.

Reading

Bellamy Foster, John, *Marx's Ecology: Materialism and Nature* (New York: Monthly Review Press, 2000).

Bellamy Foster, John, *The Ecological Revolution: Making Peace With the Planet* (New York: Monthly Review Press, 2009).

Benjamin, Walter, *Gesammelte Schriften*, Vol. IV.1 (Frankfurt/Main: Suhrkamp, 1982).

Benjamin, Walter, *The Arcades Project* (Cambridge, MA: Belknap Press, 1999).

Benjamin, Walter, *Selected Writings*, Vol. 4 (Cambridge, MA: Belknap Press, 2003).

Bonney, Sean, *Baudelaire in English* (London: Veer Books, 2008) (also at http://www.onedit.net/issue8/seanb/seanb.html).

Bourriaud, Nicolas, *Postproduction* (New York: Lukas and Sternberg, 2002).

Gladstone, David, *Setting the Agenda: Edwin Chadwick and Nineteenth-Century Reform* (London: Routledge, 1997).

Chtcheglov, Ivan, 'Formulary for a New Urbanism', in *The Situationist International Anthology*, ed. Ken Knabb (London: Bureau of Public Secrets, 2004).

Cromwell, Thomas, James Sargant Storer and Henry Sargant Storer, *Walks Through Islington: comprising an historical and descriptive account of that extensive and important district, both in its ancient and present state: together with some particulars of the most remarkable objects immediately adjacent* (London: Sherwood, Gilbert & Piper, 1835).

Dickens, Charles, *Our Mutual Friend*, ed. Adrian Poole (Harmondsworth: Penguin, 1971).

Horne, R. H., 'Dust; or Ugliness Redeemed', in *The Victorian Novelist: Social Problems and Social Change*, ed. Kate Flint (New York: Croom Helm, 1987): 223–6.

Joyce, James, *Ulysses* (London: The Bodley Head, 1960).

Liebig, Justus von, *Letters on the Subject of the Utilization of the Municipal Sewage* (London: W. H. Collingridge, 1865).

Marx, Karl, *Herr Vogt* (London: New Park Publications, 1982).

Marx, Karl, *Capital*, Vol. 3, in *The Collected Works of Marx and Engels*, Vol. 37 (London: Lawrence & Wishart, 1998).

Mayhew, Henry, *London Labour and the London Poor*, Vol. 2 (New York: Dover Publications, 1968).

Schwitters, Kurt, *Das Literarische Werk*, 5 Vols. (Cologne: DuMont Buchverlag, 2004).

Sinclair, Iain, *London Orbital: A Walk Around the M25* (London: Granta, 2002).

Trotter, David, *Cooking With Mud: The Idea of Mess in Nineteenth-Century Art and Fiction* (Oxford: Oxford University Press, 2000).

Sickening

Iain Sinclair

My general theory since 1971 has been that the Word is literally a Virus, and that it has not been recognised as such...

William S. Burroughs

Now Wash Your Hands, Please

Break out those pig masks (the ones that make everybody look like a Halloween Richard Nixon). Slaughter chickens in their hell-sheds (they're dead anyway). Cull cattle. A soup of particulates chokes the atmosphere of the Viral City. Smouldering landfill dunes, out by the airport, slither into sludge-coloured costive rivers that steam and pop with noxious gasses. Tributaries, choked with fast-breeding starflower scum, shape the broken border of the latest Grand Project: DIY stadia, hangar-malls with cliff walls smooth as fake ice, hollow retail glaciers.

Break out the parentheses, so that Vir(tu)al becomes Viral. Swallow that grunge, the lived-through oral history of ground and people, and the Virtual, condescendingly, patronisingly, gives the French kiss to future colonies floated outside history. In Virtual World everybody, no matter what their ethnic origin, smiles like a Moonie. Honorary Aryans in smart-casual leisurewear processing through planted-this-morning embankments and flowery meadows towards the threatened Great Event. There is no disease here, no discord. Among the serene generic towers of the Sponsored Estate, the viral quest for a host with blood in the veins is hopeless. All the *Midwich Cuckoos* have come home to roost. Viral City is a set: hotels, perimeter fences, triumphalist monuments. Turn a corner in Dublin and you emerge at Checkpoint Charlie, the Wall built across cobbles for the opening sequence of Martin Ritt's film version of *The Spy Who Came in From the Cold* (1965). Taken down and disassembled, the sinister guardhouse reappears as Ireland's first school for the children of travellers.

When anywhere is everywhere, only the familiar is familiar. If you can't find the postcard, you haven't arrived. Berlin's Sony Center in the Potsdamer Platz is the centre of itself, not of a district or a city. Retail centres are a manifestation of the outer ring, the former suburbs. But this Center, capitalized, does hold. That's what it's about: containment. Roof not sky. Outside tables for alfresco dining are *inside* the tent, the dome. Overhead screens play extracts from multiple-choice (no choice) industrial products, movies you don't need to see: thirst irritants, popcorn bucket stimulae.

William Burroughs, ambassador from a distant insect galaxy, laid the script out, years ago, code extracted from cut-up newsprint, T. S. Eliot, Joseph Conrad and Mayan codices:

> *Woke up sick and went across the river.*
> *Children screamed at me in the street: 'Vicioso'.*
> *Boys hung out in a bar called the Bounty where I once shot a mouse with*
> *a .22 pistol.*
> *Next set is Mexico City.*

He's right, the next set is due when everywhere is Mexico City: an infinitely extended urban organism, El Monstruo, unreadable even from the tallest vanity-project glass shard south of the Tropic of Cancer. Collect your oxygen masks at the airport. Roll back your sleeve for the business-class anti-prole shot with vitamin chaser, delivered by the glamorous hostess in Cardin uniform. Tapering towers are choked in a scarf of exhaust fumes, expectorated spray, refried beans, black cigars, mariachi migraines; they shudder, but do not crumble as tectonic plates collide in jitterbug frenzy. Out by the orbital motorway, the one linking London to Leipzig, Berlin to Beijing, you can hear, above the muted acoustic footprints, the humanoid screams of swine penned for slaughter. Fast food in no hurry to collaborate. They have a pig city in the Perote Valley on the Veracruz–Puebla border; a subsidiary, so the embedded poet/ activist John Ross tells us, 'of the U.S. hog-killer Smithfield Farms'. These boys, basing their ecological etiquette on cursory downloads from *The Naked Lunch*, were 'heavily fined for contaminating Virginia and North Carolina water sources'. Mexico offered a safe haven from environmental enforcement. Neo-liberal titans of the first world ensure, with blockbuster movies soft-selling apocalypse, that shit happens somewhere else. So we all feel bad about it. And good about them, the spotless presenters with the expensive mouths.

World City is a fold-out Len Deighton novel of the middle period, when he was writing straight television, soapy plotting plus nuggets of prime research dumped into contrived, booze-soaked midnight dialogues. Dummy characters, lightly ventriloquized, are computer-generated aliens from an Olympic pitch yet to be made. The covert apparatus of the state has only one purpose, to act as a travel agent, supplying complimentary tickets to Berlin-Tegel, Mexico City, Lisbon, Paris, Prague. Along with false passport, spending money and non-metallic weapon that doesn't show up on the X-ray scan. Eat, drink, wreck the hire car: move on. The man sitting next to you on the plane is grazing the airport thriller in which you appear. It's a world of cardboard mirrors.

In the dining room of an inn, convenient for the autobahn, convenient for the border, the generic Deighton character contemplates the fake log fire, the polished brass. *I felt at home there because I'd found the same bogus interior everywhere from Dublin to Warsaw and a thousand places in between, with unashamed copies in Tokyo and Los Angeles.*

The selling point about orbital motorways, as you discover when it's too late, is that they don't lead anywhere you want to go: they connect with other orbital motorways. Virtual World is a cat's cradle of reductive repetitions. Stuck in the loop of tedium, landscape particulars masked by earthworks and tactful screenings of tough trees, being on the road is a state of mind, not a political state. Drivers are absorbed into collective reverie, high on fumes, travel sick from junk food eaten too fast to jaunty punishment muzak. Completed orbits become the manacle shadows of the Olympic rings as projected onto the stone flags at the Osttor approach to Werner March's 1936 Nazi stadium. It was Deighton who pointed out that British Intelligence ran their operations in Berlin from that address. *When Frank said 'the office' he meant the stadium that Hitler had built.*

Remember those grave swine flu warnings of summer 2009? One hundred thousand victims, signed up for full viral participation, by August: *one hundred thousand a day.* And rising. This is a well-established politico-medical propaganda technique. Hit them with a worst-case scenario, a flash-frame from the *Revelation of St John,* and whatever actually comes along won't look so bad. The Goebbels-influenced spinmasters of New Labour, adept at burying bad news, arranged an elegant equation between the proliferation of third-world bugs bringing fever-sweats and unkind death to the elderly and infirm, to pregnant women in their third trimester, to innocent schoolchildren returning from foreign holidays, and the steepling curve of mortality statistics from the warfront in Afghanistan. The stock-market plunges, property prices collapse, cases of swine flu crampon deliriously up the charts. The brand is Orwellian: would you want to pick up a socially transmitted disease from a pig? A *Mexican* pig? A shit-eating, garlic-chewing, fifty-to-a-room pig from the barrio? Gordon Brown, prime suspect, in his increasingly manic and lockjawed exposures to the media, has started to look like a banker wrestling swine flu and losing. But still carrying on, kept upright by the stiffness of his committee-designed suit. And the applause of the crowd that only he can hear.

John Ross, a specialist on 'dread and redemption in Mexico City', pointed out that bog-standard flu kept the population in check, by culling ten thousand of the weaker brethren every year. But this new brand was promiscuous, offering love-bites to teenagers, underagers and fighting-fit visitors checking in to safe hotels. President Felipe Calderón, concerned about US tourism, kept the bad word in-house for as long as possible. He had unwinnable drug wars to pursue, sex-crime victims stacking up so fast and so visibly, along the perimeter fences and wastelots of factory towns, that they formed a major element in the novels of the latest South American literary sensation, Roberto Bolaño. And, worse than this, six-foot-plus of Barack Obama was due in town to inspect the Anthropology Museum. The pristine yanqui president was escorted through the excavated glass skulls and feathered serpents by Dr Felipe Solís: who died a week later from 'flu-like symptoms'. One of the spooks-in-shades from Obama's entourage, so Ross reports, returned home with porcine symptoms. Citizens were advised to stand six feet apart when holding street conversations. Masked prostitutes refused to exchange oral fluids with clients.

However, the usually jam-packed Metro, a logical incubator of contagion, remained open—it was joked that you could get a seat if you blew forcefully into a wad of Kleenex while munching on a handful of chicharrones *(fried pork rinds).*

The viral element was not the swine flu but the media panic, the way shock-horror headlines multiply and reproduce themselves. Rumour cannibalizes rumour. Roche, the Swiss pharmaceutical giant, went into overdrive on the production line: Tamiflu may sound girly, homeopathic, beige-pink, but it works. Even when it's as unnecessary as the monograms on Roger Federer's racket case, on his tailored white blazer. (Do they have swine flu in Switzerland? I'm sure that spare viruses are stored in secure bank vaults against the threat of future invasion by peasant nations.) The more feverish the newspaper panic, the faster units fly from the shelf. Tamiflu tabs are the silver bullets of the global pandemic that never quite was.

Alfred Döblin, in his stupendous 1929 novel, *Berlin Alexanderplatz*, makes much of the status of slaughterhouses. Doomy biblical prophecies, war hymns, newspaper headlines and cattle-killing statistics underwrite the psychosis of a vibrant and fast-moving metropolis. Citizens are too busy hustling the next drink to brood on viral infections. Herds are put to the knife. Patched-up veterans, communists and fascists, gnaw on trotters, grease dripping from military moustaches into steins of beer.

They told me in Berlin, when I set out to walk the city, that foxes made their homes in the basements of undemolished Nazi ministries. That stoats occupied cars parked for more than one night in the same place. They gnawed wires, pissed acid on leather. Wolves, coming out of the forest, roamed the suburbs. Wild boars mated with domesticated pigs in edgeland allotments. Allotment shacks were the only sort of private property comrades were allowed to own in the former East Germany.

When the horror was unavoidable, the Mexican authorities issued blue surgical facemasks called *tapabocas*, useless as a preventative (unless replaced every few hours), but striking as a science-fiction effect. Mask-wearers in the business districts resemble extras looking for an enervated Stanley Kubrick orgy, left over from *Eyes Wide Shut* (1999). Londoners didn't bother. They commuted, not having much choice, in their viral torpedoes: coughing, spluttering, wired to Nuremberg headsets and implant earpieces. The middle classes, obedient to celebrity mayors and spivvish Etonian politicians, don masks to cycle through mayhem. Bodypart donors in branded lycra. Some of them disaster manage by cushioning the inevitable impact of flesh on metal with infants, kitted out in hard-shell kiddie helmets, fore and aft. Traffic junctions, where east–west tributaries run straight across major north–south routes, are marked by ghost bicycles, wired to the fence. Flowers in the spokes, handwritten memorials.

Tramping down an ancient greenway, mesh-fence dressed with bindweed, surveillance cameras and agitated plastic ribbons, I advanced on Manchester Airport. It was the eve of the Champions' League Final in Rome. And the flow was outward. The various terminals, when I explored them, were deserted inconvenience stores, offering the sensation of being trapped beneath the Old Street roundabout. Waiting for my connection with the coach heading back to the Premier Inn circuit, I spotted the first demonstration of surgical masks in the north of England. Emerging from the terminal building, marching in step, were a group of Koreans who had flown to Manchester to pay homage to their ineffective, battery-driven compatriot, the winger Park Ji-Sung. Rather than witness inevitable humiliation at the feet of

Barcelona, they would visit the club shop at Old Trafford. Then photograph themselves, draped in new shirts, flags, caps, beneath the statue of that mythical three-headed beast, CharltonLawBest.

Gauze masks gleam in the airport twilight: as if huge Mancunian moths had settled across their screaming faces. With no other travellers on the coach, the driver detoured to drop me off at his favourite Italian restaurant. I dined, accompanied by Dean Martin, under a photograph of the ruined Colosseum.

When my wife asked, next morning, if I could feel a stiffness in the shoulder, a tightness in the neck, I denied it. Without a moment's hesitation. I'm fine. It's a bright morning and we're going to walk across an unknown city, from the latest urban vanity project at the revamped centre, over canals, through retail parks, railway lines and rivers, to the airport fringe. But my wife's suggestion has lodged itself in my consciousness. A viral parasite. Rupert Sheldrake was on to something with his morphic resonance thesis: one person feels a twinge, mentions it, and their partner suffers the same ache before the day is out. There are disease fashions promoted by the media, sponsored by pharmaceutical enterprises who have staked out liminal territory with convenient access to orbital motorways, alongside secure research establishments that don't register on Ordnance Survey maps. The virus is a fad. Don't read about it and it doesn't work. Those nifty surgical masks are covering the wrong half of your face. Keep the blindfold secure: Zorro without the peepholes. Not the bandana across the mouth like a road agent from a Hopalong Cassidy programmer.

And don't touch those tabloids! 'Men are pigs, darling', oinks Michael Winner, prime-cut interview subject, from his ballroom-size solo bedroom.

Two years ago, he caught a rare virus that nearly finished him off ... He caught the virus after eating an oyster at the five-star Sandy Lane hotel in Barbados ... He almost had his left leg amputated and now he is quite frail, physically, at least half the man he was. His hands shake and he can no longer drink as he has cirrhosis of the liver.

There are a lot of folk hobbling about with legs that were almost amputated. Once you have grazed the Winner interview, you start to experience pins and needles below the knee. Certain geographical locations, by morphic resonance transmitted through weather forecasts on local TV, laminated menus in fast-food franchises, incubate viral clusters. Michael Moorcock, the London laureate, exiled to Bastrop, Texas, remarked, early on, that he'd witnessed healthy folk running about doing communal things, putting up barns, organizing square dances or lynchings, and then seen them again, a year later, in wheelchairs, on crutches. It's the nature of the place. Trying out a new pair of cowboy boots at a line dance, Moorcock developed blisters ambitious of becoming a serious wound. The skin never healed. This is called the Bastrop syndrome: a place where specialist, backwoods viruses hang out like yokels in *Straw Dogs* waiting for another incomer to spook with their gothic yarns and nasty habits.

There is a nice traffic photograph in *The Dialectics of Seeing: Walter Benjamin and the Arcades Project*, a 1991 assembly by Susan Buck-Morss. A high-angle streetscape. Tree-lined boulevards zeroing in towards a stalled whirlpool of urban nuisance. Viral forms trapped on a petri dish. Cars face all directions, toys laid out by the hand of a bored child. None of the momentum by which metropolitan life is characterized is present. The image is forensic. The idealized traffic island, pumping like a heart, is hopelessly inadequate. The more veins and arteries you open up, the larger the clot. Focus in this anonymous street portrait is sharper, but you can contrast the impression of bug-like cars with Yoshiro Kawaoka's plate, from the University of Wisconsin-Madison, displayed in the *New York Times* as an illustration of the swine flu virus: 'seen as elongated strands'.

Viral traffic is heavy. 'Getting a jump on the next outbreak', boasts the sub-editor. With no relief from the business pages: 'For smartphones, a virus-free ride (mostly)'. Burroughs would have made something of the random conjunction. Like J. G. Ballard, he spent time as a medical student and never lost his taste for a whiff of formaldehyde in the morning.

An odd feature of the new virus is the lack of fever in a significant portion of documented cases.

Lab technicians sift warm stools, freshly delivered and still steaming on the plate, to determine how often the virus is present. The decent, old-fashioned literary viruses you appreciate in Conrad, Robert Louis Stevenson and Burroughs are malarial and recurrent. They boil the blood. And from nightsweats and convulsions come vision: *The Strange Case of Dr Jekyll and Mr Hyde* (1886), *Heart of Darkness* (1899), *Cities of the Red Night* (1981). HEAT. Without fever, swine flu lacks artistic merit. It's just another gridlocked junction in an autopsy studio. The flash from a traffic-monitoring junction box converting a speed violation into a metaphor of the body in crisis.

Quacks in Epsom, that quintessential English town where half the population once lodged in asylums, proposed the interesting notion that malaria might work as a cure for schizophrenia, narcolepsy, catatonic depression.

Malarial fever, when it has passed, helps sufferers from 'general paralysis' to recover their sanity... Malaria is supposed to kill the spirochetes: in the way that decapitation could be said to cure the common cold. Malarial therapy was developed in Germany. In England, experiments were conducted in the Epsom hospital colony, at Claybury and Horton. The laboratory at Horton became the leading mosquito-breeding centre in the British Isles. Seventy per cent of those treated survived. Three out of every ten died.

The Wall comes down, there is no distinction between hard science and junk fiction; somnambulists jerking through cake-walk trances, zombie jazzers and computer-generated predictions of death wards in privatized hospitals. All of this stuff is fed, indiscriminately, into YouTube, into pirate websites: as viral hooks for invisible product.

MEXICAN SWINE FLU HAS REACHED LONDON.

MAYOR MEETS WITH HEALTH AND KEY PUBLIC SERVICES TO DISCUSS SWINE FLU. THE MAYOR SAID: 'I'D LIKE TO THANK THE POLICE, FIREFIGHTERS, TRANSPORT WORKERS... TfL ARE CONFIDENT THEY WILL BE ABLE TO KEEP SERVICES RUNNING.'

CITY IN GRIP OF VIRAL SCOURGE. THERE'S NO MORE DENYING IT, H1N1 IS ENTRENCHED IN THE CITY.

ANTI-CASTRO TERRORISTS (CIA) INTRODUCED AFRICAN SWINE FEVER VIRUS INTO CUBA IN 1971. THE

U.S INTELLIGENCE SOURCE SAID THAT EARLY IN 1971 HE WAS GIVEN THE VIRUS IN A SEALED, UNMARKED CONTAINER AT FORT GULICK, AN ARMY BASE IN THE PANAMA CANAL ZONE. THE CIA ALSO OPERATES A PARA-MILITARY TRAINING CENTRE FOR CAREER PERSONNEL AND MERCENARIES AT FORT GULICK.

THE CONTAINER THEN WAS GIVEN TO A PERSON IN THE CANAL ZONE, WHO TOOK IT BY BOAT AND TURNED IT OVER TO PERSONS ABOARD A FISHING TRAWLER OFF THE PANAMANIAN COAST. THE SOURCE SAID THE SUB-STANCE WAS NOT IDENTIFIED TO HIM UNTIL MONTHS AFTER THE OUTBREAK IN CUBA. HE WOULD ELABORATE NO FURTHER.

So who made the viral introduction in England? John le Carré. 1979. Year of Margaret Thatcher's accession: the acceptable face of pestilence. *Tinker, Tailor, Soldier, Spy* (1974) was adapted for television by Arthur Hopcraft and directed, with measured precision, by John Irvin. Quality, the commissioners decided—enough budget for a minor government department—would be demonstrated in these films by a species of leisurely travelogue: Paris, Berlin, Bern. Sepulchral end credits showcasing an honour roll of British character actors, sub-nobility, with churchy trilling by boy soprano and limestone Oxford backdrop (anticipating the Morse franchise). Alec Guinness could take an eternity to remove his spectacles. (The Smiley part might have gone, without le Carré's veto, to Arthur Lowe.)

Now with the advent of DVD we can freeze the action to isolate the hidden signifiers. Peter Guillam, interpreted (this time) by Michael Jayston, has been brought before the wise men of the Circus to be interrogated over sightings of a rogue agent, Ricki Tarr (skittishly embodied, eyelashes and fat lips, by Hywel Bennett). Michael Aldridge, vigorously pipe-semaphoring, pronounces the man a 'defec-tor'.

'But why is it all so hot?' Guillam protests. 'What kind of a plant can he be, when we know everything about him, down to his last attack of swine fever. From which he's only partly recovered, in my opinion.'

Fever. Flu. Establishment spooks and mandarin cuckolds. A virus in service of the class war. Lower ranks too feeble to throw off infection. Despite his Wyndham Lewis surname, the wretched Ricki lives down to his blowdried christian name. While a Russian agent, impersonated in high tweed-jacket camp by Ian Richardson, does his best to look like Sir Anthony Blunt. The pig was well and truly out of sty. And over the wall of *Animal Farm*. Into the culture at large. By the turn of the millennium, porky trans-species aliens would be preying on hitchhikers, on lonely Scottish roads. See *Under the Skin* (2000) by Michael Faber.

Three days later, Isserley woke from a dream of sexual release, clutching fur in her fists.

El Hombre Invisible

Tall, gaunt, high-shouldered inside a slept-in white suit, William Burroughs was always the dishonoured consul, the struck-off doctor in the saloon: the premature Mexican. He was John Huston's awkward cameo from *The Treasure of the Sierra Madre* (1948) returned, on a loop, to the life of the streets. *El Hombre Invisible.* He walked briskly, tourist camera dangling on a strap, sunlight glinting from mean spectacles. And he evolved a technique, based on what he'd been taught by an old Mafia Don in Columbus, for staying out of shot. He saw you first. He logged your position. He read what passed for your thoughts.

The Word is literally a Virus.

And a sponge-brained regiment of pigs in suits are nudging us closer to the precipice every day.

By 1953, in *Niagara*, a Henry Hathaway film that looks better every time I see it, the war-damaged and psychotic Joseph Cotten, pushed over the edge by his wife's teasing availability, the orgasmic rush of the falls, the bells the bells, launches into a furious monologue of denunciation. Killing is kindness. The world is populated by swine.

Hunter S. Thompson, on a retainer from *Rolling Stone*, would line up his cigarette-holder, shoulder the magnum, and pound the keys like a crazy ape. The white Masonic temples of Washington, he asserts, are nothing more than a sty for Nixon, his bagmen, plumbers and wiretappers. American politicians of every stripe are 'a generation of swine'. So exit gracefully by the Hemingway route.

I decided, early on, that there was a viral lineage of writers who knew what writing was. And what it cost. They would recognize each other, but there was absolutely no requirement to get along. Burroughs endured what he described as a 'half-hour consultation' with a preoccupied Samuel Beckett. A duplex, stripped of furniture, overlooking the Tiergarten in Berlin. No drinks were offered, the Irishman was otherwise polite. 'It was apparent', Burroughs said, 'that he had not the slightest interest in any of us, nor the slightest desire to ever see any of us again.'

Ballard, reviewing *The Adding Machine* (1985), describes how Burroughs spent a lifetime 'probing some of the most feverish pulse-spots in the western world'. Medical metaphors establish common ground between two men who appreciated but never truly understood the nature of their rival's strength. Burroughs, Ballard concluded, was 'a demented neurosurgeon inside his patient's nightmares'.

When the hard-pressed gentleman junkie took up residence in London, first at the Empress Hotel in Lillie Road, and then in a featureless St James's flat, it changed English culture. It was a moment like that famous description of Lenin, returning to Russia in a sealed railway compartment: a germ, a lethal bacillus.

Pushing his viral project, Burroughs hit the streets, with tape-recorder and camera, cutting and scrambling reality; revenging himself on tradesmen who slighted him. A frothy-coffee bar, the Halifax on Frith Street, closed down, bereft of clients, in October 1972, after Burroughs played back random incidents from elsewhere. He switched soundtracks on *The Man from U.N.C.L.E.* serials. He mused on methods for editing archive to provoke riots in the street. He understood that news is written before it happens. If you want to track swine flu back to source, play Russian roulette with '70s television. Loop language. Slice image. Go Mexican.

Near the bottom of the tar pit, even before he shot his wife, Burroughs was transfixed by the memory, an engram or blockage according to Scientologists, of a horrible Mexican weekend. A bunch of wedding guests, 'elevator-shoe drunks', shooting cats with hand-guns in a locked room.

The Word is literally a virus ... It has achieved a state of relatively stable symbiosis with its human host; that is to say, the Word Virus (the Other Half) has established itself so firmly as an accepted part of the human organism that it can now sneer at gangster viruses like smallpox and turn them in to the Pasteur Institute. But the Word clearly bears the single identifying feature of virus: it is an organism with no internal function other than to replicate itself.

Burroughs believed that, by 1945, we had developed, in biological warfare facilities in England, 'the doomsday bug which was a mutated virus produced by exposing such viruses as hepatitis and rabies to radiation'. My explorations, out along London's orbital motorway, would seem to confirm this. On Dartford Marshes, in a fever hospital, about to be closed down for one of New Labour's flagship disasters, I interview a retired doctor with an interest in local history. After a tour of the wards, the airing courts, the overgrown rail tracks down to the Thames, where the cholera ships anchored, he led me to a hidden burial ground. His greatest fear, he said, far beyond the stupidity of the hospital closures and vanity projects, was viral.

'Do you know that smallpox cultures have been stored in Russia and America? Total insanity. If you don't kill them, they'll kill you. One day they *will* get out. They'll be sold to any fanatic with spare change, the highest bidder. Bio-terrorism is an inevitability.'

This is where we came in, I thought. This is the script my father, a GP, suggested when I was struggling for the synopsis required for my entry to film school. The smallpox culture, so easy to transport, in a plane coming in to Heathrow.

They bought it. I moved to Brixton in 1961. It took another 39 years to get the film made. With Chris Petit, I stood beneath the flight path, under the roar of engines, babbling apocalypse. The film was called *Asylum*. Its opening proposition has the word virus devouring archive. Year Zero + 14.

A virus had been created in the protein soup of bad television with the sole aim of destroying its own memory, the last cultural traces.

Skin Rose

Hackwork is viral. Mainstream culture spits out product on the Xerox principle: only the copy of the copy of the copy is sufficiently familiar to achieve success. Take any maximum visibility airport artefact by Dan Brown, or whoever, and you can follow it backwards, step by step, through moderate recognition, *succès d'estime*, cult status, to proper obscurity: the mad-eyed intransigent in the attic. The stapled pamphlet. The green-ink notebook. Weirdness comes out in the wash. With each improved version (*hommage*, pastiche, rip-off), textual debris smoothes into silky tarmac. Originality is overrated. In the Virtual City we start with the remake.

Viral news is not news, it's newsprint. It's caffeine-twitch, telephone nuisance, internet flak. In the partitioned corner of some open-plan office, researchers and producers fillet broadsheets for sanctioned rumours, which have themselves been assembled from wire services, spook propaganda. Media reflects media: a membrane between the virtual and the actual. Viral strands form a noose, the same voices dub themselves, croaking their riffs while clipboard spinners wave or mime throat-cutting behind glass. Political basket-cases are dusted down for TV, red lips on corpse pallor. Interrogators are impatient. Radio is a speaking clock: *tick tick tick*. Time signals interrupted by horror stories, bomb outrages, football capitalism, box-ticking reports from rat holes exclusive to journalists.

It was a rare afternoon without appointments and I was working on a Berlin piece against a three-day deadline. Before I could start on this swine flu improvisation (two weeks' grace). Before I could travel to what turned out to be a Christian Revivalist Festival on a racecourse in Cheltenham. Before I could get back to the hobbled draft of a book that should have been delivered months ago.

The phone.

Had I seen an item in the paper about a projected high-speed rail service, London to Glasgow, in a couple of hours or so? Would I pass a few remarks, on radio, about what would be lost? Nothing heavy. The authentic sense of distance travelled, difficulties, delays, topographic shifts witnessed, cultural contours respected. Would I come in to the studio and do it right now?

There is a residual politeness, or vanity, imprinted in my DNA: if invited to take part, you oblige. A neurosis: turn it down and you'll never be asked again. 'Work up a nice routine', the man said. 'But don't bust a gut. You'll get a sentence. Two minutes tops.' So you ask for a car. It's too late now to walk. Notes can be written on the journey.

The car doesn't arrive. Searching the area, admittedly a complicated nexus of Victorian squares and recent estates, I find the driver, parked mid-road, riffling through the *London A to Z*, with the aspect of a man who thinks the book is trying to put one over on him. I open the door and climb in. He's not interested in my version of where my house stands. It must have been moved. It's in the wrong place.

Too put it bluntly, the car's a wreck. The driver is a pirate, a hot-seat stand-in. An accidental psychogeographer. He's navigating Old Street with a map of Lagos. Cemeteries of sleeping policemen, in Hackney and Islington, are a trial to the ruined suspension. The radio isn't doing radio, it's locked to a messianic channel, god stuff. We arrive at the wrong studio. I'm given a map, banished into a tangle of dead-ends and unpromising cul-de-sacs. I make it, panting, with minutes to spare: a solo cubicle. Where, clamped to headphones, talking to myself, I manage a brief and inconsequential conversation with a man I've never met.

Recovering my equilibrium at home, suffering flashbacks from a journey I had no good reason to make, I notice the itch. It's as if every incident glimpsed from the car window has turned into an angry mosquito bite. My exposed arms, wrist to elbow, are mirror images of scratch-soliciting aggravation. In Dublin many of the outlying cinemas lived up to their reputation as fleapits; it was an automatic gesture, on settling into the coarse seat for a mutilated Sam Fuller, the invigorating widescreen landscape of an Anthony Mann Western, to tuck trousers into socks. Fleas blood-sucked promiscuously: ankles, neck, belly, groin. They chased heat, a temperature of response to the emotional rollercoaster of the Hollywood drama. In O'Connell Street picture palaces with chipped-glitz pretensions, men in uniform walked the aisles, before matinees, pumping a perfumed spray from giant weed-killer syringes. The dull eros of disinfectant and Sweet Afton fug is a sexual trigger for Dubliners of a certain age.

An invisible creature from the radio car was soldering my veins, weals were already as prominent as churches on a painted map of the medieval city. Guilt about my unnecessary rides—in from Hackney and back again—took the form of a primitive sat-nav system burnt into my skin. Left arm, inward. Right arm, out. The precision was remarkable. The deeper my nails tore into the zones of irritation, the more lurid the picture. But there was no fever. My parasites never ventured a centimetre beyond their allocated territory, the raised blood highway. If I went back to Truman's brewery in Brick Lane now, and they checked my arms for needle tracks, as they did in 1972, before taking me on as a plumber's mate, I wouldn't have a hope. Blacklisted pariah junkie. A scalding bath, intended to kill off the creepy invaders, made the pattern glow: the moist pink of a dying rose going brittle and brown in the froth of the outer petticoat.

Neither did the map fade. Ten days on and the bites evolved into clusters. I was tattooed with a town plan of my own *Rose-Red Empire*. Burroughs was right, the word is a virus. Antihistamine cream varnished the portrait, the weals thrived on it. Analeptic recipes acted like lip-gloss on my inflamed skin chart. Steroid solutions fed the bumps and turned them into mounds. I would wake three times in the night, tormented, hearing the chomp of tiny molars as the unseen beasts chewed away: *on the inside*.

I hadn't been near a doctor in 40 years and a few insect bites seemed like a feeble reason to break the habit, but my tossing and turning, the sandpaper scrape of nails on flesh, was driving my wife mad. The surgery on the new estate was clean and efficient. An interpreter was giving her unpatronizing attention to an elderly Polish gentleman. The doctor, mildly intrigued by the persistence, the territorial specificity of my tormentors, offered a prescription for unguents I had already tried. And then she booked me to give a talk to her students, trainee GPs, about the peculiarities of Hackney, its lost hospitals and submerged history.

The solution was the English Channel, late season, a gentle swim before breakfast. I emerged from the brine like an Old Testament leper from the Jordan: white as snow. The trail of bites had washed off, like cheap Aztec-skull transfers (commodities in which this Sussex town specialized). And, with them, the memory of the courtesy car ride, that London street script was erased. The sea has its own concerns, its rhythms. It is unimpressed by trespassing humans. Walks through cities imprint viral specifics, swims dissolve them. I checked the quotes that I'd torn out of an American newspaper in Berlin. And kept for future use.

Mexican doctors found the swine influenza virus on the hands of workers, on tables next to patients' beds, on other hard surfaces and on a computer mouse.

It has been great using smartphones as de facto computers. You don't have to buy anti-virus software, or worry that devices will go haywire every time some Ukrainian crime ring finds a new way to steal data from the cloud.

The black hats taking aim at phones have already found their targets.

There are no hard surfaces off-shore, sky curves into sea. Women on the promenade mistake the dark-slick of cloud shadows for France. The virus frisking on the fat of your computer mouse infiltrates the internet like one of le Carré's burnt-out cases. Virtual plagues solicit human hosts. New technologies facilitate the transfer. So many tourists down here are worrying at the temporal membrane by holding their image-catching smartphones aloft, to fix an episode of sunset over Beachy Head, the skeleton of the abandoned pier. They collect sets in which to project memories of events that never happened.

Later that day I met the (current) film-essayist Chris Petit to collect a VHS copy of *Flight to Berlin* (1983), his first German feature. The script, he told me, had been intended for Paris but economic circumstances required a last-minute move to the east. It made no real difference, the Viral City was everywhere and nowhere. He regretted a sequence he planned to shoot, preparations for a rock concert in the

Olympic Stadium. But in the end it didn't matter, unrealized dramas make locations more poignant. The new piece he had recently completed (or abandoned) was called *Content*: to underline the fact that there wasn't any. The journey was endless, beginning in mild depression and looping back, never concluding, in managed despair. An accidental and exemplary poetic derived from the belief that what happens happens. Keep the camera running, fix the music. Pass the baton to the child in the back seat. *Alice in the Cities* (1974).

Petit was unshorn, silver-bearded: well on the sane side of later-day Howard Hughes. It was a warm autumnal afternoon and he was wearing a heavy corduroy jacket. Post-production, and even in the editing suite, interrogating hours of drift footage, he suffered from recurrent fevers and drained energy. Self-diagnosed, after an internet search, he decided that somewhere on his travels, real or cinematic, he had picked up a dose of SFL (swine flu lite). A condition that challenged medical researchers who denied malarial symptoms. Petit's flu was refined and unswinish: it was closer to classic Victorian lethargy, laudanum vapours, and best treated by taking to the couch with a heap of novels by Roberto Bolaño and Richard Yates.

The Mexican slaughter-shed plague, incubated by the media, played down, at point of origin, to maintain tourism, and then promoted to flog pharmaceutical product in the global recession, had become a fashion accessory. Petit, acutely sensitive to contemporary mores, understood that the virus, in a homeopathic dose, was a valuable ingredient in editing a film essay about a world without narrative. The Xerox principle that offered the formula for the relationship between originality and popular success could now be applied to viruses, diseases of choice. Elective addictions. Diamanté masks copy the blue *tapaboca*. Post-viral artists wander Plague City like vampires in a costume ball staged by Jean Cocteau.

This is what the style magazines are offering:

If you're going to get ill, make sure your virus is an attractive one. Thanks to artist Luke Jerram (the man who scattered London's streets with pianos earlier this year), we know that Swine Flu is actually quite pretty. Jerram has created large-scale glass models of several virulent bugs including SARS and E-coli (a particularly nasty-looking number with a tail), so you can make an aesthetic decision about which disease to catch.

The viral egg modelled by Jerram to represent swine flu is as elegant as death, a sugar skull with the meat eaten away. A delicate lacework of sacrificial teeth. The destroyer of the huddled masses has turned itself, within six months of its debut, into an expensive totem, a funerary jewel for the urban elite. One small step from the pig-pens of Mexico City to a whitewall gallery in London's heritage slaughter-house, Smithfield. The serious players, inoculated against human contact, never turn up to their own private views. The Australian barman shocks the fashion X-ray, posing at the rail. She hasn't cracked the accent: 'Do you want arse with your spritzer?'

Reading

Bolaño, Roberto, *The Savage Detectives*, trans. Natasha Wimmer (London: Picador, 2007).

Bolaño, Roberto, *Nazi Literature in the Americas*, trans. Chris Andrews (New York: Norton, 2008).

Bolaño, Roberto, *2666*, trans. Natasha Wimmer (London: Picador, 2009).

Buck-Morss, Susan, *The Dialectics of Seeing: Walter Benjamin and the Arcades Project* (Cambridge, MA: MIT Press, 1991).

Burroughs, William S., and Brion Gysin, *The Exterminator* (San Francisco: Auerhahn, 1960).

Burroughs, William S., and Daniel Odier, *The Job: Interviews with William Burroughs* (London: Jonathan Cape, 1970).

Burroughs, William S., *Ah Pook Is Here and Other Texts* (London: Calder & Boyars, 1979).

Burroughs, William S., *The Adding Machine: Collected Essays* (London: Seaver, 1986).

Darke, Chris, *Light Readings: Film Criticism and Screen Arts* (London: Wallflower Press, 2000).

Deighton, Len, *Berlin Game* (London: Century, 1983).

Deighton, Len, *Mexico Set* (London: Century, 1984).

Döblin, Alfred, *Berlin Alexanderplatz*, trans. Eugene Jolas (London: Continuum, 2004).

Faber, Michel, *Under the Skin* (London: Harcourt, 2000).

Hilton, Christopher, *Hitler's Olympics: The 1936 Berlin Olympic Games* (London: Sutton, 2006).

Ladd, Brian, *Ghosts of Berlin: Confronting German History in the Urban Landscape* (Chicago: Chicago University Press, 1997).

le Carré, John, *The Spy Who Came in from the Cold* (London: Littlehampton, 1963).

Miles, Barry, *William Burroughs: El Hombre Invisible* (London: Virgin, 1992).

Ross, John, *El Monstruo: Dread and Redemption in Mexico City* (New York: Nation, 2010).

Sinclair, Iain, *London Orbital* (London: Granta, 2002).

Waiting

Michael Sayeau

Terminal 3 and the Politics of Waiting

Like so many airport terminals around the world, Heathrow's Terminal 3 brings concretely to life the textures and sensations of our increasingly privatized public world. We have become quite familiar with such places, which are effectively shopping malls with little portals hidden amongst the over-priced shops, through which at some point, lurching under the weight of your duty-free purchases, you stumble onto your plane. It's not hard to remember a period when airport terminals, aside from the odd snack bar or news stand, mostly contained seats for sitting on as you waited for your plane to arrive and boarding to begin. Lately, especially in places like the United Kingdom, where airports have been privatized, the seats have been largely removed from the terminals—not just to make room for more retail outlets, but to ensure that passengers, marooned beyond the security checkpoints, visit these shops. Seated passengers buy no Toblerone bars, no packs of cigarettes, no men's or women's casual wear.

But Heathrow's Terminal 3, in a subtle but revealing way, exposes just how far gone we are in this experiment of locked-in shopping. And in doing so it offers a glimmer of where things might be headed —and not just in the air-transport sector of the economy. There are only a few seats scattered around the terminal. A rough estimate suggests that there are enough seats to accommodate perhaps one-tenth or one-fifteenth of the total passenger load at any one time on a moderately busy day. But the effect of this lack of seating is only intensified by another step that the designers of the terminal have taken, for along with the paucity of seats, there are also only a few screens where you can see what gate you're supposed to use when your plane starts boarding.

The cynical step taken by BAA, the private company that owns and operates Heathrow, is to have designed the waiting area so that the departure boards are not visible from a single seat anywhere in the terminal. I know this is true because the last time I was there I was bored and had an hour to kill, so I checked. You can sit, but if you sit, you'll eventually have to get up—and you'll probably have to do this more than once. It would be easy enough to position the screens so that the passengers could see them from where they were sitting. But the planners have deliberately made this impossible. Even if you are lucky enough to find a chair, you will soon have to give it up to check the screens. You will then lose your seat, given the supply/demand

Photograph: Peter Radunzel

curve in operation in the terminal, and be forced to wander the mall again until your gate is called.

From a certain angle, then, Terminal 3's waiting area starts to seem like a giant concrete and steel machine designed to reduce comfort in the service of profit. As finance capital and its offshoots swallow more and more of the public sphere and public space, our lived experience is being affected, subtly but significantly, in countless ways. Our cities have long since become instruments for controlling our time—forcing us to wait when waiting serves, urging us to rush when speed is in order. If for Michel Foucault the Panopticon was the architectural materialization of disciplinary modernity, Heathrow Terminal 3 is a concrete version of our own privatized, profit-desperate times. The *festina lente* temporality of the terminal is emblematic of so many of the ways in which today we are forever being hurried on to wait.

In subtle but encompassing ways, waiting lies at the centre of many of today's political and economic arrangements, and the lived experiences informed by them. The shop queue, the crowded train platform, the waiting room at the hospital: these are spaces in which the struggle between the market and the social provisioning of goods and services continues to be evident. Whether we think of the food queues that became such a feature of the USSR in the 1980s, or the time that it took to have a telephone line installed before the privatization of British Telecom, or Tony Blair's second-term efforts to reduce waiting times for the National Health Service, or the Ryanair-ification of council services in Britain, waiting has long been a barometer of political atmospherics.

Once the political significance of waiting is apparent, new perspectives on other areas of inquiry open up. For instance, while studies of modernity conducted from various perspectives have generally cast the characteristic temporality of the city in terms of shock, interruption and incessant novelty, there is much to be gained from attending to their dialectical obverse. In 'On Some Motifs in Baudelaire', Walter Benjamin cast the visual shocks of the big city as an emblematic experience of modernity and a form of unconscious training in new rhythms of life. He writes of optical experiences such as are supplied by the advertising pages of a newspaper or the traffic of a big city. Moving through this traffic involves the individual in a series of shocks and collisions. At dangerous intersections, nervous impulses flow through him in rapid succession, like the energy from a battery. Baudelaire speaks of the man who plunges into the crowd as into a reservoir of electric energy. Circumscribing the experience of the shock, he calls this man 'a kaleidoscope endowed with consciousness.' Whereas Poe's passers-by cast glances in all directions, seemingly without cause, today's pedestrians are obliged to look about them so that they can be aware of traffic signals. Thus, technology has subjected the human sensorium to a complex kind of training.

The jostle at the intersection, the adrenaline spike when crossing in front of an oncoming bus, have long been thought of as emblematic manifestations of the temporality of modernity. And theorizations of modernity, its perils and embedded potentialities, have long found their own structural principles in such experiences—and thus have tended to privilege suddenness and change above other modes and temporalities of urban life. But what if, given the new perspective on urban space, politics and time that is made available through the lens of waiting, we decided to rewrite the story of the modern city as an experience of restless stillness rather than the shock of the new?

The Novel and Urban Waiting

Benjamin privileged poetry as the appropriate form for rendering the new dynamics of urban experience. Baudelaire's 'À une passante' (1857), a poem which sketches an issueless chance encounter (or non-encounter) between the poet and a passing woman, features, in the essay cited above, as the ur-text of the city's interruptive temporality. As Benjamin describes it,

> The delight of the urban poet is love—not at first sight, but at last sight. It is an eternal farewell, which coincides in the poem with the moment of enchantment. Thus, the sonnet deploys the figure of shock, indeed of catastrophe.

But if lyric poetry presents the appropriate formal framework for placing shock and change at the centre of modern experience, prose fiction provides a fitting start to our investigation of an alternative temporality of attendance and stasis as modes equally characteristic of modernity.

In *The Theory of the Novel* (1920), Georg Lukács claims that the native temporality of the novel is one of waiting. Since the 'progressive unfolding' of subjectivity's struggle with and against time is at the centre of the novel as a form, it has, by virtue of its very form and the mandates of its genre, special access to duration:

> The greatest discrepancy between idea and reality is time: the process of time as duration. The most profound and most humiliating impotence of subjectivity consists not so much in its hopeless struggle against the lack of idea in social forms and their human representatives, as in the fact that it cannot resist the sluggish, yet constant process of time; that it must slip down, slowly yet inexorably, from the peaks it has laboriously scaled; that time—that ungraspable, invisibly moving substance—gradually robs subjectivity of all its possessions and imperceptibly forces alien contents into it. That is why only the novel, the literary form of the transcendent homelessness of the idea, includes real time—Bergson's *durée*—among its constitutive principles.

Lukács goes on to conclude that 'in the novel, meaning is separated from life, and hence the essential from the temporal; we might almost say that the entire inner action of the novel is nothing but a struggle against the power of time'. Time itself, time as duration, emerges in the interstices of the novel's 'reality' as it awaits the arrival of an 'idea', an idea that never seems likely to arrive, at least not in its anticipated shape. And it is worth noting that, according to the passage above, the frantic stasis of the novel as it waits for the fulfilling idea to arrive has an erosive effect upon subjectivity itself, robbing it of itself in the act of replacing what was once there with 'alien contents'.

In the chapter from which this passage from *The Theory of the Novel* is drawn, 'The Romanticism of Disillusionment', Lukács takes

Flaubert's *L'Éducation sentimentale* (1869) as his privileged example
of the novel form and its characteristic temporality. The novel centres
on the (abortive) love affair of Frédéric Moreau and Madame
Arnoux, an affair dominated by a perverse logic of fetishistic substi-
tution and erotic deferral that ultimately transforms the relationship
itself into a terminal spin-cycle of neurotic over-sensitivity and anticipation never to be fulfilled. It is, above all else, a relationship that,
consciously or not, prefers to wait rather than to consummate. In an
echo of the romantic ethos of the novel as a form, anticipatory desire
comes tinged with a preemptive sense of disgust, an awareness that
the ideality of platonic passion will be spoiled by the vulgar physi-
cality of the sexual act.

Many critics and theorists have focused on the final scenes of the
novel as a crystallization of the temporal dynamics of the genre.
There is, however, another scene that is equally important, and that
offers a splendid example of what the modern novel might have to tell
us about the relationship between urban waiting and modern experience. It comes near the end of the second section of the novel, just as
revolutionary fervour is breaking out on the streets of Paris. Frédéric
waits on a street corner to meet Madame Arnoux for what might well
be an adulterous assignation, and feels a bit guilty for avoiding the
protest march that his friends wanted him to attend. A huge crowd of
demonstrators appears, and he hides himself in a side street so that his
friends will not see him and pull him away from his appointment with
Madame Arnoux.

Still she doesn't come. He keeps one eye on the mass of demonstrators, one eye out for his lover. Despite the proximity of both
personal and public drama, Frédéric quickly becomes bored.
Waiting, here, is composed of a mixture of anticipation and frustrated
indifference. First, we overhear him imagining her journey to the
appointed *rendez-vous*:

> 'Ah! It's time!,' he said to himself. 'She'll be leaving her house and on
> her way here'; and a few minutes later: 'She'd have had time to be here
> by now.' Until three o'clock he endeavoured to stay calm. 'No, she's
> not late. Just be patient.'

With the 1848 Revolution discovering its *Jetztzeit* only a few yards away, Frédéric attempts to distract himself from the laborious passage of time by examining the goods for sale in some shop windows:

> With nothing better to do, he kept looking into the few shops on the street: a bookshop, a saddler's, a mourning outfitters. Soon he was familiar with every book, every sort of harness and every kind of material. Seeing him going up and down in front of their establishments, the shopkeepers were at first surprised and then so frightened that they put up their shutters.
>
> No doubt something had held her up and she was feeling as miserable as he was! But it wouldn't be long before they'd both be so happy! Because she was bound to come, that was sure! 'After all, she gave me her word!' But an unbearable feeling of distress was creeping over him.
>
> On an absurd impulse, he went into the lodging house, as if thinking she might be there. At that very moment she could be coming down the street. He dashed out. Not a soul! Once again he began to pound his beat.
>
> He kept gazing at the cracks between the paving stones, the lampposts, the spouts of the drain-pipes, the numbers over the doors. The most trivial objects were becoming his companions or, rather, mocking bystanders; the dull uniformity of the house-fronts seemed merciless. He could feel himself crumbling into hopelessness. The echo of his footsteps was hammering into his brain.

Once he has expended this store of visual distractions, Frédéric turns to reciting poetry to himself or doing maths problems in his head. As if in a parody of the way that detail functions in the realist novel, Frédéric seeks clues to Madame Arnoux's arrival in 'the random number of coins in his hand, in the expressions on the faces of the passers-by, in the colours of the horses; when the result was unfavorable, he tried to ignore it'. It is an experience familiar to us all, that of visually consuming every inch of our locality when we are waiting for someone. But it is the epitome of Flaubert's satiric audacity to have his character playing these games with time when, right around the corner, the political shape of France, and perhaps the world, is being transformed. The over-determining effect of Frédéric's techniques of self-distraction expands from the coins in his pocket to his perception of the revolutionary spectacle on the streets around him. When he finally does display some interest in the mob of protestors, he only does so in order to search for a sign of Madame Arnoux.

> Then he resumed his post on the corner of the rue de la Ferme and the rue Tronchet in order to be able to keep an eye on both at the same time. Looking down the street, he could see massed groups of people lurching confusedly to and fro on the boulevard. From time to time he picked out the plume of a dragoon or a woman's hat; he strained his eyes to recognize her.

Political insurrection becomes simply another spectacle, another hazy distraction, on Frédéric's path towards what will never arrive—an erotic coupling with Madame Arnoux that he hopes will somehow preserve her romantic ideality. The next day, this theme of violence as entertainment returns as he wakes up to gunfire and a battle on some half-built barricades: 'Caught between two solid blocks of people, Frédéric was unable to move; indeed, he was fascinated and enjoying himself enormously. The wounded falling all around him and the dead lying on the ground didn't seem really dead or wounded. It was like being at a show.'

But Frédéric's sense that the revolutionary proceedings have somehow receded into a 'spectacle', a staged display, isn't simply an idiosyncratic reaction on his part. Rather, what is true for Frédéric as an individual is just as valid, if in a slightly different register, for the people as a whole, who consider what is happening as an entertaining diversion rather than a world-historical event.

> Since all business was temporarily suspended, idle curiosity and nervousness drove people out into the streets. Their casual dress tended to minimize class differences; any hatred was kept in the background and hope to the fore; the crowd was all sweetness and light. Faces glowed with pride at having achieved hard-won rights. There was a

festive mood of carnival and camp-fires; it was fun living in Paris in those early days.

'As business was suspended'—rather than temporal plenitude, Flaubert shows us empty time, time off rather than full time. Taking in Frédéric's distracted attendance upon Madame Arnoux and that of the Parisian populace upon the revolution, this entire sequence seems bent on levelling out the affectual topography of the novel and the life it represents.

In a subtly dramatic way, this scene of waiting in *L'Éducation sentimental* at once captures something essential about the novel as a form and tests the limits of that form. The moment of tarrying, self-distraction—of finding something to fill the character's mind as well as the author's page—mirrors and in fact materializes the complex temporality of the literary form in which it occurs. The novel, especially though not exclusively the novel about the city, has a mandate to stop and look in the storefront windows, to fill the time even as it keeps an eye out for the beloved to arrive, or the first shot to ring out over the barricades. The genre itself requires that those who pass through it neither board their flights directly nor simply sit comfortably while they are waiting. Something always has to be happening, even if nothing is happening at all. Frédéric marks an inaugural moment in the modernist juxtapositioning of individual waiting and the historical event, later works will make it clear that there are other postures available to those who stand in the queues of history.

Constrained Time and Modernist Form

On weekday afternoons, the atrium bar of the Royal Festival Hall is crowded enough that it can be difficult to find a seat. It's a lovely building, and because it's just a block or so from Waterloo station it's a convenient place for Londoners to schedule informal business meetings or chats with friends. But the better part of the crowd that frequents this building, at least on these weekday afternoons, are solitary men and women, almost always with laptops on their tables, sometimes drinking coffee, sometimes beer or wine, sometimes nothing at all.

The regulars know the tables where secret electrical sockets are located nearby, and they never mistakenly head for the male toilets on the south-west side of the building when they need the female toilets on the north-east side, or vice versa. There is free wi-fi, but more importantly, no one will ever ask you to leave, even if you don't purchase anything to drink. Unlike Starbucks, where you can rent a seat for an hour or so for the price of a tall latte, the Royal Festival Hall is—and feels like—indoor public space in a city that has little, an enclosed park where one is free to sit and wait. In 1983, the Greater London Council declared an 'open foyer' policy for the RFH— allowing and in fact encouraging the public to make use of the building during the day, and not just during the hour or so spent waiting for a show or performance to start.

I am sure that some of these typers and emailers are out of work, and likely some simply don't have to work. But the majority, from what I can tell, are informational workers, freelance writers and journalists, consultants and programmers. Untethered from anything so concrete as a desk in an office—and in many cases from the security of a steady pay cheque too—their work outwardly resembles leisure. Further, the relationship between waiting and what, following Maurizio Lazzarato, we might call 'immaterial labour', is more than simply a matter of appearances. The temporality of this labour, which abandons the wage in favour of piece-work payment, is defined by waiting— for employment, for payment, and for yet more employment.

In an important sense, the behaviour of these denizens of the Royal Festival Hall as they perform what can neither clearly be called work nor recreation is emblematic of a more general blurring of temporal categories that has occurred over the last century or so. In *Everyday Life and the Modern World* (1968), Henri Lefebvre identifies three categories of lived time in modernity:

> Time-tables, when comparatively analysed, reveal new phenomena: if the hours of days, weeks, months and years are classed in three categories, *pledged time* (professional work), *free time* (leisure) and *compulsive time* (the various demands other than work such as transport, official formalities, etc.), it will become apparent that

compulsive time increases at a greater rate than leisure time. Compulsive time is part of everyday life and tends to define it by the sum of its compulsions.

Lefebvre saw the encroachment of compulsive or 'constrained' time upon leisure to be one of the symptoms of what he called the 'colonization of everyday life', in which 'capitalist leaders treat daily life as they once treated the colonies'. It is a new sort of enclosure, in this case of citizens' lives and their time, that Lefebvre is worried about. The time spent preparing for and getting to work (waiting for transit, waiting on transit, stuck in traffic, looking for a place to park), and keeping oneself fit for work (shopping for food and necessities, eating, caring for the next generation of workers, etc.) reorganizes what would otherwise be leisure time into a form of pseudo-labour— yet another brand of frantic stillness, busy time-off. Waiting to work comes to seem, in his vision, as important a facet of everyday life in modern economies as work itself.

'Constrained time' is one of the favourite topoi of novelistic representation—and this is increasingly true at the onset of modernism. A quick review of the canon of the literature of the modern period renders clear the increasing centrality of 'constrained time' as a category of experience. Neither at leisure nor quite on the job, Leopold Bloom's semi-employed peregrinations around Dublin structure James Joyce's *Ulysses* (1922), whose chronological organization and ultimate issuelessness suggests a temporality for modern narrative representation that is at once insistently new and, at the same time, borrowed from classical literature. Similarly, Virginia Woolf's *Mrs Dalloway* (1925) is diffusely focused on a handful of characters as they move around London, waiting for things solid and abstract, significant and trivial, to happen. It is no wonder that one of the first passages to signal the formal arrangement of the work (in particular, the fluidity with which the interior discourse will shift from one character to another) comes as Clarissa Dalloway waits to cross a street.

> She stiffened a little on the kerb, waiting for Durtnall's van to pass. A charming woman, Scrope Purvis thought her (knowing her as one

does know people who live next door to one in Westminster); a touch of the bird about her, of the jay, blue-green, light, vivacious, though she was over fifty, and grown very white since her illness. There she perched, never seeing him, waiting to cross, very upright.

And it is not only the prose of the period that takes up the matter of waiting. We might recall that one of the inaugural works in the development of poetic modernism, Ezra Pound's 'In a Station of the Metro' (1913), takes as its scene a Metro station in which passengers are awaiting the next train.

> The apparition of these faces in the crowd;
> Petals on a wet, black bough.

The juxtapositional logic of the poem, which counterposes two images without conjunctive language, mirrors the static turbulence of the aggregated passengers as they wait. What arrives, within the confines of the poem itself, is not the train but the starkest of metaphors, a typological instance of the basic building block of the poetic art. The poem, in a sense, moves forward without moving.

It is no coincidence that these scenarios of waiting and the institutions and locations that form their backdrop have a privileged place in formally experimental works. Modern mass forms of waiting yielded new psychological effects, introduced novel forms of thinking and feeling. For instance, as Georg Simmel describes, the constrained time spent on public transport, forced to wait in close proximity to strangers, may well have influenced deeper changes to the sensory and inter-personal bearings of urban subjects.

> Someone who sees without hearing is much more uneasy than someone who hears without seeing. In this there is something characteristic of the sociology of the big city. Interpersonal relationships in big cities are distinguished by a marked preponderance of the activity of the eye over the ear. The main reason for this is the public means of transportation. Before the development of buses, railroads, and trams in the nineteenth century, people had never been in a position of

having to look at one another for long minutes or even hours without speaking to one another.

The oddly distanced intimacy of the bus queue and the train, the crowded atomization of the café, the purgatorial temporalities of the bureaucratic waiting room—each of these are laboratories for the development of new modes of subjectivity, themselves the object of political and economic experimentation and exploitation. The 'attention in distraction' of the harried air traveller is harnessed by the designers of BAA and its leaseholders, just as the store-front glass windows were at an earlier stage architectural reflections of the divided, intermittent consciousness of nineteenth-century *boulevardiers* like Frédéric Moreau. The fact that modern experience was happening just as much and just as significantly where Frédéric was pacing before the shop windows as where the barricades were being erected around the corner stands as an indication of the implicit and complex politics suggested by the modern urban novel and its characteristic forms.

The Politics of the Queue

Vladimir Sorokin's novel *The Queue* (1985) is centred both thematically and formally on a modern form of urban waiting that has already disappeared along with the socio-political form that gave rise to it. The variety of waiting in question is one that played an important and highly visible role in the ideological grappling between East and West throughout the Cold War. Soviet citizens queuing for goods—at one point for bread and butter, later for Levi's jeans and Adidas trainers—seemed tangibly to represent the disadvantages of the socialist economy in comparison to the capitalist one, as the latter easily filled shops and malls to the brim with shoes and televisions for sale.

Despite the fact that Sorokin is known as a dissident writer, whose works were banned in the USSR and generally only published abroad, *The Queue* now reads, if not without ambiguity, like a nostalgic celebration of the Soviet queue rather than a dystopian satire of it.

The form of the work is adapted to the scenario that it represents. A stream of unattributed speech—conversations, arguments, negotiations—flows almost without a break. The 'characters', if that's the right word for those who wait, join the line and leave it, sometimes to return, sometimes to disappear for good. The news of the day (football scores, foreign and domestic affairs) is discussed when someone unfolds a newspaper; waiters strategize how and where to get something to eat, and air their resentments when others break into line ahead of them. A sample of the text, chosen almost at random, gives a clearer sense of the work than any description:

> – And who's on keyboard—Hensley?
> – Hensley …
> – You wait and wait, and what's it all for?
> – That quick!
> – Uh-huh …
> – I haven't had a good fuck for ages either.
> – Having a child so late, of course … difficult business.
> – He's had things in *Yunost*, I think. And then a book of his came out.
> – Interesting?
> – Yeah, not bad. Detective story.
> – Have you read *A Shot in the Back*?
> – No.
> – That's quite good too. Murder mystery. The friend kills him.
> – Look, everyone's going to start running now.
> – Are we going to move soon, d'you know?
> – I don't know. They should say.
> – They'll tell us.

In taking all of this on, and in the manner that it does, *The Queue* emphasizes the unlikely vitality of what would seem to be a powerful symptom of Soviet communism's imminent demise. What is more, it evokes a different model of the relationship between the individual and society from the one that forms the political undergirding of the conventional Western novel. In his afterword to the text, written for a new edition in 2007, Sorokin describes some of the ways in which the architecture of the queue was at once determined by and an advertisement for the political economy that produced it:

> It was after the victory of the collective body that the phenomenon of the queue appeared in Russia with all its classic attributes: numeration (the person's number in line was usually written on the hand); the periodic roll call and ruthless elimination of anyone who stepped away for a moment; a strict hierarchy (those standing behind were supposed to obey those standing in front); the quantity of goods allotted per person (this was also decided collectively), etc.

Other statements in Sorokin's afterword suggest a complex, historical trajectory in which *The Queue* (and the style of life represented in it) is seen as a primitive state from which Russians were later rudely ejected by 'the atom bomb of a market economy':

> After its raucous explosion, people standing in lines discovered three terrible truths:
> 1. Money is real.
> 2. The people standing next to you in line have different abilities.
> 3. There are not 3 kinds of sausage, but 33. Or even 333.

What makes this epiphany at the end of communism historically strange, even paradoxical, is the fact that the truths of the new world that Russians begin to inhabit in the aftermath of the queue society are precisely those that form the ideological armature of the realist novel from whose conventions Sorokin has chosen to depart. The reality of money, the difference between people, and the abundance of detail to attend to—the very stuff of the nineteenth-century novel —are what the post-Soviet citizenry begin to discover, and what Sorokin belatedly describes, in his retro-modernist novel.

What is clear today is that Sorokin's novel, and the very nearly obsolete world that it describes, preemptively invert the logic of the BAA terminal design and the political-economic atmosphere that it so vividly evokes. And it does this in the course of presenting a vision of a distribution system and its corollary temporality that are themselves inversions of the one in which we live today. An immense political contrast is reduced to a relatively simple matter of everyday urban life: where capitalism offers the rapid delivery of goods and services to those with the cash (or credit) on hand to purchase them, socialist egalitarianism depends upon making its citizens wait. Sorokin's vivification of an unlikely scenario, however satirical its original intention may have been, not only indicates an alternative pathway for the novel as a form, but also stands as a subtle trans-valuation of the act of waiting itself.

Benjamin's Anteroom

Walter Benjamin's canonical descriptions of the city as a site of inter-ruptive temporalities of shock and distraction stand as scenically grounded previews of his later, more abstract work dealing with wider matters of historical change and the politics of time. But it is worth noting in this regard that the architectural metaphorics never quite disappeared, only shifted from the busy urban street toward a different sort of space. And further, taking heed of the shift in these metaphorics can help us to understand a deeper, subtler shift in the emphases and ideas at play.

In his late work 'On the Concept of History', Benjamin repeatedly stages the distinction between social-democratic theory and his own 'historical materialism' as a difference between two forms of being in and working with time. The former believes in human improvement that is both 'boundless' and 'inevitable' and which takes the shape of a 'progression through a homogeneous, empty time'. It is a form of ameliorism, one that waits in full expectation of the gradual, incremental arrival of improvement. The historical materialist, on the other hand, waits differently. Rather than passive spectatorship of incremental change, the temporality of history is a complex affair in which moments of stasis explode into something new. History 'is the subject of a construction whose site is not homogeneous, empty time, but time filled full by now-time [*Jetztzeit*]'. The historical materialist 'cannot do without the notion of a present which is not a transition, but in which time takes a stand [*einsteht*] and has come to a standstill'.

And just as history is constituted by a rhythm of rest and sudden interruption, the intellectual practice of the historical materialist involves a corollary rhythm:

> Thinking involves not only the movement of thoughts, but their arrest as well. Where thinking suddenly comes to a stop in a constellation saturated by tensions, it gives that constellation a shock, by which thinking is crystallized as a monad. The historical materialist approaches a historical object only where it confronts him as a monad. In this structure he recognizes a sign of the messianic arrest of happening, or (to put it differently) a revolutionary chance in the fight for the oppressed past. He takes cognizance of it in order to blast a specific era out of the homogeneous course of history.

In the notes that he wrote as he prepared this essay, collected as 'Paralipomena to "On the Concept of History"' in the *Selected Works*, Benjamin deploys the metaphor of the *anteroom* in order to describe what he sees as the social-democratic misinterpretation of Marx. 'Once the classless society is defined as an infinite task, the empty and homogenous time was transformed into an anteroom, so to speak, in which one could wait for the emergence of the revolutionary situation with more or less equanimity.'

On the surface, the terms of Benjamin's distinction couldn't be sharper. But if a little pressure is applied to them the clarity of the difference begins to blur a bit—and especially when we take the measurements of this waiting room that is 'homogeneous, empty time'. Is the materialist historian truly out of the 'anteroom' of the event, or just waiting there with a slightly different posture? We might say that the difference between the two forms of waiting—ameliorist-gradualist on the one hand and messianically minded on the other—boils down to different ways of waiting for the show to start. And in fact, if we look back at the terms in which Benjamin has placed the present on the side of historical materialism, this present time 'which is not a transition', which 'has taken a stand and has come to a stand-still' in what he describes as a 'messianic arrest of happening', it might seem that the problem with the social democratic anteroom is not so much the equanimity of the waiting, but rather the fact that those who inhabit it expect the waiting one day to end. And, conversely, rather than an interruption from the outside (as per the depiction of shock in the essay on Baudelaire), or a mystical arrival, it becomes clear that it is the 'standstill' itself, a waiting that does not expect to end, that constitutes the shock, the event privileged by the historical materialist. The essay is oblique when it comes to describing exactly what the historical materialist is waiting for (Benjamin mentions at the end of the essay the Jewish prohibition on investigating the future)—as it must be to avoid falling into anticipatory stance of those that he critiques. This form of waiting, disjoined from the 'equanimity' of an expected outcome, politicizes the urgent stasis, the frenetic stoppage, which runs from Frédéric Moreau to the passengers at Terminal 3.

The history of modernity has been narrated again and again as a story of speed and anticipation, of the training that informs it and the ramifications of this training. It is a story whose telling has often started from the close reading of generic urban scenes—most fundamentally, that of pedestrians traversing a busy city boulevard. But when we brush the literature and theory of the period against its grain, we discover an alternative starting point in moments of waiting. And when we commence from the queues and the anterooms, the pauses and the patience they entail, we discover a secret indication that the best path forward may lie not with the provocation of the event, but rather with learning to wait the right way. The efforts to extract profit from waiting such as those that inform the design of our bus shelters and airport terminals bring to light the stakes of political engagement both materially and metaphorically. The waiting that we do today on the streets and in the buildings of our increasingly privatized cities is at once a manifestation of capitalism's failure to deliver on its promises and an untimely and unlikely advertisement for persistent if obsolescent forms of sociality and equality.

Reading

Benjamin, Walter, *Illuminations*, trans. Henry Zohn (New York: Schocken, 1969).

Flaubert, Gustave, *A Sentimental Education*, trans. Douglas Parmée (Oxford: Oxford University Press, 1989).

Lefebvre, Henri, *Everyday Life in the Modern World*, trans. Sacha Rabinovich (New York: Harper & Row, 1971).

Lukács, Georg, *The Theory of the Novel*, trans. Anna Bostock (Cambridge, MA: MIT Press, 1973).

Sorokin, Vladimir, *The Queue*, trans. Sally Laird (New York: New York Review of Books, 2008).

Zigzagging

Mark W. Turner

Bent City

Washington DC has always been a city of circles and squares. In the years immediately following the end of the American Revolution in 1776, when the burgeoning new republic needed a seat of government, it was to a French rationalist that President Washington initially turned. Pierre L'Enfant—architect, engineer and soldier, who fought alongside the colonists in the war of independence—designed a city of regularity, with sweeping vistas along impressively straight, wide avenues with strategically placed circles occasionally interrupting the essentially rectilinear plan. Out of land donated by the neighbouring states of Maryland and Virginia, a modern capital city was planned from scratch. It was always intended to be a monumental and monumentalizing city—not only a city designed to impress the people with the seriousness of the new democratic project, but also a city designed to accommodate the people, with stretches of open public spaces and parkland. L'Enfant planned where the grand Capitol building would sit atop a hill, he situated the White House accordingly, and his vision for the ten-miles-square that was to be the capital was unwavering. Like so many large-scale urban development projects, L'Enfant's plan for the city became stuck in the bureaucratic mire of various Commissioners; refusing to alter his plans, he was eventually replaced as chief architect. This first great architect of the new United States later died a pauper. However, the city that was eventually built was not so far from what L'Enfant had imagined, and in the centuries since it has become more rather than less like the city of radials and broad avenues he had in mind. In the circles and squares of downtown Washington today, you still feel something of the confidence and certainty of Enlightenment modernity.

Washington, most people agree, is a 'nice' city, divided neatly into quarters and with the Capitol building roughly at its centre. Usually, apart from trawling the imposing museums along the Mall, visitors only ever spend time in the north-west quarter of the city, with its elegant rows of nineteenth-century townhouses and well-proportioned *beaux-arts* apartment buildings in upscale leafy neighbourhoods and high-end retail districts. Whenever I return to Washington, and to its north-west in particular, I always want it to be something other than it is: a little less straight, a little less homogenous, a little more bent.

I know Washington pretty well, having spent the first 18 years of my life stalking the city from a distance, a few miles beyond the northernmost border in the new 1960s–'70s suburbs of Maryland. I grew up in an altogether different sort of planned environment. Our home was in a new subdivision called 'Valencia', built on land that had been an apple orchard, and the name for the model of our house was the 'Cadiz' (ours sat alongside three other styles rolled out across the subdivision, the 'Barcelona', 'Avilla' and 'Castille'). Although the name of our neighbourhood evoked eastern Spain and our particular house suggested Andalusia, the streets around us were all very Anglo—Chichester Lane, Winterthur Court, Autumn Drive. The loose grasp of Spanish geography was matched by an equally loose grasp of Spanish design since, as far as I could tell, there wasn't anything distinctly Spanish about our split-level, open-plan contemporary with a mansard roof (yes, a mansard roof in Cadiz) apart from a heavy and out-of-place Moorish iron chandelier that hung in a hallway. Our subdivision backed on to others, more established by some years, including Pilgrim Hills and Colesville Manor. My neighbourhood was planned, but without much attention to cultural consistency. It was a bit like Nathanael West's description of a Hollywood film set at the beginning of *The Day of the Locust* (1939), a mishmash of styles and references that didn't add up to any coherent whole: pilgrims and conquistadors, manor houses and mansard roofs.

As a young child, the 'District' (as older people said) or 'DC' (as younger people said) was a place to go for special events, and 'Valencia' was conveniently located just off New Hampshire Avenue, one of the major arteries into the capital. If you took a left turn out of our neighbourhood and kept driving straight for about ten miles or so, you'd eventually hit downtown. School trips to the great museums on the Mall, fireworks on the Fourth of July at the Lincoln Memorial, Christmas concerts at the Kennedy Center, and once or twice, during the Iran hostage crisis or the Native Americans' march on Washington, even a political protest—these were reasons to venture into the city for suburban children like me. After the arrival of the liberating Metro subway system, by which time I was a budding teenager, I was able to explore the city unchaperoned. That was in the early 1980s. Riding the Metro into the city, zigzagging the streets aimlessly, was about as good as life could get for this boy from 'Valencia', I thought, and certainly it compared favourably to hanging out at the McDonald's or Safeway parking lot, which were my other options.

The older I got, the queerer I got. I found less and less comfort in the normative things the suburbs appeared to do really well—family block parties, friends' birthdays with spin-the-bottle, flirting at the mall. Sensing that these probably weren't interesting for me, not in the long term, I invested a lot of psychic energy in imagining Washington, a city just out of reach. As I stored up scattered bits of information gleaned here and there, it became a place of sexual excitement in my head—a place where a Congressman got caught soliciting a teenage hustler at a bar called the Chesapeake House (I learned that from the evening news, and duly noted the establishment's address), but also a place where gay men in hot pants played volleyball at a nightclub virtually in the shadow of the Capitol building (I learned that from the lesbian family-friend who cut my hair). Other people had their own versions of the city, but as I pieced it together, Washington was where all the wickedness of the world converged in a downtown neighbourhood called Dupont Circle. When still a youth, hearing my suburban parents say 'Dupont Circle' was a little bit like hearing them say 'cancer'—it was spoken mostly in whispers. But whispers matter, particularly to curious, eavesdropping children. Dupont was, and still is to a lesser extent, the acceptable, public gay face of Washington, and as the only gay face of Washington that I knew much about in my adolescence, it was the area onto which I projected all my sexual hopes and desires. Naturally, I never actually went there, not until very late into my teens. It's not that the Metro wouldn't have taken me there—in fact, my Metro stop was on a direct line to Dupont, so it couldn't have been easier—rather, that I was terrified of what I might find once I got there. Surely, all the sins of the cities of the plain would unfold bare-assed before me. While this had a certain appeal in the abstract, the simple fact was that I had little idea what one did in Gomorrah, let alone Sodom. I stayed away in the hope of some future pilgrimage.

One of the problems with cities is that they tend never to be quite as satisfying as our projections of them, and Dupont Circle had too great a burden to bear in my fantasy life. It was, mostly, the creation of scraps of random information I picked up here and there. In the harsh light of day (and even in the much harsher gay-bar light of night), Dupont has never quite lived up to those suburban whispers, and it wasn't half as wicked as I'd allowed myself to hope. The illicit, illegal, lustful and perverse—all the stuff a horny teenager longs for, perhaps particularly a queer one—seemed strangely contrary to the charms of Connecticut Avenue and the village-feel of 17th Street, with its brass-railings-and-hanging-plants gay bars. The exciting departure from everything I had thought and known, the longed-for revelations of difference and a real sense of freedom—you won't stumble on that in the bourgeois P Street corridor, with its well-mannered, well-appointed bars and cafés.

What I came to understand about Dupont Circle, where I later lived for a year after college, perhaps still in hot pursuit of my teenage fantasies, was that, in its way, it is actually a very straight part of a very straight city. Sure, there are plenty of gay men, and these men can openly hold hands or kiss on the streets around Dupont; and of course hordes of stores and shops cater for the local 'gay community'. Still, I'm now struck by the essentially straight-down-the-line normality of Dupont. The lines that radiate out of the Circle, its grid of lettered and numbered streets, its generous but dignified proportions—all of these point to that underlying rationalism that has been part of the city from the very beginning. In a city of certainty, whose utter predictability hints at the monotony of the company town that it is, Dupont Circle confirms rather than confounds conventional expectations. No, if it's Sodom and Gomorrah you are after, you're probably better off sitting at home fantasizing in the suburbs.

But 'nice' Washington isn't all the city has to offer. There are other Washingtons, other parts of the city, less prosperous, less presentable neighbourhoods that I never knew anything about as a teenager. These places existed behind the whispers. I only came to know them, to seek them out in the dark, in my twenties. The illicit and perverse city of sexual adventure was there (and still is, though increasingly in peril), but not in one of the most expensive neighbourhoods of the capital, not in the media-friendly gay-guidebook versions of the city. The queerer, more uncertain city was elsewhere: in parking lots after dark where men drove around in a circuit of gas-guzzling automotive cruising; in the green and grassy edges of the city, across the river, at the iconic Iwo Jima Memorial or in Lady Bird Johnson Park, where men fucked in bushes at night; among the warehouses of south-east, not far from the Navy Yard, where a row of sex clubs and bathhouses ('The Follies' and 'The Glorious Health Club') would welcome a surprisingly wide range of men, of different races, generations and backgrounds; in the old-school leather-and-denim bars ('The Eagle' and 'The Leather Rack') that wouldn't have much right to exist in the more hygiene-conscious streets of Dupont. These spaces have their traces, too. Police records across many years provide a public record of these spaces; stories told by friends, passed on by word of mouth, provide another kind of record. Washington, like all cities, I learned in time, has its bent side, though it may take some wandering and a certain amount of luck to find it.

Curved Line

Though nowadays Washington seems almost quaint, with its low-rise cityscape, continental feel, and huge monuments, L'Enfant's original plans—almost fully realized during the twentieth century—are strikingly modern. His circles and squares relied on the sort of geometry and precision that we have come to expect in the modern city. In his manifesto, *The City of To-Morrow and Its Planning* (first published as *Urbanisme* in 1926), the architect and urban visionary Le Corbusier boldly announced a new kind of urbanism, a set of principles that would build a clean city of virtue in the wake of nineteenth-century industrialism's corrupt city of vice. For Le Corbusier 'a town is a tool', and by the early decades of the twentieth century, the tool was no longer being put to proper use: 'The lack of order to be found everywhere in them offends us; their degradation wounds our self-esteem and humiliates our sense of dignity. They are not worthy of the age; they are no longer worthy of us.' Here and elsewhere, the architect searches for a language in which to express his belief that a radical change to the built environment is the only hope for saving the soul of man in the modern age. The city is a tool, but also a machine and a workshop for the spirit. The call to build is fervent, and, as he puts it elsewhere, the choice is stark: architecture or revolution. It is through architecture and the machinery of the modern age that the progressive values of the Enlightenment city, the sort of rational city suggested in L'Enfant's plans for the new democracy, can be renewed. By rebuilding our cities in more rational ways, we can begin to regain some of that lost self-esteem and live in greater dignity than the world of the nineteenth-century city allowed.

For Le Corbusier, in the 1920s, modern man is living in a mess, 'a perpetual state of instability, insecurity, fatigue and accumulating delusions'. Like other diagnosticians of damaged modernity—Freud and Simmel, say—Le Corbusier finds the man on the street to be anxious and neurotic, 'brutalized and battered' by the increasing speed and pace of modern life. The mess of the modern condition needed cleaning up and straightening out, and if there is a guiding principle in Le Corbusier's vision of the future it is the absolute value of the straight line. At the beginning of the first chapter of *The City of To-Morrow*, we are introduced to the lazy pack-donkey, an aimless creature curiously responsible for the dysfunctional urban world we have inherited:

> Man walks in a straight line because he has a goal and knows where he is going; he has made up his mind to reach some particular place and he goes straight to it.
>
> The pack-donkey meanders along, meditates a little in his scatter-brained and distracted fashion, he zigzags in order to avoid the larger stones, or to ease the climb, or to gain a little shade; he takes the line of least resistance.

It is this pack-donkey, 'who thinks of nothing at all, except what will save himself trouble', who is 'responsible for the plan of every continental city'. It is this pack-donkey who has produced the labyrinthine cities that develop by accident rather than by design and who has made our cities unliveable. It is a medieval, rather than a modern, sort of creature. The Left Bank of Paris, the City of London, even New York below Washington Square, all have the pack-donkey to thank for their curved and clogged streets. 'Function', 'order', 'geometry', 'exactitude' and 'perfection' will be the keywords that will keep the pack-donkey in check. Straight, not bent. Direct, not meandering. This will be the route of the new modern man.

As polemical manifestoes go, this is all stirring stuff, and it makes a lot more practical sense than, say, the Futurists' or the Surrealists' ideas for revolution, which remain at the level of jest and gesture. We feel Le Corbusier's sense of urgency and ambition in his plan for a 'Contemporary City of 3 Million People'—to say nothing of his plan to raze Paris and start building afresh—which is elegant, bold and audacious, with its glass, cruciform skyscrapers, wide boulevards and open spaces. One almost longs to cheer the bulldozers on as they clear out the Left Bank! Almost, but not quite. There is a lot that is disturbing about the city of tomorrow. What seems so wrong about a vision of modernity organized around straightness? It's simple really: I prefer a city made in my own image, imperfect and bent. If it's true that our understandings of ourselves are in part the result of our understandings of and relationships to the environments we build, and if it's true that the fantasies we project onto those spaces tell us something about who we are, then the straightened city does not leave me much room for my particular kinds of fantasies. What about ambiguity, contingency, or (one of the things Le Corbusier most objects to) capriciousness? In the modern world, he tells us, 'we struggle against chance, against disorder, against a policy of drift'. But what if chance, disorder and drift point to alternative experiences of modernity, in which altogether different, queerer urban experiences might be enabled and explored? What if there are other kinds of connections, interesting and significant ones, that not only cannot be made along the straightened line, but are actually hindered by it? What if there is a version of the city that cannot be rationalized, determined and understood always already?

The chance encounter, the uncertain and random accumulation of knowledge, the wandering urban journey: this is how I like to experience my cities, and this is the urban experience of a figure I know well. The cruiser—in his way a kind of pack-donkey who follows the curved line, unsure but curious about who might wait around the bend, avoiding the straight line which reveals itself all at once. The cruiser (usually a man, but not always and not necessarily one)—who takes to the streets of the modern city in search of, or at least open to, a reciprocal moment of contact with another. The body, of course, is important: its gestures, the signals it sends out, the way it inhabits the streets and moves or remains still. Certainly there is a special contact that takes place in the eyes, in the moment when an anonymous other's eyes meet one's own, when, in the time that it takes to blink, a kind of understanding is breached and a queer sort of connection made. Maybe it's sexual, maybe not. The cruiser is Whitman rather than, say, Baudelaire, the Whitman who writes:

> as I pass, O Manhattan, your frequent and swift flash of eyes offering
>   me love,
> Offering response to my own—these repay me,
> Lovers, continual lovers, only repay me.

He is the Whitman who asks, 'Stranger, if you passing meet me and desire to speak to me, why should you not speak to me?'

Though I am particularly fond of and admire the meandering cruiser, he is only one kind of wanderer, one sort of man of the crowd among many in the modern imagination. Passing him in the streets we find the somewhat alienated and endlessly objectifying figure of the *flâneur*, a tired figure by now, exhausted surely at having to bear the burden of so many discussions of urban modernity. There's also Simmel's 'stranger', a wanderer who arrives but refuses to leave, a figure who 'comes today and stays tomorrow', whose strangeness (not to say estrangement) is a sign both of nearness and distance. There is also the playful, nearly anarchic Situationist for whom a whole new mode of urban movement, the *dérive*, challenges our assumptions about the daily stroll. 'In a *dérive*', Guy Debord tells us,

> one or more persons during a certain period drop their relations, their work and leisure activities, and all their other usual motives for movement and action, and let themselves be drawn by the attractions of the terrain and the encounters they find there. Chance is a less important factor in this activity than one might think: from a dérive point of view cities have psychogeographical contours, with constant currents, fixed points and vortexes that strongly discourage entry into or exit from certain zones.

The dérivist wanders, propelled forward by the psychogeographical variations that direct him, open to all possibilities, with no predetermined goal. The cruiser, the *flâneur*, the stranger, the dérivist—there are many who resist the logic of straight lines and who are at home in the curved and even broken lines of the bent city.

Perhaps we might think of these different strategies for wandering as modes of resistance against all those attempts to plan and to order our lives. Michel de Certeau, in *The Practice of Everyday Life* (first translated into English in 1984) suggests that we must find new 'ways of operating' to counter those organizing, normative institutions that regulate and regularize society. For de Certeau it is the 'clandestine forms taken by the dispersed, tactical, and makeshift creativity of groups or individuals'—what he calls 'tactics'—that help us to move against the discipline of the straight line. A tactic 'operates in isolated actions, blow by blow', with

> a mobility that must accept the chance offerings of the moment, and seize on the wing the possibilities that offer themselves at any given moment. It must vigilantly make use of the cracks that particular conjunctions open in the surveillance of the proprietary powers. It poaches in them. It creates surprises in them. It can be where it is least expected. It is a guileful ruse.

I like the idea of experiencing a city blow by blow. A good tactician knows when to take his chances. Maybe not all pack-donkeys are as scatterbrained as they seem, as they zigzag their way across our cities.

The city of circles and squares, of order, geometry, exactitude and perfection, has produced its own forms of creative resistance to the normativity of everyday life, perhaps particularly for marginalized people for whom resistance may mean survival. Certainly, this was the case for David Wojnarowicz (1954–92), a writer, painter, photographer, collage artist, graffitist, band member, performance artist, AIDS activist and hustler. Along with friends including Kiki Smith, Nan Goldin, Peter Hugar and Keith Haring, he was a central figure in the East Village art scene that became prominent in the 1980s. Essentially 'a lot of struggling, ego-willed artists, musicians, writers, performers and entrepreneurs who were living and working in an area of town that was affordable', as the artist Keiki Bonk puts it, the East Village scene was not so much like an organized movement as a loose group of artist-neighbours who sometimes collaborated and shared makeshift gallery spaces. Although his work is found in major collections and is increasingly praised, today Wojnarowicz is probably still best known in the annals of art history for the controversy he caused as an angry spokesman for the dispossessed in the time of AIDS during a period of right-wing backlash against sexual freedom. Like the photographer Robert Mapplethorpe and other queer artists in the late 1980s and early 1990s, Wojnarowicz fell foul of the National Endowment for the Arts, the government funders, who found his work obscene and overly politicized. In a much-quoted passage from a catalogue essay he wrote for a group exhibition organized by Nan Goldin in 1989, Wojnarowicz tells of his fantasies to 'fuck somebody without a rubber' and 'to douse [Senator Jesse] Helms with a bucket of gasoline and set his putrid ass on fire'. Such provocations by an HIV+ man, in a national climate of fear and loathing, were not read by Republican politicians as the 'radical gestures of the imagination' Wojnarowicz believed them to be, rather as obscene, anti-family and overtly political calls-to-arms. Wojnarowicz became one of the poster-boys for creative resistance, for beating the system at its own game. In a high-profile and landmark court case, he sued the Reverend Donald Wildmon of the American Family Association for infringing his artistic copyright. Wildmon had cut and pasted the dirty bits from various of Wojnarowicz's works of art, creating a flyer that presented 'an orgy or drugs and sex', as Richard Meyer describes it, that was mailed out to tens of thousands of people on the Christian Right. The artist triumphed in the 1990 case of *David Wojnarowicz v. American Family Association and Donald E. Wildmon.*

Wojnarowicz was a man of the streets and the open road. He turned his first trick at the age of nine, dropped out of high school and left home aged 16, and took to living on the streets shortly thereafter. His life wasn't one of direct routes and straight lines. He zigzagged his way through New York, but, importantly, he also zigzagged his way through different media—photography, writing, video, graphic pop art, paintings, collage—never settling or fully embracing a single mode of expression. This unwillingness to be seen as only a painter or photographer or filmmaker or writer was precisely what many art critics came to object to in his work. The same is true of many queer artists who refuse to work in a single medium—Derek Jarman springs to mind. Wojnarowicz was as promiscuous in his artistic practice as he was in his personal life, and there was a purposeful refusal to be pinned down, to focus, to remain in the same place. In part, Wojnarowicz learned from the queer writers he had read closely, Arthur Rimbaud and William Burroughs, for example, who haunt his work and suggest different urban tactics for the bohemian artist. Indeed, an early series of photographs, *Rimbaud in New York* (1978–79) imagines the poet transposed to contemporary New York. Here, a man wearing a paper mask with Rimbaud's face is seen shooting up, masturbating, standing under the West Side Highway, riding the subway and generally inhabiting spaces of urban alienation. The sense of displacement continues in the posthumously published *Waterfront Journals* (1997), a series of short monologues written in the voices of people he meets during his movements through the city or across the country. Titles of chapters include 'Guy on Second Avenue 1:00am', 'Young Boy in Times Square 4:00am', and 'Elderly Transvestite on Second Avenue (Evening)'. Individual encounters are located precisely in time and space, and while a subcultural mapping takes place—Times Square, the YMCA, the Lower East Side, for example—there is a randomness to the assembling of chance encounters. Glimpses and traces of urban life rather than patterns of existence.

In the Shadow of the American Dream (1999), a posthumously published selection of Wojnarowicz's diaries and journals, takes us from his adolescent experiences hustling in the mid 1970s to his death in 1992. We see him lighting out for the territories (he imagines himself as Huck Finn at one point), a victim of wanderlust that takes him across the United States and to Canada and France among other places. But most of the selection is comprised of extended, lyrical narratives that map his particular downtown New York, from the underpass of the West Side Highway, to the nearby parking lots, docks, abandoned warehouses and piers, extending from the West Village up to the meatpacking district, around 19th Street or so. The waterfront on the west side of the city was historically a busy and important commercial port, with a booming business until the second half of the twentieth century, when economic decline hit and the import of commodities dried up. By the early 1970s, just after the Stonewall Riots in the West Village that marked a turning point in gay activism, commercial business on the west side had almost completely disappeared, and in its place a queer subculture began to flourish—queer not simply because there were lots of gay men fucking in abandoned warehouses, but because of the way it brought together all kinds of marginalized people: trannies and truckers, leather boys and sissies, addicts and artists who converged in the night.

'So far my life has been filled with a variety of situations and circumstances where I have ended up roving through scenes that are very removed from scenes most people commonly go through,' Wojnarowicz writes in 1978, 'and as a result I have developed a keen sense of the awareness of the darker areas of society and its characters.' These piers and warehouses, where he once lived rough, are a significant location in the landscape of his artistic imagination; he paints graffiti murals on the walls, takes photographs of men there, writes about it, has sex, and generally hangs out. In journal entries from the late 1970s, we see him trying to articulate his own kind of urban practice, a practice that suggests something more active and engaged than simply meandering or wandering, something less defined and direct than the immediate connections of sexual cruising. Here, he recounts one long evening among many by the piers, from 8 October 1979:

Visited the river again this evening, red traces of dusk far behind the sea green walls of Jersey shipping warehouses, red aura glow inside the pier warehouse walking from room to room, dusk through busted walls getting cruised by lanky queens, searching for the man from Texas, looked through the blue night halls, the warm rooms with pale filmic images of men in boots fucking other men in corners, the ghosts of leather jackets and boys with pasty faces behind concrete walls slow movements extending from shoulder to elbow to wrist, drifting images of desire range rogue desire in the irises immersed in shadow like the folds of river water over the face, seas in fading light, the dead man falling fathoms, the live man falling fathoms, the long lingering sight, the stare into folds of depth of unbreathing moisture, the erotic sense of withdrawal behind misty walls of concrete, the image of sense seen in their eyes not invisible to me, the scene obscured by walls and shadow, the man from Texas wasn't there. I drifted ...

This is sensuous, evocative language, and we catch in Wojnarowicz's voice the haunting echoes of urban sexual outlaws from the past— not only Burroughs and Rimbaud, but also Baudelaire, Whitman and Genet. As he drifts through the scene, his camera-like eye sees bodies in a scene of dissolution, in which red and blue, fire and water, light and shadow are brought together. In another passage, from 6 March 1980, we read:

> Restless walks filled with coasting images of sight and sound, cars buckling over cobblestones down quiet side streets, trucks waiting at corners with swarthy drivers leaning back in cool shadowy seats and windows of buildings opening and closing, figures passing within the rooms, faraway sounds of voices and cries and horns that roll up and funnel in like some secret earphone connecting me to the creakings of the city. There's a discreet pleasure I have in the walking of familiar streets, streets familiar more because of the faraway past than for the recent past, streets that I walked down odd times while living amongst them, seen through the same eyes but each time the eyes belonging to an older boy, spaced by summers and winters and geographical locations. Each time different because of the companions I had previously while walking those streets. I can barely remember or recall the senses I had had when viewing the streets years earlier, my whole change in psyche, I mean. Yet there's still a slight trace of what I felt left, a trace filled with the unconcerned dreams and tragedies and longing that make up thoughts before the seriousness of age sets in.

There is an excess of language throughout the passage, a groping to express his experience of the city. Passages such as this, in which memory, time and place are bound up with a walk through the city, are familiar enough from the classic literature of the modern city— we might think in their different ways of John Harmon's frantic search for his identity as he walks through London in Dickens's *Our Mutual Friend* (1865) or Clarissa's expedition in search of flowers in Woolf's *Mrs Dalloway* (1925). However, unlike those texts, in which the walker accumulates meaning by walking, Wojnarowicz's writing seeks to resist rather than establish meaning, to evade precision and definition. These brief, often surreal, glimpses or traces eradicate boundaries even as the built environment around him endlessly seems to suggest them.

Thought about another way, Wojnarowicz simply refuses to pause; movement must be continuous, like his prose that is never tempted by the lure of the full stop. In another passage from 8 October 1979, he writes:

> Really it's this lawlessness and anonymity simultaneously that I desire, living among thugs, but men who live under no degree of law or demand, just continual motion and robbery and light roguishness and motion, reading Genet out loud to the falling sun overlooking the vast lines of the desert receding into dusk and darkness, drugs and aimlessness, the senselessness striving to be something, the huge realization of the senselessness of that conscious attempt in the midst of the way this living is really constructed, the word *constructed* not even being sensible, unreal, the endless forms of chance and possibility as an alternative to construction, the free floating in time/space/image, the futility and impossibility in even subscribing to the definition of it for even in the definition in the construction of words is the inherent failure to obtain the living sense of the desire.

Continual motion, lawless anonymity, the attempt to live beyond construction—in his romanticization of the outlaw, Wojnarowicz longs for a way of living beyond the constraints (architectural, aesthetic, social, sexual, legal) of the everyday. Perhaps this is the logic of the zigzagging pack-donkey, refusing to heed simple directions. For him, a deserted pier is a nocturnal playground; a disused warehouse is an artist's studio, a sex club, a home. Wojnarowicz's city is not rational or tidy. Function doesn't really figure. His zigzagging drifter engages in an exploratory and self-determining process that depends on endless movement. It is in the uncertainty of what lies ahead that the possibility for change and difference arises, at least imaginatively. The *flâneur* gets bored; the dérivist completes his mission; the cruiser connects—but the pack-donkey zigzags on, resisting the straight and narrow.

Le Corbusier believes that the curved line is 'ruinous, difficult and dangerous'—he senses the disruptive potential of the bent mind. But what happens in the city of tomorrow when all space is thought through and rationalized in advance? What happens when there is no such thing as uncertainty? What happens when it all becomes predictable? People will create their own alternative geometries, strategically, tactically, finding new ways of moving, new ways of operating. There will always be the opportunity to create danger.

In one of his late interviews, Foucault discusses what he describes as the most common fear among straight society:

> that gays will develop relationships that are intense and satisfying even though they do not at all conform to the ideas of relationships held by others. It is the prospect that gays will create as yet unforeseen kinds of relationships that many people cannot tolerate.

Foucault doesn't get much more specific than that in his hope for new queer ways of living, of 'new life-styles not resembling those that have been institutionalized'. But the gay lifestyle that has emerged since Foucault's death in 1984 and Wojnarowicz's in 1992—a mainstream, consumer-driven, hopefully married and pretty normal looking urban 'Gay Lifestyle', of the kind we find in, say, Dupont Circle—has not developed along the (not-so-straight) lines Foucault had in mind. We need more zigzagging. Washington DC, like so many examples of the rational city, may be dominated by circles and squares, by a geometry that we think we know, by a plan that appears to tell us all we need to know; but it too is a bent city. If we wander and meander, drift and cruise, if we follow the zigzagging packdonkey to the warehouses and parking lots, to the parks and piers, we find that there are tactics afoot and people taking their chances.

Reading

Debord, Guy, 'Theory of the Dérive', in *Situationist International Anthology*, ed. Ken Knabb (Berkeley, CA: Bureau of Public Secrets, 2006): 50–4.

de Certeau, Michel, *The Practice of Everyday Life*, trans. Steven Rendall (Berkeley, CA: University of California Press, 1988).

El Kholti, Heidi, Chris Kraus and Justin Cavin (eds), *David Wojnarowicz: A Definitive History of Five or Six Years on the Lower East Side* (New York: Semiotext(e), 2006).

Foucault, Michel, *Politics, Philosophy, Culture: Interviews and Other Writings 1977–1984*, ed. Lawrence Kritzman, trans. Alan Sheridan (London and New York: Routledge, 1990).

Hornsey, Richard, *The Spiv and the Architect: Unruly Life in Postwar London* (Minneapolis: University of Minnesota Press, 2010).

Le Corbusier, *Towards a New Architecture*, trans. Frederick Etchells (New York: Dover Publications, 1986).

Le Corbusier, *The City of To-morrow and Its Planning*, trans. Frederick Etchells (New York: Dover Publications, 1987).

Meyer, Richard, *Outlaw Representation: Censorship and Homosexuality in Twentieth-Century American Art* (Boston: Beacon Press, 2002).

Turner, Mark W., *Backward Glances: Cruising the Queer Streets of New York and London* (London: Reaktion Books, 2003).

Wojnarowicz, David, *The Waterfront Journals* (New York: Grove Press, 1996).

Wojnarowicz, David, *In the Shadow of the American Dream: The Diaries of David Wojnarowicz*, ed. Amy Scholder (New York: Grove Press, 1999).

Wojnarowicz, David, *Rimbaud in New York 1978–79* (New York: PPP Editions, 2004).

Notes on Contributors

Matthew Beaumont is a Senior Lecturer in the Department of English at University College London. He is the author of *Utopia Ltd.: Ideologies of Social Dreaming in England 1870–1900* (2005), and the co-author, with Terry Eagleton, of *The Task of the Critic: Terry Eagleton in Dialogue* (2009), published by Verso. He has edited or co-edited three collections of essays: *As Radical as Reality Itself: Essays on Marxism and Art for the 21st Century* (2005), *The Railway and Modernity: Time, Space and the Machine Ensemble* (2005) and *Adventures in Realism* (2005).

Marshall Berman is Distinguished Professor of Political Science at the City College of New York. He is the author of *The Politics of Authenticity: Radical Individualism and the Emergence of Modern Society* (1970), *All That Is Solid Melts Into Air: The Experience of Modernity* (1982) and *Adventures in Marxism* (1999). His most recent book, *On the Town: One Hundred Years of Spectacle in Times Square* (2006), has recently been republished by Verso.

Kasia Boddy teaches in the English department at University College London. Her most recent books are *Boxing: A Cultural History* (2008) and *Let's Call the Whole Thing Off: Love Quarrels from Anton Chekhov to ZZ Packer* (2009), co-edited with Ali Smith and Sarah Wood. Her current research interests include American fiction in both its long and short forms.

Iain Borden is Professor of Architecture and Urban Culture at the Bartlett School of Architecture, UCL. His research includes explorations of architecture in relation to critical theory, philosophy, Henri Lefebvre, Georg Simmel, film, gender, boundaries, photography, bodies and spatial experiences. His authored and co-edited books include *InterSections: Architectural Histories and Critical Theories* (2000), *The Unknown City: Contesting Architecture and Social Space* (2001), *Skateboarding, Space and the City: Architecture and the Body* (2001), *Manual: the Architecture and Office of Allford Hall Monaghan Morris* (2003) and *Bartlett Designs: Speculating With Architecture* (2009). He is currently working on a history of automobile driving and urban experience.

Rachel Bowlby has written books on the history of shopping and on changing forms of identity. Her books include *Just Looking* (1985), on department stores, *Shopping with Freud* (1993), *Carried Away* (2000), on supermarkets, and *Freudian Mythologies: Greek Tragedy and Modern Identities* (2009).

Gregory Dart is a Senior Lecturer in the Department of English at University College London. He is the author of *Rousseau, Robespierre and English Romanticism* (1999), a study of the influence of the French Revolution on the English Romantics; and a short book, *Unrequited Love: On Stalking and Being Stalked* (2003). He has produced a number of articles and book chapters on William Hazlitt, Pierce Egan, John Soane, B. R. Haydon, John Martin and Thomas De Quincey, and edited two collections of Hazlitt's works, *Metropolitan Writings* (2005) and *Liber Amoris and Related Writings* (2008). He is currently completing a book-length study of early nineteenth-century art and literature entitled *Cockney Adventures*.

Geoff Dyer is the author of many books, including *But Beautiful: A Book about Jazz* (1991), winner of the Somerset Maugham Prize; *Out of Sheer Rage: In the Shadow of D. H. Lawrence* (1997), a finalist, in the US, for a National Books Critics' Circle Award; and *The Ongoing Moment* (2005), winner of an Infinity Award from the International

Center of Photography. He considers himself an expert in the field of urban studies on the grounds that two of his novels—*Paris Trance* (1998) and *Jeff in Venice, Death in Varanasi* (2009)—have the names of three cities in the titles.

Patrick Keiller's films include *London* (1994) and *Robinson in Space* (1997), a study of the UK's landscape extended as a book in 1999. He studied architecture at University College London and fine art at the Royal College of Art, where he began making films. Recent works include 'Londres, Bombay', an exhibition at Le Fresnoy: Studio national des arts contemporains, Tourcoing (2006), featuring a 30-screen moving-image reconstruction of Mumbai's Chhatrapati Shivaji Terminus, and 'The City of the Future', at BFI Southbank, London (2007–8), a five-screen navigable landscape of the UK c. 1900. A forthcoming film was photographed during 2008.

Esther Leslie is Professor of Political Aesthetics at Birkbeck, University of London. She is the author of *Walter Benjamin: Overpowering Conformism* (2000), and *Walter Benjamin: Critical Lives* (2007). Other books include *Hollywood Flatlands: Animation, Critical Theory and the Avant-garde* (2002), published by Verso, and *Synthetic Worlds: Nature, Art and the Chemical Industry* (2005). She is an editor of *Revolutionary History*, a co-editor of *Historical Materialism*, and a member of the editorial collective of *Radical Philosophy*. Together with Ben Watson she runs the website www.militantesthetix.co.uk

Michael Newton is the author of *Savage Girls and Wild Boys: A History of Feral Children* (2002) and a book on *Kind Hearts and Coronets* (2003) in the BFI Film Classics series. He has also edited Edmund Gosse's *Father and Son* (2004), Joseph Conrad's *The Secret Agent* (2007), and *The Penguin Book of Ghost Stories* (2010). He lectures at the University of Leiden, in which town he rents a flat that's all his own.

Chris Petit is a writer and filmmaker. His films include *Radio On* (1979) and *Chinese Boxes* (1984). Television work includes *Unrequited*

Love (2006), documentaries on weather and air stewardesses, and several collaborations with Iain Sinclair, including their film about the M25, *London Orbital* (2002). Novels include *Robinson* (1993), *The Psalm Killer* (1996), *The Hard Shoulder* (2001), and *The Passenger* (2006). His most recent work is *Content*, a film essay and ambient twenty-first-century road movie.

Michael Sayeau is a Lecturer in the English department at University College London, where he works on modernism and literary and cultural theory. He is currently completing two projects: one on the 'everyday' in modernist literature, the other on modernism and simplicity.

Michael Sheringham is Marshal Foch Professor of French Literature, University of Oxford, and a Fellow of All Souls College. He has been Visiting Professor at several French universities and at UC Berkeley. He has written extensively on Surrealism, modern and contemporary French poetry and fiction, and on autobiography and related genres. His publications include *Beckett: Molloy* (1986), *French Autobiography: Devices and Desires* (1993) and *Everyday Life: Theories and Practices from Surrealism to the Present* (2006). He has edited *Parisian Fields* (1996) and, with Johnnie Gratton, has co-edited *The Art of the Project* (2005).

Iain Sinclair has lived in Hackney, East London, since 1969. His novels include *Downriver* (1991), winner of the James Tait Black Prize and the Encore Prize, *Radon Daughters* (1994), *Landor's Tower* (2001) and, most recently, *Dining on Stones* (2004), which was shortlisted for the Ondaatje prize. Non-fiction books, exploring the myth and matter of London, include *Lights Out for the Territory* (1997), *London Orbital* (2002) and *Edge of the Orison* (2005). He has also edited *London, City of Disappearances* (2006). He and Chris Petit have co-directed four documentaries, one of which, *Asylum* (2000), won the short-film prize at the Montreal Festival. His most recent book is *Hackney, That Rose-Red Empire: A Confidential Report* (2009).

David Trotter is King Edward VII Professor of English Literature at the University of Cambridge. He was co-founder of the Cambridge Screen Media Group, and the first Director of the University's MPhil in Screen Media and Cultures. His most recent books are *Cinema and Modernism* (2007) and *The Uses of Phobia: Essays on Literature and Film* (2010).

Mark W. Turner is a Reader in the English department at King's College London. He teaches courses on urban modernity, nineteenth-century literature and media, and Anglo-American queer culture. His books include *Trollope and the Magazines* (2000) and *Backward Glances: Cruising the Queer Streets of New York and London* (2003), and he is currently co-editing an edition of Oscar Wilde's journalism. He has written and reviewed for a range of publications, including the *Independent*, the *Observer*, *Blueprint* and *Vogue*.

Index